OUT OF
SIGHT
OUT OF
MIND

OUT OF
SIGHT
OUT OF
MIND

Abuse, Neglect and Fire in a
London Children's Workhouse
1854–1907

JOHN WALKER

By the same author:

The Queen Has Been Pleased – The Scandal of the British Honours System –
Secker and Warberg 1986, Sphere Books 1987.

Writer, editor, publisher: *www.E7-NowandThen.org* – Forest Gate local history blog

Typeset in Garamond & Goudy Old Style
by riverdesignbooks.com

Dedicated to the memories of Irene Alice Walker, who survived, and John Lathwell, who didn't

Among other public buildings in a certain town, which for many reasons it will be prudent to refrain from mentioning, and to which I will assign no fictitious name, there is one anciently common to most towns, great or small — to wit, a workhouse.

Opening lines to *Oliver Twist* by Charles Dickens

Table of contents

Some subsequent lives

ACKNOWLEDGEMENTS

This book was inspired by delving into my family history and through running a local history website about Forest Gate in east London (www.E7-NowAndThen.org), which is where I live. Some of my relatives spent time in workhouses and children's homes over the last 150 years – about which I knew little – and I wanted to find out more. There was a similar dearth of information, locally, about an impressive building which had once been a 'workhouse school', and is located about half a mile from my home. I was intrigued.

I soon discovered that relatively little has been written about workhouse establishments – which collectively housed many millions of British people over the centuries – beyond the work of the indefatigable Peter Higginbotham. His books are cited throughout the text and his website (www.workhouse.org) is a huge fund of information about so many poor law institutions. I am greatly indebted to his enormous efforts.

Little of the story outlined in this book has previously been told – and certainly not in a joined-up sense. It relies heavily on contemporary press reports and archive materials. The British Newspaper Library Archive, with its sophisticated search engine (www.britishnewspaperarchive.co.uk), has been indispensable; and this work could not have been written without it.

Fortunately, many shelves of documents relating to the Forest Gate institution survive in the National and the London Metropolitan Archives, and staff in these wonderful places have been unfailingly helpful in digging them out for me. Smaller collections of documents and fragments at the London School of Economics, the Tower Hamlets Local History Library and Archives and Newham's Archives and Local Studies Library have all been of some assistance. I thank the staff for their time and understanding, in pointing me in the right directions. I am also deeply appreciative of the staff at the British Library, whose patience and helpfulness in times of reader uncertainty is very comforting.

Although the Newham Local Studies Library does not hold much relevant material, I would like to place on record my thanks to its former archivist, the late Jenni Munro-Collins, for her help and support over an eight-year period with this project and my website. Apart from some volunteer help, she was, effectively, the entire public-facing staff of the archives for much of that time. She did a sterling job of work and will be much missed.

I would also like to thank my wife, Sandra, and children Rose, Owen and Jack for their advice, comments and encouragement as I have beavered away and paid them less attention than they deserve. I am very much in the debt of fellow 'Forest Gate History Boys', Mark Gorman, Peter Williams, Robert Nurden and Tony Morrison for their support, guidance, observations and general good blokeness, as I have wittered to them about the obsession that has become this book. Thanks are also due to my fellow Crystal Palace sufferer and historian, Jim Chrystie for his helpful observations. I am particularly grateful to John Webb and Paul Norton for providing me with previously unpublished information and images concerning the fires on Training Ship *Goliath* and in the Forest Lane buildings.

I wish to apologise to our dogs for not taking them out as much as I had promised, but they can rest assured that their lives are more comfortable than those of any of the children featured within these pages.

Many thanks are due to my copy editor, Kate Bohdanowicz whose insight and eye for detail has sharpened the text, and to my creative designer Latte Goldstein, who has pulled together 70,000 plus words and a jumble of images into what feels like a coherent publication.

All errors in the book are, of course, my own.

The photographs and illustrations included are, for the most part, old and every reasonable attempt has been made to track copyright owners. Anyone wishing to assert copyright to any untraced photos is invited to contact me, via the blog, below.

If you have additional information, or stories about relatives or incidents relating to the institution, please feel free to add them to the E7 website, (www.E7-NowAndThen.org), in the comments section. My hope, as ever, is that this book, like all good history writing, should be part of an iterative process, informed by the insight of as many commentators as possible.

John Walker,
September 2021

ABBREVIATIONS AND TERMINOLOGY

To put many of the organisations listed below into a historical context, readers may find it useful to cross reference them with their appearances in the Timeline produced on page 226.

CCHF – Children's Country Holiday Fund. This was a scheme initiated in 1877 by Henrietta Barnett to offer workhouse children an annual holiday and experience life outside the institutions in which they were brought up.

CofE – Church of England, the 'established' religious denomination of England following sixteenth-century reformation.

FGDS – Forest Gate District School(s) – see section on terminology below.

FGSD – Forest Gate School District – see section on terminology below.

GER – Great Eastern Railway, which provided a rail link between Forest Gate and both the City of London and the Essex countryside; first opened in Forest Gate in 1841.

LCC – London County Council, the first proper London-wide local authority, established by the 1888 Local Government Act.

LGB – Local Government Board, the government body that succeeded the Poor Law Board (see below) in 1871, taking over responsibility for supervision of the poor law in England.

LMA – London Metropolitan Archives, host of archives relating to London poor law unions and institutions such as the FGDS.

JFS – Jews' Free School, independent Jewish school, established in 1732, moved to Whitechapel in 1822.

MAB – Metropolitan Asylums Board, established under the 1867 Metropolitan Poor Law Act to have supervisory powers over asylums and hospitals, was given responsibility for TS *Goliath's* successor ship, TS *Exmouth*, in 1876.

MABYS – Metropolitan Association for Befriending Young Servants, established by Jane Senior in 1876, with significant input from Henrietta

Barnett, to provide an after-care service for girls leaving poor law schools in London.

MCPLF – Metropolitan Common Poor Law Fund, established by the 1867 Metropolitan Poor Law Act, to help fund education in poor law schools.

NA – National Archives, host to archives relating to the LGB and PLB (see above and below).

PLB – Poor Law Board, central government body responsible for supervising the administration of the poor law in England between 1847 and 1871.

PLC – Poor Law Commission, established as the central government's agency overseeing workhouses and other institutions established by the 1834 Act, until replaced in 1847 by the Poor Law Board.

SDF – Social Democratic Federation, an early socialist political party in England, established in 1881, and in some respects a forerunner to the Labour Party, established in 1906.

A NOTE ON TERMINOLOGY

The Forest Gate School District (FGSD) is the name of the organisation which ran the Forest Lane 'school' – when it operated as a district school under the control of the guardians and unions of the area. The Forest Gate District School(s) (FGDS) was the name of the buildings themselves. Sometimes these were described by outside bodies in the singular – as just one 'school' – and sometimes in the plural – acknowledging the fact that technically there were three on the site – one for boys, one for girls and one for infants, all under the same management.

The school district, as a legal entity, was run by unpaid representatives of the controlling unions (Whitechapel, Hackney and Poplar, at different times), together with some ex-officio appointees nominated by the government (Poor Law Board and Local Government Board, at different times). Today these people would be described as governors. They were, however, described as 'managers' and what we would today recognise as the institution's managers – the superintendent, matron and heads – were described as 'officers'. To avoid confusion, the book refers to the 'governors' rather than 'managers' when describing the governing committee. A simple transposition of those words would be understandable to the nineteenth-century reader.

ILLUSTRATIONS

The alternative to the Forest Gate workhouse school, for many East End orphans and abandoned children in 1872.
Line drawing by Gustave Dore entitled Wentworth Street, Whitechapel from his publication London, a pilgrimage.

CHAPTER 1

1066–1854: CHILDREN AND THE POOR LAW

The poor, and their children, may always be with us, and how they are treated are yardsticks for judging the state and values of the nation in which they live. This book is the story of how more than 50,000 pauper children were treated in an east London institution during the second half of the nineteenth century. It examines how conditions and lifestyles for them altered, during that relatively short period of time – and who and what were the agents and inhibitors of those changes.

It should be stated, at the outset, that although the institution has always – contemporaneously and historically – been referred to as a 'school', it was not. It was quite simply a workhouse for children, aged from two to usually 14 or 15. It was residential, with the youngsters living 24 hours, seven days a week under workhouse conditions, and attending its own inferior school for barely 10 per cent of the time.

It was run, locally, by workhouse bodies and was supervised, nationally, by the government department responsible for administering the poor law. At the same time, local school boards supervised education and a government department of education looked after the interests of non-workhouse children.

As will be become clear, conditions in the 'school' replicated workhouse life for the youngsters; but instead of the back-breaking work their parents and other people undertook there, the children performed 'industrial' tasks, aimed at running their institution as cost-effectively as possible. This on-the-job training embraced not just housework, but tailoring, carpentry, boot making, gardening and repair work, at no charge. Although the boys' training was frequently denounced as offering unsatisfactory preparation for future work, management persevered with it because it kept costs down.

The framework for the children's treatment was outlined in legislation passed by a parliament elected by neither women nor the poorer half of the male population. The details of their existence were determined by representatives of a relatively small number of affluent local property-owning ratepayers who, by definition, were never likely to require the services of the institution for either themselves or their own children.

Their unsympathetic, harsh, penny-pinching provision was only over-turned once a small number of determined women and working-class advocates and guardians were able first to reform, then finally overthrow, the oppressive and inhumane regime the children endured.

BEFORE THE 1834 POOR LAW AMENDMENT ACT

Until the early years of the nineteenth century, England had been an over-whelmingly rural country in which travel and geographic relocation were rare. National government was relatively minimal in ambition and played little part in trying to regulate social relationships.

Religious houses, such as monasteries and abbeys, provided huge financial and social support to the impoverished, old and infirm from the Norman Conquest until the dissolution of the monasteries in the 1530s. The effective closure of upwards of 800 of these institutions resulted in significant hardship for people unable to support themselves. A large void was left by the removal of this formerly vital social safety net and uncoordinated, essentially local, ad hoc arrangements emerged to plug the gap.

These soon proved deficient, and the unmet needs of the destitute, aged and sick became a national problem, which the 1602 Poor Law Act sought to address. Under the terms of the Act, responsibility for meeting their needs was left to local people, and the institutional vehicles adopted for addressing them were based on the parish – Church of England (CofE) – based authorities.

Although the secular state intervened, in the form of Acts of Parliament, it still regarded the responsibility for addressing poverty as a religious, quasi-charitable function of the Church. The state dissolved the monasteries and its supporters benefited, but it still expected the reformed Church to continue to accept responsibility for the administration of support to the poor, locally, thereafter.

Most towns and villages were small by modern standards and their parishes correspondingly so. The general absence of migration meant that a sense of community prevailed, and the 'unfortunate' poor were often widely known. Sympathetic customised solutions were frequently adopted to meet their individual and specific needs. Local able-bodied poor were regularly found work of community or marginal economic value to perform in exchange for 'outdoor relief', or payments in goods or kind, to keep them from starvation and total destitution.

The costs of caring for the poor were met from local rates, imposed on local landowners by the parishes, via the offices of the (unpaid) overseers of the poor, first established in 1597. Glances at parish records throughout England from the seventeenth until the early-nineteenth century routinely indicate a local familiarity with the needs and fates of individual applicants for 'poor relief', and grants and assistance were often customised to meet individual circumstances.

The itinerant poor were usually discouraged from settling in a non-home parish for fear of becoming a financial burden. Those who sought relief from a parish for which they could not prove an established connection, such as place of birth, marriage, lengthy residence or long-held employment, were sent back to their parish of origin to receive support or assistance required, under various Acts of Settlement dating from 1662.

Considerable variations in poor relief provision and practice prevailed from place to place, and over time. The treatment offered and received often depended on seasonal or economic circumstances, and the attitudes of those dispensing relief, as well as that of the local gentry, who effectively funded the system. A rather crude, and unspoken, social contract existed within most communities which, for the greater part, were content to 'look after their own'.

Patrician traditions of noblesse oblige, often encouraged by the Church, nurtured charitable approaches and attitudes towards the sick, geriatric and unfortunates. At a more mercenary and mechanistic level, many landowners knew that poor relief suited their own economic purpose, even though they were its principal funders. At harvest, lambing and other busy times in the agricultural calendar, additional cheap casual labour from the ranks of the able-bodied poor would be required in farms around the country.

They would be hired for short periods, to help farmers garner crops and nurture livestock, ready for market.

To have a pool of reasonably fit, under-employed local people to call upon as casual agricultural labour was a convenience for many rate-paying farmers. If no poor relief were provided during down times, the pool of quasi-surplus labour would perhaps have migrated or evaporated and harvests would have rotted, or the newborn farm animals would have been left unattended and for dead in the fields.

Such labour could be hired to undertake a specific job and then be laid off, and the parish would be left to maintain them and their families, at subsistence levels, until they were needed again. For landowners this offered a seasonal workforce that was easier and cheaper to fund than having to retain marginal labour on an estate payroll, doing nothing between peaks in demand.

The same principle was adopted for other work in the village – repairing the church roof, primitive maintenance of highways, burying the dead etc. It was simply what, in today's terminology, would be regarded as the pre-industrial gig economy – with the safety net being the parish rather than the welfare state. Cheap, casual, readily available labour had its advantages to the local economy, and miserable poor relief was a small price for local people of substance to pay for it.

The world of poor law administration, of course, was often more complex than this in practice, and its history is peppered with scandal, colourful characters and tyrants who defied the norm. The foregoing description does, however, offer a generalised picture of an era of small settled communities, church-dominated life, casual employment, lack of geographical mobility and of established social relationships. Together, these maintained a social cohesion and addressed some of the economic needs of the rural poor in customised ways and at most times.

However, rapid developing economic changes in the late-eighteenth and early-nineteenth centuries were to transform this landscape and blow away these fragile, mutually dependent, rural relationships.

The agricultural revolution, with its mechanisation, scientific method and enclosures, reduced the demand, and indeed dependency, in many areas, for seasonal labour. With this often came a reduced sympathy for many of the rural casually employed, during their periods of economic inactivity. Early nineteenth-century rural unrest, most notably the Swing Riots of

1830 when agricultural workers protested about mechanisation and harsh working conditions, are testimony to some of this dislocation of traditional interdependent village relationships.

This gradual erosion of social stability resulted in an increased vulnerability, uncertainty and anxiety among many of the rural poor. Their insecurity often manifested itself in urban drift, with the prospect – or more accurately desperate hope – of employment and some minor economic relief in the factories and other work opportunities spawned by urbanisation and the forward march of the Industrial Revolution.

Rural families took advantage of the easier transport means, which had resulted from the development of turnpike roads, canals and railways, and moved to alien urban environments where they knew nobody. They were soon to find that the streets they encountered, far from being paved with gold, were often not paved at all. Insanitary conditions were rife and life expectation rates plummeted.

Housing development in the rapidly developing towns and cities was uncontrolled and living conditions were cramped, poor and unhygienic. There was not even the consolation of a small patch of land on which to grow food, which many of the new urban poor had left behind in the countryside.

No, little, or pitifully paid work, together with insanitary and over-crowded housing conditions proved to be too great a problem for many of the new townsfolk. The small ecclesiastical parishes that existed in the rapidly developing towns were overwhelmed and unable to dispense parish relief adequately, or address the emerging chronic social problems caused by urban dysfunction.

The construction armies that created the new transport networks often turned into large gangs of dispossessed poor, unable to fend for themselves when the projects they were working on came to an end. The builders were usually away from their home communities when ill-health, economic down-turns and industrial injuries struck, and they simply added to the growing problems of urban poverty and deprivation.

Until the early years of the nineteenth century, local overseers of the poor were left with almost total discretion in the ways in which they treated applicants for poor relief. It was usually exercised by providing outdoor relief, or, less frequently, imposing a residence in one of the few small work-houses that operated in the country. The parish, particularly in fast-growing towns, was unable to cope with the unprecedented rise in local population, economic distress and demand for assistance. Repatriating the destitute to their parish of birth simply became impractical, given the ever-increasing scale of the problem.

Some parishes, from the seventeenth century, had established workhouses as a partial means of meeting the needs of some categories of their local poor; but there was no obligation for any parish to build them. Such work-houses were usually small by latter-day standards – often accommodating at most a few dozen people. The rules on whether or not to establish a workhouse, who would be eligible for support within it, and the nature of the support offered were entirely parish matters.

Most of the workhouses treated child inhabitants in a similar way to the adults; they would see their families regularly, or even live and eat in the same cramped rooms. Family life for the pauper young, until the early decades of the nineteenth century, would not have been significantly different from that of poor children outside the workhouse, other than to the extent of their economic destitution.

As far as outdoor relief was concerned, parish children would also have been treated pretty much the same as their parents and other adults, except they probably only received pro rata payments or relief, because of their age. Many children were regarded as important parts of the rural economy and were often as likely as their parents to be employed when seasonal labour was required in villages and farms.

One parish solution, in some rapidly expanding towns, was the con-struction of larger workhouses. They resulted in many children being accommodated under the same roof as a considerable number of adults, with very different needs. Whitechapel's workhouse, for example, became one of the country's largest, with a capacity of 600 inmates in 1777.[1]

Institutions of this size were seen by some as providing unsatisfactory and inappropriate accommodation for children. The sheer scale of the new, larger workhouse populations, however, meant that it was possible to develop cost-effective solutions for treating the young separately. Consequently, a number of more appropriate and customised institutions were developed to address their needs.

A prevailing belief was that the young would be adversely affected and 'contaminated' by a culture of pauperism and what were often regarded as the feckless poor within workhouses. Children-only institutions were gradually promoted as an antidote to this 'contamination'.

Jonas Hanway (1712–1786) was an English trading merchant with a considerable interest in child welfare; he helped Thomas Coram establish the Foundling Hospital in 1739.

Intense lobbying on his part in the 1760s resulted in the passage of legislation, subsequently known as the Hanway Act. This 1766 law was the first to directly address the needs of London's pauper young. It required metropolitan parishes to remove workhouse children, aged three to six years old, from the institutions and relocate them at least six miles away from the capital. The intention was to take them from the poor public health conditions of the metropolis and place them in the care of rural nurses.

Jonas Hanway (1712–1786), whose work inspired countryside locations for London orphanages and training ships.

Historian Dorothy George called the Hanway Act 'The only piece of eighteenth-century legislation dealing with the poor which was an unqualified success.'[2] Hanway, himself, estimated that his law saved 1,500 lives a year during his lifetime; a claim that has never been convincingly refuted.[3]

The intention of the Hanway Act was that young pauper children should be raised in what were, effectively, privatised baby farms. The hope was that they could be encouraged to embrace different cultures, lifestyles, behaviours and attitudes that would see them rejecting a workhouse way of life when they became adults. The nursing and care charge was set at 2 shillings 6 d per week per child – to be paid for by the despatching parish to the homes accepting the youngsters.

Gradually the Hanway principle was extended to embrace the establishment of purpose-built schools and homes to accommodate the metropolitan pauper poor. The most famous institution to emerge was Frederick Aubin's school in South Norwood – the Norwood School of Industry – then in Surrey, now South London. It opened in the early 1820s and grew to accommodate upwards of 650 young people, sent from a variety of inner London parishes.

The landmark Hanway legislation set a precedent for what was later to become the Forest Gate School District (FGSD). In another related development, in March 1786, Hanway established a training ship for young naval recruits, via the Maritime Society, of which Training Ship (TS) *Goliath* – a significant offshoot of the FGDS – was an exemplar.

Widespread failures of existing poor law legislation and its application during the early decades of the nineteenth century led to the establishment of the 1832 Royal Commission on the Poor Law. It was created to address the inadequacies of the existing crumbling and ineffective system of poor law relief, and address the attendant problem of the rising costs of caring for the poor, particularly in urban areas.

The commission was greatly influenced by the thinking of the utilitarian Jeremy Bentham (1748–1832). Although he died before it reported, his objective was to minimise the poor's reliance on outdoor relief, for both economic and moral reasons. He believed it was moral weakness rather than economic necessity that drove the poor to seek help from the poor law system, and this lack of moral strength should be punished by the system. He opposed the culture of dependency, which he felt the prevailing system encouraged, as he believed it rewarded fecklessness. Instead, he argued that the poor should be accommodated in hostile, punitive workhouses, which would be run on the principle of 'less eligibility' – where conditions would be worse than anything that could be encountered outside the institution, by even the poorest, and thus act as a deterrent to apply for entry.

AFTER 1834

The subsequent 1834 Poor Law Amendment Act accepted these Benthamite principles and effectively nationalised the system of poor relief by creating central government poor law commissioners and assistants, each responsible for overseeing the application of the law's principles in smaller geographic areas. They eventually formed a new government department, the Poor Law

Board (PLB), whose job was to establish, and then ensure conformity to, nationally determined standards of behaviour, regimes and treatment within all workhouses – down to the nature of diets, uniforms, work practices and accommodation arrangements.

The commissioning regime's objective was to enforce the principle of 'less eligibility' by discouraging poor people from turning to workhouses as a safety net, and make the conditions within them as intolerable as possible. Those forced to succumb were, consequently, looked down upon and demonised as feckless individuals.

Since it was difficult to give inmates less food than the meagre amounts on which those below the breadline outside the workhouse lived, or provide them with worse accommodation than the damp hovels which many people inhabited, other means of humiliation had to be found. Families were split up, with men and women forced to live in separate wards and children living apart from their parents, with only irregular visiting permitted.

Workhouse inmates were required to wear uniforms, as reminders of their lack of independence and dignity. Nationally prescribed diets were kept simple and tedious and aimed at offering little more than minimal subsistence. Arduous, mind-numbing and back-breaking work, together with tyrannical regimes and oppressive overseers, were imposed on those who entered the workhouses – all as deterrents to would-be applicants.

The Royal Commission envisaged that different types of institution could be created to accommodate different classes of poor, with children and the sick cited as examples; although this recommendation did not feature prominently in the legislation that immediately followed the report's publication.

The less eligibility principle presented a dilemma as far as the treatment of children was concerned. They were clearly too young to be blamed for indolence and their own fate, and thus could not be treated as unworthy recipients of support. Equally, however, they could not be seen to be looked after too favourably. If they were, it was argued, parents outside would be tempted to treat the institution as a refuge and provider of a better life, and so send the children there; thus defeating the objective underpinning the institutions.

This quandary was played out tortuously throughout the institutions that were constructed to accommodate many of the children. It was most apparent when it came to providing education at a time when it was neither compulsory, nor universally available for those outside poor law establishments. It was argued that the 'pauper children' who were taught to read and write were, in fact, being treated more favourably than their illiterate counterparts in the outside world. Some workhouse guardians adopted bizarre compromises in order to address the dichotomy, such as teaching children to read, but not to write.

The most widely adopted compromise seemed to be to give children the absolute minimum of support and comfort in barrack-like institutions – children's workhouses – offering a rudimentary education and some practical job training, which was often substandard. This provided a watered-down version of the Hanway principle, which it was claimed would give children the tools to enable them to be differently motivated than their 'feckless parents', and at the same time address the less eligibility principle.

These conditions, it was felt, would encourage the emerging generation to be independent and discourage them from turning to the workhouse for support when they became adults. By providing the youngsters with some skills, workhouse schools, it was argued, would provide a foundation for them to gain employment as adults, and so break the cycle of poverty.

The 1834 Act also heralded the establishment of poor law unions – essentially a bringing together of a number of local parishes into much larger single bodies, under the watchful eye and guidance of a poor law assistant commissioner. Each union (managed by a board of guardians – comprised of representatives from each of the constituent parishes) would be large enough to apply economies of scale in dealing with growing numbers of dependent paupers, and establish different types of institutions for different classes of people.

These included, as we shall see, 'separate schools' – or more accurately children's workhouses – and a variety of asylums directed at accommodating people with different forms of illness, both physical and mental. They were called separate schools because they were built away from the workhouse itself, as separate institutions.

The Whitechapel Board of Guardians – the subject of much of this book – was established in 1837, by combining 16 former parishes into a single union. The Hackney Union was created the same year, by the merger of two previous parishes and the third part of what was later to constitute the FGSD; Poplar's board had been established the previous year by the merger of two former parishes. When the FGSD was established, it was to cater for a number of poor children who, less than 30 years earlier had been spread over 20 separate poor law parishes, each too small to be able to offer a customised facility for children.

Responsibility for children had become a significant problem for poor law authorities by the 1830s. Orphans and sick and abandoned children emerged in unprecedented numbers within the new urban sprawls. Many were left to roam the streets to fend for themselves in extremely vulnerable circumstances, while others found their way to workhouses for shelter and sustenance. It was estimated that in 1838 half the population of workhouses was under the age of 16.[4] Conditions within them for the children were totally inadequate. When fever attacked the Whitechapel workhouse in 1838, poor law inspectors found four or five girls sleeping in one bed and infants sleeping in a room they seldom left.[5]

The plight of pauper children began to capture public and institutional consideration in the 1830s. *Bentley's Miscellany*, in 1837, ran a series of articles under the title of 'The Parish Boy's Progress'. This was the first draft of what was to become Charles Dickens' *Oliver Twist*, with its infamous depiction of workhouse conditions for children. The hitherto little acknowledged problem of armies of urban pauper children was beginning to be thrust into the very centre of the public's reading and consciousness.

The treatment of the young poor provoked consideration and innovative responses elsewhere in Europe. In 1833 – midway through the deliberations of the Royal Commission on the Poor Law – the Rauhe Haus (rough house) scheme was created in Hamburg. These were homes for groups of 10 to a dozen parentless children who would be treated like a family, under the care of a 'brother', instead of in large, anonymous institutions. The system later become something of a template for the cottage homes network that gained widespread adoption in the UK, from the 1870s (see Chapter 5).

In 1839, in the village of Mettray, near Tours, France, an influential agricultural colony was opened aimed at reforming delinquent boys. Its underpinning philosophy was that rural surroundings, contact with the land and communal living and farming, within a pleasant architectural environment, would provide positive influences on disturbed young boys, and improve their sociability and character. The experiment was widely regarded as a success and, just like the Rauhe Haus system, it was to later influence thinking on the institutional care of young people in Britain.

Rauhe Haus, an 1830s German experiment in providing family-type living for orphaned children.
(Credit: Mary Evans/Peter Higginbotham collection)

Both of these successful European schemes were founded on the principle of accommodating relatively small groups of youngsters within caring, family-like environments. It took British poor law administrators half a century to appreciate, and widely adopt, their principles – to the detriment of hundreds of thousands of British pauper children who suffered in the interim.

Instead, by the later 1830s, a combination of circumstances in Britain pointed poor law administrators in the opposite direction: to construct larger-scale homes – children's workhouses – as the preferred response to dealing with the growing army of young paupers.

Dr James Kay (later Sir James Kay-Shuttleworth) (1804–1877) was an educationalist who saw at first hand the plight of the poor in newly industrialised towns. He was appointed an assistant poor law commissioner in 1835 and four years later became England's first educational civil servant. He inherited a system where most unions outside of London kept their children in the workhouse and educated them in a variety of school-type settings, many with work or industrial training added to their schedule.[6]

In 1838 he proposed housing pauper children away from the workhouse, in what he termed 'district schools'. Unlike separate schools, which were run by a single union, district schools were to be run by a group of unions.

He saw them as servicing a number of the recently established poor law unions, and he commissioned architectural drawings to illustrate how they could work in practice. Their principal benefit, he suggested, would be to offer education and training for the young people, away from the 'polluting association of workhouses'.

He had been influenced by Aubin's school in South Norwood, in which he had worked to improve the conditions and education of the young people. That institution offered industrial training, banned corporal punishment and was seen to improve the morale of the children. It was a widely heralded public educational establishment, in the days before the compulsory education of British children.

Kay envisaged there being 100 similar district schools, nationwide, each accommodating and educating around 500 children. He felt that the children would be weaned away from a culture of dependence and have it replaced with a 'spirit of hopefulness and enterprise'. He said they would be 'better fitted to prepare the children for conflict with the perils and difficulties of a struggle for independence than anything which their present situation affords.'[7]

Kay's proposals were incorporated in the 1844 Poor Law Amendment Act, which permitted unions within a 15-mile radius of each other to co-operate and establish a school district, for the purpose of establishing joint schools. The advantage of these school districts, he argued, was to offer economies of scale in teaching large classes and industrial training in a wide range of crafts. They also offered the benefits of cost savings on furniture and staff for the sponsoring unions, as well as providing an opportunity for attracting better quality staff. His vision, unfortunately, was corrupted, when put into practice.

Only three district schools were initially established in 1849 – the North Surrey, South Metropolitan and Central London schools. The latter was a renaming of Aubin's school in Norwood, which had been purchased in order to become a guardian-controlled entity. The institution was moved to Hanwell in Middlesex in 1857.

The following year, Charles Dickens described the poverty of the children attending the Norwood school, immediately after its redesignation as a district school as:

> Little personifications of genuine poverty … compounds … of
> ignorance, gin and sprats. Generally born in dark alleys and back
> courts, their playground has been the streets, where the wits of

many have been prematurely sharpened at the expense of any morals they might have. With minds and bodies destitute of proper nutriment, they are caught, as it were, by the parish officers, half-wild creatures, roaming poverty-stricken amidst the wealth of our greatest city; and half-starved in a land where the law says no-one shall be destitute of food and shelter.[8]

In 1849, an outbreak of cholera in Mr Drouet's private school in Tooting killed 150 of its 1,400 pupils. Like Aubin's Norwood School of Industry, Bartholomew Drouet's establishment for pauper children aimed to mop up some of the London youngsters Hanway's Act said should be sent to the country. Dickens was so horrified that he described the school as 'brutally conducted, viley kept, preposterously inspected, dishonestly defended, a disgrace to a Christian community and a stain upon a civilised land.'[9] The epidemic instilled the fear of the rapid spread of contagious disease within big institutions and put a temporary halt on the building of others. Drouet was charged with manslaughter but was subsequently acquitted. His school did not survive the outbreak.

Mr Drouet's school in Tooting, a private school used by London guardians for workhouse children.
(Credit: Mary Evans/Peter Higginbotham collection)

Dickens' observations and that of journalist Henry Mayhew's in his book *London Labour and the London Poor*, published in 1851, paint terrible pictures of the conditions in which the capital's needy lived, as did Charles Booth's *Life and Labour of the People of London* published 40 years later. Booth described destitute children outside of workhouse institutions, often abandoned or orphaned and living on their wits, as 'street arabs' – see a copy of a Dore print of Whitechapel in 1871 on p. xiv for a contemporary representation. It is perhaps a sign of how dehumanising life in the poor law schools was that these street children preferred to chance their luck leading semi-feral lives in the city than submit to the indignities the workhouse regimes presented.

―――――――――

So the lessons of the successful European childcare models were not heeded, and the dangers to health the large-scale children's institutions posed were soon forgotten. From the 1850s, boards of guardians in the metropolis rushed to erect large, impersonal, uncaring institutions for their pauper young. Perhaps the most notorious of these 'barrack schools', as they later became branded , was the Forest Gate District School (FGDS).[10]

What was to become the FGDS started its life as Whitechapel's separate school, on Forest Lane, Forest Gate in 1854. When a second wave of multi-union London district schools was created – three in 1868 – Whitechapel's school in Forest Gate became one, as its guardians joined with those of Hackney and Poplar to establish a joint, or district, school for a large area of east and north-east London.

The institution was, in fact, an enormous children's workhouse, whose intake, at the time of its opening, accounted for almost quarter of the population of Forest Gate. Nevertheless, as we shall see, it barely got an acknowledgement in the contemporary annals of the locality. These Victorian children, for the most part, were out of sight and out of mind.

The FGSD's journey during its five decades of existence was a brutal and uncaring one, dominated by oppressive and corrupt management, poorly qualified and exploited teachers and an almost total disregard for the health, care and social needs of the youngsters who crossed its threshold.

At any one time, upwards of 900 children lived there, in conditions that the Canadian sociologist Erving Goffman would, a century later, describe as a 'total institution'. It resembled a prison more than a home, but its occupants' only 'crime' was to be born into poverty.

From the outset, the institution did not nurture its pupils as potentially useful members of society, to be educated, socialised and empowered; they were abused as anonymous wretches and treated with contempt. Following workhouse practice, they had their hair shaved on entry, wore impersonal uniforms, were not addressed by their names, were separated from their siblings and were rarely allowed out into the local community. If they were lucky, they would receive a visit once every three months from a relative.

Food was dull and often contaminated; mealtimes were conducted in total silence. Strict, uninspiring and unchallenging lessons were taught, initially, by the untrained, in grossly overcrowded and unhealthy rooms. There was no formal recreation or pleasure for the inmates – a more accurate description of the children. It was a soulless institution, obliged to impart an Anglican upbringing in a cold and unsympathetic way to its charges, who were trapped, brutalised and ignored.

It was dangerous too. In a 15-year period (1875–1890), the FGDS and its associated training ship TS *Goliath*, which was stationed on the River Thames in Grays, Essex, both suffered serious fires. Three years later, the Forest Lane establishment endured a scandalous bout of food poisoning, and there were frequent health epidemics.

A number of previously unsung heroes emerge from this story, as do some previously untainted villains of poor law administration. The slow-moving tectonic plates of British nineteenth-century politics and public administration gradually enabled significant, but previously excluded, sections of society to have an influence on the way society was ordered. The FGSD was a huge beneficiary, principally from the determination and impact of two pioneering women – who brought empathy – and two equally groundbreaking working-class men – who brought experience of workhouse living and poverty.

They were able, initially, to influence and introduce minor reforms to the establishment's culture, but all came to conclude that these institutions were organisationally and culturally inappropriate places for raising young people to become fully rounded, socialised future citizens.

Their efforts, inside and outside the institution, played a huge part in bringing to an end the system of barrack schools, which for 50 years FGDS was a prominent and rather dreadful example.

NOTES

[1]   Peter Higginbotham, *Workhouse Encyclopaedia*, The History Press, 2012, p. 323

[2]   George, Dorothy, *London Life in the Eighteenth Century*, 1966, p. 47

[3]   *Oxford Dictionary of National Biography*

[4]   Higginbotham, *Encyclopaedia*, p. 60

[5]   Alexander Michael Ross, *The Care and Education of Pauper Children in England and Wales*. PhD thesis, University of London 1955 – *www.core.ac.uk/download/pdf/1882891.pdf*, p. 31

[6]   Peter Higginbotham, *Children's Homes – A History of Institutional Care for Britain's Young*, Pen and Sword, 2017, pp. 196-8

[7]   Higginbotham, *Encyclopaedia*, p. 83

[8]   Charles Dickens, *Household Words* Vol 1, No 23, 1850, pp. 549-552

[9]   *The Examiner*, 27 June 1849

[10] The Appendix provides an outline summary of the institutional provisions adopted by poor law unions in east and north-east London from the 1850s onwards. Almost all of these unions established some kind of 'school' for their young in nearby Essex.

CHAPTER 2

WHITECHAPEL'S CHILDREN'S WORKHOUSE

The population of London rose from one million to two and a half million during the first half of the nineteenth century; its seams were bursting and overspill land was needed.

The 1844 Poor Law Amendment Act replaced and built on the philosophy of the 1766 Hanway Act, which had established a direction of thought for public policy relating to poor law children. The new legislation facilitated the development of customised institutional care for London's pauper young, in rural areas. Schools, children's homes and orphanages were soon founded in Lewisham, Hendon, Merton and Barnet – all then outside the metropolitan boundaries – established by London unions to accommodate their workhouse children.

West Essex, a largely agricultural and part marshy land to the east of the River Lea, provided a safety valve for accommodating East End pauper children from the 1850s. East and north-east London poor law unions established institutions in the territory for their impoverished young. Shoreditch, having initially established a school in Enfield in 1848, developed a larger one in Brentwood in 1854.[1]

St George in the East Board of Guardians (effectively Wapping) purchased eight acres of land off Gipsy Lane (now Green Street) in Plashet, west Essex in 1849 'sufficiently capacious for the reception of the pauper children of that union', in order to build an institution. The land was agricultural in nature and just a mile from Forest Gate.

Whitechapel guardians entered into discussions with St George in the

East's about accommodating their children within the new facility.[2] In the event, they could not agree on terms and withdrew from the discussions. They started to look for similar land, close by, upon which to build their own establishment.[3]

Whitechapel, the most westerly of the east London unions, is situated on the borders of the City. Historically it had been home to the many trades and industries that serviced the affluent area – breweries, Spitalfields Market, silk weaving, slaughterhouses and the Whitechapel Bell foundry among them – to such an extent that it came to be known as 'the other half' of London. It was also home to many London wharves and early docks.

As a port, it attracted waves of immigrants: Huguenots in the late seventeenth and eighteenth centuries, sailors working for the East India Company, German and Dutch Jews in the early nineteenth century and a huge number of Irish immigrants from the 1840s fleeing the Great Famine.

By the middle of the nineteenth century, the once prosperous Huguenot population was squeezed, economically, by the industrialisation of other textile trades, and fell on hard times. Many of the subsequent tranches of immigrants entered the area impoverished, and sought refuge in the casual industries that proliferated within the district. By the 1850s, Whitechapel was a rapidly expanding but poor area, increasingly characterised by economic insecurity, grossly overcrowded slums and a high dependency on poor law support in times of economic downturn.

As a result, its union had one of London's largest workhouses and its guardians sought a separate site to house its pauper young – which accounted for its discussions with St George in the East.

LONDON 'OVER THE BORDER'

West Essex was adjacent to Epping Forest and before the mid-nineteenth century it had been sparsely populated. The land adjoining the banks of the Thames, to the south, was marshy and had been of little economic value, while that further north, including Plashet and Forest Gate, east of the Lea, was more fertile and agricultural in nature.

The whole area experienced a huge lease of non-agricultural life from the 1850s, which accounted for the creation of the borough of West Ham – the fastest growing urban area of Britain in the second half of the nineteenth century. The banks of the rivers Lea and Thames offered land for the location and relocation of services as well as factories from the rapidly expanding metropolis, and became the industrial catalyst for the complete transformation of the area. The northern part of the emerging borough eventually became a massive sprawl of late-Victorian housing, but not before the establishment of Forest Gate's workhouse school within its boundaries.

Edwin Chadwick (1800–1890) played a significant role in the development of West Ham, both north and south, quite unwittingly. He worked for the Poor Law Commission that set the framework from which eventually emerged the FGDS. Then, from the late 1830s until 1854, he was mainly associated with public health reform, and recommended moving burial grounds out of metropolitan areas into the countryside, a policy formally adopted in 1850, which was to help define the area.[4]

Six cemeteries, covering almost 400 acres, were built around this less marshy northern part of what is now Newham, all within a five-mile radius of Forest Gate. The City of London cemetery, itself covering 200 acres, was constructed between 1853 and 1856 and is within a mile of the site of what was simultaneously developing as Forest Gate's poor law school. Bodies could be buried in these cemeteries safe in the knowledge that they would not resurface during bad weather, as they may have done in the boggy marsh lands closer to the Thames.

The riverside parts of West Ham were also affected by Chadwick's public health work, which had inspired the passage of the 1848 Public Health Act and various Metropolitan Building Acts. These, collectively, encouraged and directed the establishment and transference of a number of industrial functions, which were prejudicial to London's public health, to those riverbanks.

Many so-called obnoxious industries – chemicals, tanning, food processing and the like – moved from inner London to these areas, on land which, 150 years later in 2012, was to form the basis of Stratford's Olympic Park.[5]

It became convenient to dump London's public health problems on west Essex. Civil engineer Joseph Bazalgette (1819–1891) looked to the Thames at Beckton, which was within the area, for the destination of his central London sewerage system, established in response to the Westminster 'great stink' of 1858. The nearby Abbey Mills pumping station – later dubbed the cathedral of sewerage – was part of his elaborate system and opened in 1866. In a separate venture, by 1870, adjacent Beckton became the home of the largest gas works in Europe.

The pressures on London as an expanding mercantile centre, brought such a demand for increased ship-building capacity and docking facilities, that their traditional local home – the Pool of London – was no longer able to cope. The Victoria Docks were constructed on what was previously the uninhabited Plaistow Marshes and soon became Europe's largest dock.

The land two or three miles further north of the Thames and a mile east of the Lea could not accommodate water-based industries, or those requiring good river links, but did offer cheap solutions for some of London's other unwanted problems.

One local man who spotted the great potential that well-connected, rural Forest Gate land offered to the rapidly expanding metropolis was shrewd businessman, Norfolk-born Samuel Gurney (1786–1856). In 1812 he had acquired, through marriage, Ham House, a large country seat in the then hamlet of Upton, to the south of the area. He was Britain's pre-eminent financier, known as the 'banker's banker' and his country house was a relatively easy carriage ride to his place of work in the City.[6]

He was also a significant social reformer, and actively assisted his sister, Elizabeth Fry with her prison reform work, as well as his in-laws, the Buxton family, with their anti-slavery campaigning. He fought to establish Liberia as an African colony for freed American slaves and financially supported many of those affected by the Irish hunger of the mid 1840s. He opposed capital punishment, and put his own liberty at risk by providing an alibi for a man who otherwise would have faced the noose.[7]

His philanthropy in east London and Essex funded a hospital to deal with industrial accidents in Poplar (that later became St Andrew's) and provided land, without charge, for the construction of church-based schools in Forest Gate, before the establishment of board schools. He is remembered in nearby Stratford by a large obelisk, erected in his honour by 'Friends', a reference to both his fellow Quakers and his wider social and business circles.

When it came to land acquisition, however, Gurney wore his business rather than philanthropic hat. He had started buying land in the latter stages of his life after scaling back his involvement in banking. He had purchased more than 600 acres of local agricultural land, in various parcels from the mid-1840s (Woodgrange, Greenhill and Hamfrith farms among them) in the Forest Gate and Little Ilford areas. To put this in context, the total acreage of Forest Gate today is only about 800 acres. The 'going rate' for these land purchases was around £135 per acre.[8]

One of the plots he purchased was to the north of Forest Lane, almost adjoining the Great Eastern Railway (GER) rail track. An 1821 survey by James Clayton indicated that it had been owned by the Peacock family, and Gurney bought it from them in 1846, just after the adjacent railway line had started servicing the area. He soon set about reselling it, at a handsome profit, to public bodies that appreciated the benefits of easily accessible and low-cost undeveloped land, a short distance from the City.[9]

It was to Gurney that the Whitechapel guardians turned when their negotiations about co-locating an institution with St George floundered.[10] The union's headquarters in Charles Street would have been on Gurney's route from his home in Upton to his offices in the City's Lombard Street. In 1852, he sold the Whitechapel guardians 12 acres of his recently purchased Peacock plot for £220 per acre – a 60 per cent premium over his purchase price. It was on this that they built their poor law school.

Forest Gate had the advantage of being rural and less than six miles away from the Whitechapel workhouse. It was easily accessible by rail, with a station just three stops away on the GER. Forest Gate Station originally opened in 1841, although it closed between 1844 and 1846 due to a lack of passengers.

Having sold the land on which the workhouse school was to be built, Gurney moved to cash in on the out-of-the-metropolis cemeteries boom. He sold a plot of land adjacent to the school site to the New Synagogue, in 1856, for the construction of a Jewish cemetery. He had also set in motion the sale of 12 contiguous acres to the West Ham Burial Board, to build West Ham cemetery before his death later that year.[11]

And so it was that west Essex became a repository for many of the metropolis' unwanted problems, whether stinky industries, effluent, dead bodies or unwanted children, earning itself the title promoted by Charles Dickens as London 'over the border'.[12]

Gurney's heirs, over the next 40 years, continued the land disposal programme, which was hastened by financial difficulties the family bank encountered after his death. They sold much of the land for property development and established the basis of what is largely the late Victorian suburb of Forest Gate. The population of West Ham rose almost fifteenfold, from 18,817 in 1851 to 267,358 over the next half century.

WORKHOUSE SCHOOL FOUNDED

The *Essex Standard* tracked the construction of the Whitechapel institution in Forest Gate. In April 1853, it reported that rapid progress was being made in building the facility 'intended for 400 children'. The paper was of the opinion that the Forest Lane establishment, like its Plashet counterpart, would 'form a new and important feature in the treatment of the pauper children of the metropolis'. It asserted confidently that the training regimes proposed at the two establishments 'cannot fail to meet the approval of those who feel an interest in the welfare of the juvenile portion of the pauper population of the metropolis.'

Six months later the paper was able to report that the West Ham Gas Company was extending its reach 'to supply the Whitechapel Industrial Schools with 250 lights, as in every portion of that establishment gas will be used, including sleeping and living rooms, inner and outer offices etc.' [13]

After a further five months the same newspaper reported that construction was developing apace for the Whitechapel union, who had more pauper children than any other metropolitan parish. The buildings stood in 12 acres and its gardens were to be cultivated by its 'inmates'. Like its St George in the East neighbour, Whitechapel's 'receptacle' would be open for inspection by the public, every day of the week, a visit to which the newspaper recommended its readers. [14]

The choice of language in the short article is indicative of the way in which the pupils were regarded at the time, and confirmed that it was seen as a junior workhouse. They were referred to twice as 'pauper children', who were 'inmates' of a 'receptacle', words which suggest an undesirable underclass, a widely held social response to the children of the poor. It was this prevailing attitude that enabled much of the callous treatment of those children to go unchecked in an institution created to accommodate them.

The children's workhouse opened its doors for the first trickle of youngsters, with no fanfare, in May 1854. [15] A week later, *The Standard* was able to wax lyrically about its virtues, which it felt would soon be copied by other metropolitan districts and by unions further afield. The language used again pointedly reflected prevailing attitudes, including a reference to the children as 'the inmates of such asylums'. It reiterated its invitation to readers to visit the buildings, where they would be made most welcome. [16] As will become evident, the welcoming open door to visitors was soon closed. It quickly became clear that conditions there were pretty scandalous and not suitable for public inspection.

The establishment had capacity for more children than Whitechapel required, so its guardians sublet space to other unions, in order to subsidise their own requirements. St Pancras was the first to sign up and its guardians agreed to pay a fixed annual sum to accommodate up to 150 of their poor young, irrespective of the use they made of it.[17]

For 14 years, the Forest Gate facility operated as a Whitechapel-owned institution, with surplus space sublet to the guardians of other unions. Hackney, Poplar and West Ham joined St Pancras in sending their children, under contract. The story of those 14 years was of one minor scandal after another, and of a lack of care and compassion towards the 700 or so children accommodated within it – highlighted most clearly by some of the contracting unions.

The children from St Pancras had their own teachers in the institution, although the rules governing them were decided by Whitechapel. In September 1856, a St Pancras teacher, Mr Potter, wrote to his guardians about corporal punishment inflicted on their boys. He said that seven of them had been flogged, by order of the governors, receiving an average of five lashes each, most resulting in the letting of blood. The punishment he reported was 'inflicted by the [Whitechapel] schoolmaster on the children's naked persons, when laid across a desk, with a bunch of birch rods.'[18]

St Pancras ordered an inquiry, and put Whitechapel on notice that the arrangements between the two unions were in jeopardy. The inquiry reported four weeks later and concluded that although there were beatings, Potter had exaggerated their extent. It would not be the only time that the whistleblower was sacked for raising a matter of concern. Several St Pancras guardians, however, took the opportunity to 'express their strong opposition to corporal punishment in any form'.[19] It would be easy to dismiss complainant Potter as an embittered troublemaker, for which he paid a heavy price, if it were not for the fact that within a month, other serious allegations emerged.

The PLB had previously been very critical of St Pancras because of the very cramped conditions in which its children were kept in its own workhouse. In particular its medical officer had reported that the children had an inadequate 450 cubic feet of space each in their dormitories. Following a visit to Forest Gate in 1856, a St Pancras guardian found that the dormitories were even more crowded than that, with each child having an average of 250 cubic feet, and that, 'Moreover under the windows was the most pestiferous cesspit he had ever smelt.' 'A reference, presumably, to an open, unplumbed-in toilet in the sleeping quarters,' opined the *Northern Daily Times*.[20]

Within a year, St Pancras guardians were told of 'the disgraceful state in which the poor pauper children's clothes – but more especially the shoes and stockings were in.'[21] Guardians were so appalled by what they saw that they brought samples back to show their colleagues. The *Marylebone Mercury* took the story up:

> Several of the children's boots and socks were produced before the Board and aroused the indignation of everyone present. The shoes were completely worn through, they were soleless, and the socks were in a filthy condition and in complete tatters ... one boy informed the committee that they had not had clean socks for three weeks ... . The rough worsted stockings were in the most filthy state, the feet being rotted, almost, away.[22]

One of the visitors, a Mr Stockton, urged the St Pancras guardians to erect its own facility, for the protection of its parish's children. The Whitechapel guardians defended themselves, claiming that matters weren't as bad as had been reported, and blamed junior staff for the problems identified. They said, 'As to the bad stockings ... any neglect in this matter arose from the fact there being two nurses who were not conversant with their duties, and through the temporary absence of the superintendent.' They also blamed deficiencies on the part of their suppliers for some of the shoddy clothing.[23]

Having absolved themselves of responsibility, the Whitechapel guardians attacked their St Pancras opposite numbers for 'allowing the discipline of the school to be subverted, by questioning the children as to their diet etc.' Unadvisedly, they then 'invited the directors of that parish [St Pancras] to attend at mealtimes and judge for themselves.'

And they did just that. One St Pancras guardian, Mr Tomlinson, reinforced earlier objections, complaining that he 'was then dissatisfied with the slovenly appearance of the children and the way in which the meals were served up', and another, Mr Cameron, repeated the plea for St Pancras to build its own establishment. Although the chairman of the guardians was sympathetic to these requests, he 'expressed his fear that, at the present time, they could not think of laying out a sum, of perhaps £10,000 for parish schools.'[24] The writing was on the wall for the future of the arrangement between St Pancras and Whitechapel, which was of concern to Whitechapel because St Pancras was paying over a quarter of the institution's running costs.[25]

A bizarre court case, the following year, confirmed the neglect suffered by some of the youngsters in Forest Gate. A mother who had tried to track her missing daughter down found her in the establishment, where she was 'In such a dreadful state from filth and disease ... the forefinger of her right hand had been cut off ... the stump appeared diseased.' The girl also had open abscesses on her face.[26]

An altogether separate concern related to the treatment of its Catholic pupils. The 1845 Act For The Further Amendment Of The Laws Relating To The Poor In England decreed that a CofE chaplain, who was approved by the local bishop, should be appointed to all workhouse schools. His job would be to oversee the religious instruction of all pupils. The Act required that creed registers be kept and made provision for children of other faiths and denominations to be attended to by their own ministers.

Irish immigration to Whitechapel, following the hunger of the 1840s, was considerable; they were overwhelmingly poor and Roman Catholic. Many second and third generation people of Irish heritage continued to live in poverty and ended up in the Whitechapel workhouse, with their children sent to Forest Gate – they accounted for up to 15 per cent of the inmates. According to the 1845 legislation, they were entitled access to Catholic priests. However, the establishment, in common with other child work-houses in London, came under repeated attack from the Catholic church for sidestepping this obligation. The issue became a long running saga at the school and later at its spin-off establishment, TS *Goliath*.

In April 1859, *The Tablet*, reported a public meeting in Whitechapel, where priests criticised the lack of access and facilities offered by children's workhouses to the 'hundreds' of Catholics resident in them, along the lines of 'we pay our taxes, we want equal access to our children'. Speaking of Forest Gate, one participant said that he had sent six letters there asking about Catholic children from his parish and not had a single reply, and that 'a Catholic priest had not been allowed to visit any of the cases.' He maintained the law was not being upheld, nor would it be until a Catholic priest was appointed there. He concluded by saying that as 'they paid their poor-rates, they had a right to a share in the proceeds of the common fund.'[27]

A year later the *Essex Standard* illustrated how much more care and attention was paid to meeting the faith needs of the school's CofE pupils, when it reported that up to 100 of them were taken each week for services to the two nearest churches.[28]

Despite the complaints from the Catholic community, the Whitechapel guardians were unmoved and failed to address their concerns. Two years later similar criticisms were aired by priests about the Forest Gate establishment, in the Irish press. The Rev James Macguoin said that he had visited the facility and although there were in the region of 100 Catholic children resident, he was only given access to eight or nine of them in a cold, crowded room. He also complained that many of the books he had left with them became defaced and mutilated and that he was abused and called names, such as 'papist' and 'Romanist' by other children 'and they were not chided for it.'

He continued: 'in many instances the children said they would become Catholics whenever they left the school, but that they were afraid to be Catholic while in the school, lest the other children would ill-use them.' He quoted examples of children's and parents' religious wishes – even when put in writing – being ignored; and cited that as a final rebuff and insult to his faith, after he 'gave catechisms to the Catholic children, and when the guardians heard of it they suspended me.' The Catholic children issue was not satisfactorily resolved at Forest Gate, by a clearly discriminatory and hostile set of managers and governors, and was to return in a significant way a decade later.

Two months after this controversy, St Pancras' guardians agreed, in principle, to establish their own children's workhouse in Finchley, on land they owned, at a cost of £8,000. The savings of £3,000 per year, charged by Whitechapel for Forest Gate, were seen as partial compensation for the costs of its construction.

During the debate about building this, St Pancras' guardians expressed more concerns about Forest Gate, including that it had 'lost' 15 of their children, as they could no longer account for them. The guardians were told that children kept running away from Forest Lane, and one of their number pronounced that he did not believe the location was a healthy one for the children.[29]

A year later, the Whitechapel union advertised for a new 'Master and Matron' of its Forest Gate establishment, with salaries of £80 and £50 respectively, plus rations and furnished apartments. The advert said the couple needed to be married and gave some indication of the duties of the master, but not of the matron. The first quality required was an ability to keep the books, as demanded by the PLB, and secondly to 'superintend the cultivation, by the boys, of the grounds attached to the school, about 9 acres; and the industrial training of the children in the establishment.'[30]

No mention was made of the educational needs or the care of the children. A couple, James and Elizabeth Barnett, were appointed, but their presence had no immediate beneficial impact on conditions. Just two years later, a visit by some Poplar guardians found 30 of their children were ill, and that they saw 'nine children eating their dinners with their fingers, no spoons or anything being supplied to them.'

The visitors commented that, 'There were fully two-thirds of the whole of the children at the Forest Gate institution who were suffering from some kind of disease.' So horrified were they with what they saw, they resolved unanimously to take immediate steps to find another facility 'so that the whole of the children might be removed from Forest Gate school, and that the Whitechapel Guardians be informed of the cause of these proceedings.'[31] Three months' notice was required to terminate the 'arrangement which has for so long existed between the boards.'[32]

In a strongly worded editorial, the *East London Observer* commented that it was only the vigilance of Poplar's guardians that had brought the matters to light: 'If the evil be as bad as we are led to believe it is by these reports, then vigorous steps should be at once adopted to remedy them and to visit on their authors the inevitable penalties.'[33]

However, while the paper expressed concerns about the health of the children, it had greater worries about the impact of Poplar's decision on Whitechapel's ratepayers: 'If Poplar removes 130 children, and other parishes also remove, we shall have an enormous establishment, kept up at the same salaries, for a comparatively few children, thus, materially enhancing the cost of each child.' In the event, Poplar guardians did not proceed with their threat because of the contractual obligations with Whitechapel. In any case, they soon discovered that there was no suitable accommodation available elsewhere to house their children.

St Pancras' resolve to leave Forest Gate was reinforced by its own rapidly growing population and workhouse numbers. The Finchley land on which it had considered building its facility proved to be insufficient to meet the union's needs. So, the guardians switched their plans further north and began constructing an establishment in Leavesden, near Watford, which they opened in 1870 with 700 residents.

Meanwhile, the population of West Ham was also growing rapidly, and its union began a search for accommodation for its pauper children, and prudently sought a competitive price for a bulk placement in a local institution. They were quoted six shillings per week per child at Plashet, but only 5s 6d at Forest Gate.[34] They chose the latter, and sent 60 children there from March 1864.[35]

The Whitechapel guardians were in uncomfortable territory. There was a demand from other unions for the surplus places at their establishment but they had to manage it better, or their contracts could be terminated, leaving their own ratepayers with the financial burden. In order to regularise this, and minimise their exposure to fluctuations of demand, they wanted West Ham to enter into a longer-term arrangement for placing their children in Forest Gate. The West Ham guardians had no such desire.[36]

Poplar and Hackney, meanwhile, also had a dilemma. They faced unwanted competition from other unions for the space in Forest Gate, but depended upon a less-than-satisfactory institution in which to house them.

The 1867 Metropolitan Poor Act provided a solution for Hackney, Poplar and Whitechapel; it encouraged the creation of district schools to be managed by a committee of representatives of participating, London, unions. The move was welcomed by much of the press, The *Illustrated Times*, for example, commented that:

> Nothing destroys the independence of character and engenders the pauper spirit so effectively as associating with paupers. The race of workhouse children if reared away from workhouses, may be so trained as to cease to be in their turn, as they have hitherto generally been, the propagators of pauperism.[37]

The Act created an all-London body, the Metropolitan Common Poor Law Fund (MCPLF), to be financed by contributions from all London poor law unions to effectively pay for the education and maintenance costs of pupils attending the establishments. The Act also gave the PLB the right to appoint up to a third of the members of the governing committees, so that a wider range of views and experience could be brought to their administration.

West Ham was not eligible to join such a district, as it was not a 'metropolitan union'. So, from Poplar and Hackney's perspective, a would-be competitor for places at the establishment was eliminated. From Whitechapel's position, the costs of running the facility would be shared with the London body and two other unions. Additionally, any future complaints received would be delegated to a 'Board of Managers' [henceforth referred to as governors[38]] consisting largely of representatives of the three unions.

The unions had to agree to the coalition, and the compensation the new body would pay Whitechapel for taking over its premises. The figure was fixed at £34,000, with unions contributing pro rata to their rateable values. This meant: Hackney 41 per cent (£14,000), Poplar 37 per cent (£12,500) and Whitechapel 22 per cent (£7,500). Hackney and Poplar paid their contributions to Whitechapel, to buy it out of sole ownership of the institution.[39]

Having agreed the details, the three unions applied to the PLB for its approval, which it gave, under its newly acquired powers, and the Forest Gate District School was founded. The *East London Observer* explained the position succinctly:

> A letter was read [to the Poplar guardians] from the Poor Law Board stating that at present there was no separate school for the Poplar children, and that the union should be included in a school district. The children of Poplar district and Hackney parishes were at present at Forest Gate in the school belonging to Whitechapel. The PLB therefore, under the power given to them by the Act of 1867, had determined to issue an order to combine the three parishes into one district, for school purposes, and the order would be transmitted forthwith.[40]

And so, with the establishment of the FGDS, everyone got what they wanted. It seemed like a match made in heaven, except the numbers didn't add up.

Within weeks of the establishment of the district school, the PLB told its governors it was overcrowded. Other problems surfaced and Hackney soon wanted out. The three-union district lasted just eight years.

NOTES

[1]   For a more detailed account of solutions adopted by the east London Unions, see Appendix

[2]   *Essex Standard*, 30 May and 3 Jun 1851

[3]   *Essex Standard*, 30 May 1851

[4]   *Oxford Dictionary of National Biography*

[5]   For an excellent account of the history and process, see: Jim Clifford, *West Ham and the River Lea – A Social and Environmental History of London's Industrialised Marshland,* *1839–1914*, UBC Press, 2017

[6]   www.e7-nowandthen.org/2017/12/samuel-gurney-1786-1856-forest-gate.html

[7]   Ibid

[8]   He bought the 131 acre Hamfrith estate in 1851 for £17,710

[9]   E. R. Gamester, *The History of Forest Gate Hospital,* published by Friends of Forest Gate Hospital, 1954

[10] Alan Palmer, *The East End – Four Centuries*

of London Life, John Murray 1989, p. 68

[11] *Essex Standard*, 4 Jul 1855

[12] The rapid uncontrolled development of West Ham provoked its own public health problems and the government appointed Alfred Dickens – Charles' civil engineering brother – to examine the jerry-built housing and cholera-inducing state of the area in 1855, and make recommendations for their future amelioration. The findings were shocking as recorded in the *Report to the General Board of Health on a preliminary enquiry into the sewerage, drainage and supply of water and the sanitary conditions of the inhabitants in the parish of West Ham*, Her Majesty's Stationery Office 1855. Two years later, Charles Dickens published an article in *Household Words*, a weekly paper he edited, pointedly called 'Londoners over the Border'. The article had been penned by Henry Morley (*Household Words*, 12 Sep 1857), and its title, as a description of the area, stuck, and is still cited to this day (e.g. in the title of Neil Fraser's 2012 book *Over the Border – The Other East End*).

[13] *Essex Standard*, 18 Nov 1853

[14] Ibid, 17 Mar 1854

[15] Ibid, 31 May 1854

[16] Ibid, 2 Jun 1854

[17] *Northern Daily Times*, 4 Nov 1856

[18] *The Morning Advertiser*, 18 Sep 1856

[19] *Wiltshire and Gloucestershire Standard*, 11 Oct 1856

[20] *Northern Daily Times*, 4 Nov 1856

[21] *The Morning Advertiser*, 28 Oct 1857

[22] *Marylebone Mercury*, 31 Oct 1857

[23] *Marylebone Mercury*, 28 Nov 1857

[24] Ibid

[25] *The Globe*, 26 Dec 1857

[26] *Morning Chronicle*, 27 Sep 1858

[27] *The Tablet*, 2 Apr 1859

[28] *Essex Standard*, 13 Apr 1860

[29] *Marylebone Mercury*, 14 Jun 1859

[30] *East London Observer* (*ELO*), 4 Aug 1860

[31] Ibid, 6 Sep 1862

[32] Ibid, 13 Sep 1862

[33] Ibid

[34] *The Essex Herald*, 17 Jan 1865

[35] Strangely, the West Ham workhouse was not within the boundaries of West Ham but the two institutions they sought quotes from were, although they were run by non-West Ham unions.

[36] *Chelmsford Chronicle*, 3 Mar 1865

[37] *Illustrated Times*, 16 Feb 1867

[38] See a Note on Terminology, p xii, above.

[39] London Metropolitan Archives (LMA): FGSD-001

[40] *ELO*, 13 Jun 1868

CHAPTER 3

DISTRICT ESTABLISHED

To give an indication of the nature of child destitution at a time the school district was established, fewer than a quarter of its original pupils had parents in a workhouse; almost a half were orphans and over a quarter had been deserted. Unsurprisingly, Whitechapel, as the founder union of what had become the Forest Gate School District, provided the largest number of pupils – 389 (43 per cent), with Poplar supplying 257 (30 per cent) and Hackney the fewest, with 213 (25 per cent).

The original intake of the school, by gender, union and category of child was:

	Orphans[1]		Deserted		Parents in workhouse		Total
	M	F	M	F	M	F	
Whitechapel	122	76	44	60	39	48	389
Poplar	45	45	46	52	42	27	257
Hackney	62	41	20	28	33	29	213
Total	**229**	**162**	**110**	**140**	**114**	**104**	**859**
Orphans: 391; Deserted: 250; Parents in Workhouse: 218							

REGIME RULES

The PLB launched the FGSD with a 10-page, tightly printed memorandum which defined who the child recruits were to be and what was expected of them. It also provided detailed job descriptions of all categories of staff and outlined the functions and relationships between every part of the institution.

The establishment was to have a managing committee, elected from each of the three constituent unions, but the participating boards themselves were to have no direct control. To be eligible for governorship, a candidate was required to occupy a property in the area with a rateable value in excess of £40 per annum – which effectively excluded anybody but comfortably middle-class people. Women were not excluded from membership, but mid-Victorian property ownership patterns meant few were eligible.

Funding of the district was to be shared between the unions, in proportion to their rateable values. The cost of the maintenance of the children and staff salaries were to be paid by the recently created MCPLF. Salaries were to be determined by the PLB, who kept a tight rein on all staffing and spending matters.

This arrangement provided an ongoing source of tension between the governors, who often wanted to increase salaries, and the PLB, who usually denied the request in the interest of frugality. A consequence was that staff at all levels were poorly paid, which, in turn, affected their quality, competence and effectiveness.

Economist and Poor Law Commission advisor Nassau Senior crystallised the complexity of the problem, when he wrote in 1861:

> The position of the workhouse schoolmaster is peculiar. He is appointed by the guardians and paid by the Treasury, according to a scale fixed by the Poor Law Board. His rank on that scale, which regulated his emoluments, is decided by the Privy Council Inspector and he is dismissed by the Poor Law Board. Those who appoint him do not pay him and cannot dismiss him. Those who pay him know nothing of his qualifications, and those who assign to him his salary are not his employers.[2]

All contracts for goods and services, as well as job vacancies, were to be externally advertised, to ensure transparency and avoid obvious corruption – a frequent complaint about many previous poor law institutions.[3]

Children could be admitted from any of the three unions, accompanied by an admission form. Typically, the age range was from two to 14. In 1873, for example, in a note of guidance, the Local Government Board (LGB – successor to the PLB) wrote to the FGSD: 'As a general rule, the children should be received into the infants' school as soon after two years of age as … they are fit to be removed from the nursery in the workhouse.'[4]

There was pressure on the establishment to release children once they had reached 14, as their home union wished to save on the cost of sending them there. Sometimes, the 14 year olds were sent straight back to the workhouse, but the institution frequently attempted to launch them into the outside world, unsupported. Advertisements were regularly placed in the local press seeking positions for the youngsters, such as 'several boys and girls … who have attained the age of fourteen years and upwards and are considered to be adapted for learning trades and employment as servants … . Applications sought, in writing, or in person.'[5] It was not until 1876 that after-care arrangements were adopted, and then initially, only for girls.

On admission, the children were placed in the reception ward and examined by the medical officer. If they were unfit or unwell, they were placed in a sick ward. If fit, they were sent to a class appropriate to their gender and age (i.e. girls seven – 14; boys seven – 14 and infants – under seven). No child was to be kept in the reception ward longer than necessary.

On admission, the child's clothes were to be taken, disinfected and stored ready to be returned on departure. The child was then strip searched, to prevent forbidden objects entering the place.

Once assigned to a class, the child was to remain there, in its own classroom, day room, dormitory and yard 'without contamination with those in other classes'. In other words, in a punitive act, siblings could be separated, with little prospect of ever meeting up again until they finally left the institution.

An exception to enforced separation was that some older girls could be asked to assist with housework in the infants' section, as part of their industrial training as domestic servants. Some seven to nine year olds could be held in the infants' section until their educational attainment allowed them to progress to the older-aged classes. In very exceptional cases, and only with the prior permission of the superintendent, mixed sex classes could be undertaken for the oldest pupils.

The PLB was responsible for determining the maximum number of children and it, and the governors, had to be informed immediately if that figure were exceeded. Much governor and PLB time was spent addressing this issue.

Options examined for dealing with excess numbers included building additional accommodation and placing 'surplus' children elsewhere. In some cases the children would have to remain in the home workhouse until places in the school became available – thus partially defeating the object of establishing the institution.

Although children could be admitted to FGSD as young as two, and would occasionally remain in Forest Gate until they reached 16, they would be discharged if their parents left the sponsoring union's workhouse. As parents moved in and out of workhouses, the children followed them in and out of the establishment.

The problem with the 'ins and outs' as these children were to be known, caused ongoing difficulties. Children could be returned to their workhouse of origin if they were deemed disruptive.

The governors established the daily timetable, subject to ratification by the PLB. All significant changes of activity during the day were to be undertaken in silence, after a peal of a bell. A register of pupils was taken each day, half an hour after the set time for rising, and was accompanied by an inspection of each child for cleanliness. The governors determined the children's clothing and uniforms.

Children were only allowed into their dormitories during assigned sleeping hours. Conditions were cramped. No more than two children over the age of seven could share a bed (implying that below that age a greater number was permissible) and that boys over the age of 10 had to have sole occupancy of one. Cramped as these conditions appear today, they were far better than those experienced by many children living in slum housing, outside the workhouse system.

All meals were to be taken in the dining room, unless a child was in the sick ward, and 'during the time of meals silence, order and decorum shall be maintained.' The children were fed in accordance with a dietary table prescribed by the PLB, and there was to be no deviation from it, except in cases of sickness and on Christmas and some saints days. The superintendent (for boys) and matron (for infants and girls) assigned industrial training to each pupil and 'every child capable of working shall be trained and instructed in some branch of industry, or in agricultural or household work.'

The establishment had to ensure that each child received a minimum of 18 hours per week instruction in the three Rs and 'the principles of the Christian religion', together with whatever else the superintendent and governors deemed suitable. If any child left to work for an outside employer and later returned, they were not permitted to continue with education but were expected to be occupied exclusively on industrial training.

Children could only be visited by parents and relatives with the prior approval of the superintendent, and only once every two months.[6] The visits were similar to those currently conducted in modern prisons. Visitors were searched before entering the buildings and forbidden substances (including all food and drink) were removed. Visits took place in a room established solely for that purpose, and always under the supervision of a member of staff.

No books were allowed, unless explicitly approved of by the governors, except for religious books introduced by non-CofE clergy, for the sole use of their flocks. No cards, dice or any other games of chance were permitted. There was to be no non-essential work undertaken by the pupils on Sundays – a day set aside for religious services and reflection.

Misbehaviour was punished by a bread and water diet for up to 48 hours. Bad behaviour was defined as lying, swearing, insulting, being unclean, being inattentive at school, gambling, not obeying orders, attempting unauthorised departures and misbehaving during religious services or worship.

Repeated or escalated bad behaviour could be punished by 24-hours solitary confinement on a bread and water diet, or by corporal punishment. Only the superintendent or teaching staff were permitted to inflict corporal punishment. It had to be administered in the presence of a witness and could only be inflicted two hours after the commission of the offence for which it was imposed. A punishment book was kept, in which all measures were recorded, and this was available to the governors for inspection and comment.

The governors were expected to appoint a 'Visiting Committee', from among themselves, whose job was to inspect the establishment at least once a week and report back to the other governors. It was to report on the state and cleanliness of all parts of the buildings, suitability of education provided, training offered, medical provision supplied, and religious observance fulfilled. It was to hear any complaints from pupils or staff, and report its findings to other governors. It was delegated responsibility for ensuring that the PLB-defined maximum roll was not exceeded.

The superintendent was required to be at least 21 and be able to maintain a set of accounts; there was no requirement for him to have any education, care qualifications or experience. If he were married to the matron, and one of them resigned, the other was required to leave too. The marital status of the superintendent was taken very seriously, as will become clear, and when it changed, postholders were expected to resign, and seek re-appointment under the changed status. This was not always sanctioned.

He was responsible for all admissions and for the care and welfare of all boys over the age of seven. He was expected to 'enforce industry, order, punctuality and cleanliness', and was required to ensure that prayers were read each day at breakfast and supper. It was also his job to inspect all rooms, each day, for cleanliness and to ensure that all meals were delivered appropriately.

The superintendent oversaw the industrial training of the boys and visited them in their dormitory each night, before lights out, to satisfy himself that calm prevailed. It was his job to see they were properly clothed and that their clothes were repaired, when necessary.

He had certain public health responsibilities: managing the medical officer, ensuring sickness records were maintained and reported to the PLB, ensuring that relevant authorities were informed of illnesses, and that appropriate arrangements were made in the event of the death of a child. He was responsible for ensuring that the roll did not exceed the maximum permitted number.

He was ultimately responsible for the execution of all regulatory and administrative procedures and that the institution had appropriate provisions, which were to be adequately accounted for. He was required to maintain a register of all children leaving the establishment for work in industry.

The superintendent was expected to ensure the cleanliness and smooth running of the kitchen and food preparation areas, and was required to operate a complaints system, accessible to the pupils, reporting its details to the governors. He was to maintain the minute book and keep governors and visitors informed of the state of the institution. He was ultimately accountable to the governors for its smooth running. It was quite clear that in all matters in the establishment, the buck stopped with the superintendent.

The matron was the superintendent's deputy and was expected to supervise, for the girls and infants, what the superintendent did for the boys: their behaviour, dormitories, cleanliness, industrial training etc. In addition, she had full establishment responsibilities for ensuring that all clothes were clean, repaired and labelled with the institution's name. She had to see that the children's linen was clean and changed regularly and that the laundry was properly managed. She had responsibility for all female staff.

The medical officer was expected to attend the establishment each day and be available if called out during out-of-hours periods. He was responsible for maintaining all medical records, issuing medicines, vaccinating children and recommending diets for sick children. He was to report any potential public health issues to the superintendent and governors and keep treatment records up to date and available for inspection by governors and the PLB.

The nurses worked for the medical officer and were required to keep the superintendent and matron informed on all health matters. They were responsible for the sick wards, ensuring that they were well-ventilated and warm and had lights on at night, and they were paid between £14 and £17 per annum. Fortunately, the nurses were required to show they could read the instructions on a bottle of medicine, and the medical officer had to hold (unspecified) medical qualifications.

The school masters and mistresses were required to teach for at least 18 hours per week and to accompany the children for all periods of exercise and on any trips away from the premises. They were to inspect the children daily, to ensure cleanliness and discipline were maintained and were to enforce compliance with all rules. They were expected to report to governors when anything untoward occurred during school hours. There was a significant gender pay gap between the women and the men appointed to these posts. All the teachers and nurses were residential, and in addition to their salaries, they received free board, lodging and laundry.

The chaplain's appointment was subject to the ratification of the local CofE bishop; he was responsible for overseeing religious instruction. He was also required to conduct a religious service each Sunday, and on certain other Christian holy days, and was expected to attend daily and give religious instruction. He had to produce a regular 'chaplain's report' on religious observance and to maintain a creed register of all pupils. He was expected to visit and minister all sick children and ensure that non-CofE children's ministers were informed when any of their flock was ill.

The porter was the gatekeeper and had to maintain a record of all people entering and leaving. He was responsible for examining all parcels that came in and ensuring that no prohibited goods, such as alcohol, unauthorised books or food not supplied by a contractor were brought in. He was required to lock the external gates at 9.00 pm and unlock them at 6.00 am. He was paid £30 a year. Following a number of attempted 'escapes', in 1872 the governors were permitted to pay a police officer 2s 6d per night to patrol outside the building between 6.00 pm and 8.00 am and ensure that boys did not abscond (there is no mention of girls making similar attempts).[7]

All staff disciplinary matters had to be reported to the PLB. Governors were able to make temporary appointments, in the event of illness of any permanent member, and had the authority to request a security bond from people appointed to the posts of clerk or treasurer. The appointment of all permanent members of staff had to be approved by the PLB, who kept detailed personnel records of each of them.

All 'professional staff' were on one month's notice. Nobody disbarred from office by the PLB could be employed at the establishment. Resignations were often sought, rather than dismissals imposed, meaning staff could leave with a clean employment record, and be employed in other poor law institutions. This enabled bad apples to remain within the system and repeat their inappropriate behaviour elsewhere.

In addition to the detailed memorandum outlining the responsibilities and relationships between the various people associated with the institution, the PLB published 30 pages of pro-forma documentation for the regular submission of statistics to both it and the governors. These required details of the numbers of pupils broken down by age and union of origin, staffing composition and levels, disciplinary issues, diet sheets and arrangements for dealing with sick children, together with timetables and scholastic records.

Although the PLB had been meticulous in establishing ground rules and accountability procedures, there was a serious lack of foresight about the institution's fitness for purpose, which became apparent from its inception.

It was responsible for determining the composition of the board of governors, but exercised this duty clumsily. The institution was to have a board of nine, representing the constituent unions; four from Poplar, three from Hackney and only two from Whitechapel, despite it being the founder union with the largest number of children.

The logic behind the distribution was never made explicit, but it sowed the seeds of dissent from the start. The composition also flew in the face of the 1865 Union Chargeability Act. This said that the financial contribution was to be made by unions engaged in joint projects (children's workhouses, asylums etc.) and based on the rateable value of the participating unions, rather than on the usage made.

HACKNEY WANTS OUT

Hackney was the richest of the three unions and was required to contribute most to the institution's running costs, but this was not reflected in the number of governors it was allocated. Within a year of the establishment of the FGDS, it expressed its dissatisfaction to the PLB because, as reported in *The Clerkenwell News* in May 1869, it 'paid two-thirds of the expenses of the establishment, they ought to have a similar share of representation, whereas they had at present the election of only one third of the managers.'

The PLB replied sympathetically six weeks later and intimated that it would deal with the matter in due course. But the concern was not resolved until April 1871, when the PLB increased Hackney's representation to four governors. That two-year period, however, led to a festering resentment in Hackney about the way it was being treated. Not only did its union pay the largest portion of the running costs, it had the fewest pupils. The upshot was that its ratepayers were paying almost 50 per cent more per child at Forest Gate than Poplar's and almost double that of Whitechapel's. Its guardians wanted their grievances addressed.

The position when the district school was founded was:

Union[8]	Hackney	Poplar	Whitechapel
Rateable Value	£536,121	£487,576	£267,139
% of establishment costs borne	41%	37%	22%
Number of children attending	222	303	257
Average cost per child per week	11s 4d	8s 4d	5s 10d

When it was established, the PLB set its maximum roll at 770, but it opened with over 850. Quite why the board sanctioned this excess at the outset is not clear. In the summer of 1868, it sent a letter to the governors explaining how bad the problem was:

> The dormitories are very crowded ... . The school rooms, as well as the dining hall, are too small for their present occupants. 700 children completely fill the dining hall. There is an average of only 235 cu ft space for infants; 222 for girls and 227 for boys. If each child were given even just 300 cu ft, there would only be room for 609 inmates, instead of 803. If they were given an average of 250 cu ft each, there would only be room for 732.[9]

One solution would have been to have removed one of the three unions from the district, but the PLB did not have authority to do this. Despite Hackney's unjust treatment, its guardians did not wish to leave until they had found another location for their children.

In June 1869, Hackney proposed sending some of its children to an establishment in Margate. The FGDS' governors vetoed this, as the cost would have come from their budget, and not Hackney's.

The PLB noted that the nearby St George in the East Union's children's workhouse was underused and it took in 220 pupils from other unions in south and west London to mop up its spare capacity. The PLB suggested that the Plashet establishment should be incorporated into an expanded FGSD. This would enable the excess numbers of Forest Lane pupils to be sent to Plashet, and thus create a neat, all-east-London solution. The non-East London unions would have to find new locations for their Plashet children, but that was hardly a concern for the east London guardians.

This seemed an ideal solution; the Plashet and Forest Gate buildings were a mile apart. A streamlined, more cost-effective system of management could operate across the two and east London's pauper children, from four separate unions, could easily be accommodated in two buildings under a common board of governors. London's long-serving poor law schools' inspector Edward Carleton Tufnell (working from 1847 to 1874) strongly backed the suggestion.

Hackney's guardians were wary, for financial reasons. They feared they would have to pay even more to buy into the St George facility in order to accommodate the surplus Forest Gate children.[10]

Drill at St George-in-the-East school, Plashet

In the event, St George's guardians would not agree the merger; they wished to maintain their independence, and vetoed the proposal.

The PLB's next favoured option was for the FGSD to build additional accommodation on the Forest Gate site, and effectively run two establishments – one for orphan children and those who were likely to be permanent at the institution, and a second, and new facility, for those children who were more likely to be transient – the aforementioned 'ins and outs'.

The PLB commissioned an architect to cost the additional accommodation on the site and floated an estimated figure of £20,000. The FGSD unions – who would have had to pay for it – rejected the proposal on the grounds of cost.[11]

THE INS AND OUTS

The problem of the ins and outs that the PLB sought to address was caused by the constant churn of children created by some of the principles of 'less eligibility'. The policy of offering 'no outdoor relief' to the very poor, which was vigorously adopted by Whitechapel, meant that for many families living on the margins of poverty in the area, there was no safety net or alternative to destitution on the streets or admission to the hated workhouse.

Families with no savings or possessions had to turn to the workhouse for food and shelter in times of extreme hardship, with a view to leaving as soon as they saw opportunities for a meagre independent existence outside. Their children would be kept in the main workhouse until their accommodation and educational needs were assessed, and a place found in the FGDS. Once sent to Forest Gate, the child would be placed in the quarantine/reception ward before being permitted to join the mainstream classes.

This process could take a minimum of six weeks, during which time the parents may have left the workhouse. At this point, the child, who would have received almost no formal education in the school during that time, would also be extricated.

Within days the adults may have been forced to seek readmission to the workhouse, in which case the process for the children began again but still without access to proper schooling. These children – the ins and outs – had severely disrupted educations.

Central District school, Hanwell, where Charlie Chaplin was an 'in and out'.
(Credit: Mary Evans/Peter Higginbotham collection)

The problem dated back to at least 1814, and although firm figures for its scale are difficult to establish, the rapid turnover of children was indicated in the FGDS' 1887 annual report. At the year's end, there were 660 children in the establishment; during the previous twelve months 597 had been admitted and 542 discharged, indicating an annual turnover rate approaching 90 per cent.

As almost three quarters of the children (the orphans and the deserted) were long-term pupils, the huge turnover indicates an average stay of potentially 400 ins and outs to be as little as four to six weeks, probably repeated many times in any year.

This problem was exacerbated by the governors' attitudes to parental visits. These were restricted to one afternoon every two months in Forest Gate until 1892. Many parents who wished to visit their children more frequently withdrew them from the institution for relatively short periods, for social contact, before returning them soon after. The children, on their return, faced the same induction procedures again.

Charlie Chaplin was, perhaps, the country's most famous district school inmate, and described the ins and outs problem in his autobiography.[12] In

1896, aged seven, he entered Newington Workhouse with his mother Hannah and brother Sydney. The two children went through the admissions process at Newington, had to wait for a place at the district school in Hanwell (the former Central London District School) and to be despatched there, where they were placed in the probationers' isolation ward for two to three weeks before being admitted to the school proper. The two brothers were then separated, Charlie being allocated to the infants' department and his older brother, Sydney to the boys' department. They did not see or have access to each other.

Two months after first entering the institution, Hannah, desperate to see her boys, left Newington Workhouse and took them out of the Hanwell school for a day. The boys were not allowed to return to Hanwell at night but had to re-register at the workhouse and go through the same admissions procedure, from workhouse to Hanwell, again. The boys spent 18 months at Hanwell and their education during that time was severely disrupted by this process.

Having had their proposal for additional accommodation for the ins and outs in Forest Gate rejected in September 1869, the PLB continued to express their concern about chronic overcrowding. It now housed 903 children, compared with the prescribed upper limit of 600. Places needed to be found for 300 elsewhere.[13]

A number of cheaper, alternative quick fixes were investigated, but all failed to fully address the overcrowding issue.

In 1869, the FGSD decided to take advantage of a recently enacted piece of legislation and acquire a training ship, *Goliath*, with a capacity of 550 boys, to be moored off Grays in Essex to help. From the FGSD's perspective, it was a cheaper option to building additional premises, as it would only cost £6,000.

The PLB approved the move and told the governors in December that no further building was required at Forest Gate. They thought they had achieved their objective and the three boards of guardians were happy that a solution had been found at less than a third of the cost of new construction in Forest Gate.

Four months later, the governors agreed another cheap, short-term fix. The 'receiving' ward was to be extended. The existing single-storey building accommodated 24 children, 12 of each sex. The PLB approved £1,600 to construct a second storey and increase its capacity to 52, which barely addressed the scale of overcrowding. Yet the proposal, predictably, created an overcrowding problem in the receiving ward itself. Under the new arrangements there was an average ground square footage of 36 per bed, which worked out at a bed plus two feet on all four sides for movement in the new dormitories.

Within two years of the foundation of the district school, it was clear that the accommodation arrangements were not fit for purpose, and the governors were incapable of addressing the problems they faced.

NOTES

[1] National Archives (NA), MH27/101

[2] Ross, p. 108

[3] NA, MH27/101

[4] NA, MH27/104

[5] *ELO*, 29 Jan 1870

[6] *Hackney and Kingsland Gazette*, 14 Aug 1869

[7] NA, MH 9/22

[8] LMA , FGSD 001

[9] NA, MH27/101

[10] *The Clerkenwell News*, 5 Jun 1869

[11] NA, MH27/101

[12] Charlie Chaplin, *My Autobiography*, Simon and Schuster, 1964, pp. 21-23

[13] NA, MH27/101

CHAPTER 4

TRAINING SHIP *GOLIATH*

———

Anthony Ashley-Cooper, the 7th Earl of Shaftesbury (1801–1885), had a distinguished political and philanthropic career, particularly relating to the welfare of the young poor. He is perhaps most associated with the factory and allied acts of parliament, which attempted to limit the hours of work and reform some of the worst aspects of the emerging factory system for the very young. He also served as president of the Ragged School Union – which aimed at providing education for the very poorest, during the 1840s.

A century after Hanway's 1756 training ships' proposal, Shaftesbury persuaded the Admiralty to provide him with a redundant frigate. He sought a vessel that could accommodate up to 1,000 youngsters, who otherwise would have been in workhouses, night shelters, or on the streets, to train them for the Royal Navy or merchant marine.

The Admiralty agreed to his request and provided him with HMS *Chichester*, moored off Greenhithe, Kent. It was fully fitted out to accommodate 250 trainees, but it experienced mixed fortunes. Conditions on board were undisciplined and harsh. In 1869, for example, its first superintendent was dismissed for drunkenness – and his crew left with him. It emerged that birching of miscreants was common, and the boys were treated impersonally, only being known by numbers and not by names.[1]

Almost certainly inspired by Shaftesbury's initiative – but before its major deficiencies emerged – the 1869 Metropolitan Poor Law Amendment Act made provision for the establishment of training ships as a poor law facility. It permitted any union or district school, to purchase, or hire, such a vessel, subject to PLB approval, for training boys for service at sea.

The Admiralty granted the MCPLF, supported by the PLB, the use of HMS *Goliath*, a redundant 2,596-ton, 84-gun, man-of-war ship, two years later. She was originally constructed in 1833 and saw service in the Crimean War. From the Admiralty's perspective, the arrangement got an unwanted ship off its books and, based on the *Chichester's* early success, offered the potential of training difficult-to-recruit young sailors in the future.

The FGSD made a to bid to manage the ship, as a cheap way of addressing some of its overcrowding problems. But it could only accommodate a fraction of the district's demand for places. No girls could be sent, and only the older boys – mainly aged 12 and over – were suitable for recruitment. This represented only about 100 boys, which was around 15 per cent of the FGDS population. Nevertheless, it was better than nothing and the district was prepared to pay the £6,000 refitting costs, as a cheaper alternative to constructing new buildings in Forest Lane.[2]

In the event, the FGSD only sent 58 boys in the first year of the ship's operation – almost 250 short of the places needed to address the overcrowding issue. The move was not universally welcomed. Eton and Balliol-educated, Edward Tufnell, the government inspector for London poor law schools, was highly sceptical of the ship's potential effectiveness.

He wrote to the PLB on 19 June 1869 to say the navy's requirements were such that it was unlikely any boy brought up in a workhouse institution would ever be fit enough to qualify for naval selection. His statement was damning of the general physical health of London's poor children and reflected his own low expectations of those for whom he had a supervisory responsibility. Naval regulations, he said, stipulated that recruits needed to have a minimum height of 4ft 10ins and a chest measurement of at least 29ins. These, he declared, 'no London pauper can attain to ... a stunted growth being the characteristic of the race.'[3]

He stated that the teaching accommodation likely to be available on board would be inferior to that in a land-based district school, and that the vessel would be too expensive to run. Grudgingly, however, he conceded that the experiment would be 'worth a trial, but I should be far from guaranteeing a success.'

The MCPLF agreed to place Training Ship (TS) *Goliath* under the management of the FGSD, because the organisation appeared large enough to supervise the initiative and 'Two of the unions [Poplar and Whitechapel] included in the district were waterside Unions and therefore cognisant of the business to be undertaken.'[4] The ship was to be governed by what was effectively a sub-committee of the FGSD.

THE SHIP TAKES SHAPE

In March 1870, the district advertised in the *Pall Mall Gazette* for a 'Captain/Superintendent of a Training Ship'. The terms were: 'Until the boys are placed in the ship, £150 pa – thereafter £300 pa – without any other allowance for rations.'[5]

William Sutherland Bourchier was appointed; he was 46, Greenwich born, and of 'well-known naval stock'.[6] He took residence on board with his wife Mary and their three teenage daughters. The couple appointed two resident female servants (a cook and a housemaid) to look after their domestic needs.[7]

Bourchier was an experienced sailor, having started his naval career in 1841, as the master's assistant on the Royal Navy vessel, HMS *Impregnable*. He rose through the ranks, subsequently becoming a navigating sub-lieutenant, lieutenant, and finally, sail commander in 1866. He served in the Mediterranean, off the West Coast of Africa and in South America, in the West African squadron (a small unit established by the navy to prevent the illegal transporting of slaves), before retiring in 1870.[8]

Bourchier had TS *Goliath* moved to Grays, in Essex, where she was close to TS *Chichester*, moored on the opposite bank of the Thames. He recruited a crew of predominantly former seamen as instructors, trainers and support staff, in advance of welcoming the first boys to the training ship – and thus doubling his salary to £300 per year.

In August 1870, Bourchier and the FGSD advertised for four posts; all the successful candidates were to have free rations and residence on board, in addition to their salaries. The positions were for a chief officer, with an annual salary of £80; a chief seaman instructor, also on £80, who was required to 'be qualified to teach the art of swimming'; a carpenter, on £75 and a cook on £50.[9] Although they were to look after a much smaller number of youngsters, the salaries of most staff were almost double that of their opposite numbers in Forest Gate.

From the outset, both the PLB and FGSD kept a very close eye on conditions on board and were prescriptive about many aspects of its management. For example, they stipulated, to the very last thread, the clothing that was to be worn.

William Sutherland Bourchier, 1823–1904. (Source: The Graphic, June 1904)

On 27 July 1870, they agreed that each boy on board should be issued with:

Cloth trousers – 1; serge [a strong woollen cloth] trousers – 2; **canvas trousers** (to wear over serge in cold weather and also for working aloft) – 2; **serge frocks** [long loose outer garments] – 2; **white frock** – 1; **cotton shirts** (for night shirts) – 2; **flannel shirts** – 2; **stockings** – 2; **comforters** [bed covers] – 1; **caps** (to be worn with the name of ship on ribbon on Sundays and when on shore or leave etc.) – 1; **scotch bonnets** [flat cap] – 1; **neck tie** – 1; **knife** (to be allowed after making a certain number in progress book) – 1; **clothes brush** (between three boys) – 1; **black painted bag** – 1; **bed** – 1; **blanket** – 1; **coverlet** [bed cover] (for winter months, when necessary) – 1; **thread; needles; combs** – 2; **little bag** [for keeping needles and thread] – 1; **canvas jumpers** (to be worn over serge frocks in winter) – 2; **towels** – 2; **pocket handkerchief** – 2; **scrubbing brush** - 1; **Seaman's catechism** [a manual, including instruction in use of onboard weaponry, published in 1868]; **ribbon**, with name of ship (to be worn on cap) – 1.[10]

Unlike the children in Forest Gate – who had no clothes of their own – the boy sailors were issued with their own garments. They were held responsible for their safekeeping and mending, hence the appearance of needle and cotton in the kit issue. The importance of looking smart and tidy at all times was drummed into them and they would have been punished for untidiness or having ragged clothes.

This discipline and culture fostered self-respect and developed personal responsibility – qualities that were not sought and barely recognised in the district school itself.

In August 1870, immediately prior to its opening, the PLB determined that the diet for TS *Goliath's* boys, aged 12 to 16, should consist of:

BREAKFAST (each day)
6oz bread or biscuit, 2/3rd pint of cocoa, with sugar.

DINNER
Sunday: *5oz fresh cooked, roast beef, 8oz potatoes, 3oz bread, 4oz flour, 3/4oz suet or dripping, 1 1/2oz raisins.*
Monday: *1 pint soup, 5oz boiled beef, 8oz potatoes, 3oz bread, 1/4 pint peas or equivalent.*
Tuesday: *5oz fresh cooked roast beef, 12oz potatoes, 3oz bread.*
Wednesday: *6oz cold meat, 8oz potatoes, 3oz bread, 6oz flour.*
Thursday: *1 pint soup, 3oz cold meat, 8oz potatoes, 3oz bread, 1/4 pint peas or equivalent.*
Friday: *5oz roast or baked meat, 12oz potatoes, 3oz bread.*
Saturday: *9oz bread, 2oz cheese.*

SUPPER (each day)
6oz bread or biscuit, 2/3rd pint of cocoa, with sugar.[11]

Although the food served to the boys was monotonous and starch-based, it was substantial enough to enable most of them to develop physically and to meet the naval entrance standards that inspector Tufnell felt were unlikely to be achieved. However, Bourchier was concerned about the food's quality. He was on record complaining in the strongest terms about the supply of unfit meat to his ship, and returning it to its supplier twice, in November 1871 and again six months later.

The boys would have had half a dozen decent mid-day meals a week, but relied heavily on bread for the rest of their sustenance. Between dinner (lunch) time on Fridays and dinner time on Sundays, for example, they would only have had 37oz of bread (a little over a current standard UK loaf), 2oz of cheese (about 4 cu cm) and two $^2/_3^{rd}$ cups of cocoa.

The Forest Gate governors queried this diet, not for its lack of variety, but because they feared the boys were being given too much bread. It was agreed that its consumption would be kept under scrutiny, with a view to reducing it, if any were left unconsumed.

Because TS *Goliath* was part funded by the MCPLF, it was not intended for the exclusive use of the FGSD unions. Initially only about 20 per cent of the boys on board came from them. On 4 March 1871, the *Hackney and Kingsland Gazette* reported that only 21 of its boys were recruits and there were only 33 from Whitechapel, a little over a year later.[12] This ship did little to provide the additional accommodation FGDS so desperately needed.

A circular letter in August 1870 was sent to boards of guardians in London, inviting them to send youngsters to TS *Goliath*[13] whom they would be required to part fund. Within weeks of launching, boys from other unions were recruited and it was up and running as a training ship in November. By December, Clerkenwell's guardians had agreed to place boys on it, at a charge of 8 shillings per week.[14] The guardians of Camberwell, Holborn, Islington, St Olave's, Strand, Shoreditch, Wandsworth and Clapham unions soon followed. At the first prize-giving day for the boys in 1871, certificates were awarded to boys from 16 different London unions and 13 unions outside the capital.[15] This pattern of widespread recruitment continued throughout the life span of TS *Goliath*.

As the number of boys on board increased, other staff appointments, mainly ex-sailors, were made. By April 1871, in addition to Bourchier, the crew and instructors on board were: Richard John Fenn, single, aged 27, head schoolmaster (trained and certified); Henry Finn, single, 28, assistant schoolmaster (trained and certified); Joseph Church, married, 38, seaman instructor; John Hall, single, 27, schoolmaster (seaman instructor); John Pratt, married, 46, schoolmaster (seaman pensioner); Uriah Dickens, widower, 45, schoolmaster (seaman pensioner); Thomas Norris, married, 35, schoolmaster (seaman pensioner), and John Faulkner, married, 51 schoolmaster (seaman pensioner).[16]

This complement of eight teachers and instructors in 1871 was better than in the Forest Gate establishment; giving a teacher to pupil ratio of 1:50, compared to 1:76.

It took little over a year for the training ship to receive high level recognition for its qualities. A leader in *The Times* of 11 October 1871 was fulsome in its praise:

> We are told, and we can well believe, that the training supplied on board the *Goliath* – education not only in books, but in work – transforms with astonishing rapidity and completeness even the facial and bodily characteristics of the street arabs who have the good fortune to be drafter to the school ship at Gravesend. Dull eyes brighten, narrow chests expand, stunted figures erect themselves, and the mental and moral nature partakes of the health change. In this metamorphosis we have a promise for the future.[17]

Bourchier was assiduous in his cultivation of unions sending boys to TS *Goliath*, as his contact with Croydon's guardians illustrates. Although the union only had ten to 12 boys on board at any time, he bombarded it with details of their progress, via an extensive, unremitting correspondence. He provided them with details of crew members, boys' achievements, successful placements, vacancies on board the ship, and details of triumphant visits made and plaudits gained. He was regularly at pains to show that few, if any, boys left the ship to become further burdens on the ratepayers of the despatching unions, and that the training vessel was well-regarded by the PLB and its successor, the LGB.[18]

In correspondence, Bourchier told the Croydon's guardians that between 14 Aug 1872 and 30 April 1873, 127 TS *Goliath* trainees had joined the sea service, 35 had enlisted in the army or obtained situations on shore and 16 were taken charge of by friends or relatives. This was a total of 175 who had a brighter future after their spell of training on board. All 35 of those who joined the army, he said, were either unfit for sea service, expressed a strong desire to join a military band, or declined to go to sea.

He was proud to share one quote in particular, coming as it did from George Sclater-Booth, president of the LGB:

> I am satisfied that there is no institution in or near London productive of greater or more unmixed good and that the ratepayers of the metropolis as well as those of the district itself are deeply indebted to the managers for their untiring exertions in maintaining its efficiency.[19]

Croydon was only one of literally dozens of supplying unions, and Bourchier would have maintained that level of contact with most, if not all – without secretarial help in an era without access to duplicators or photocopiers. A punishing correspondence schedule, on top of his other superintendent responsibilities kept Bourchier a busy man.

Anxious to maintain the flow of recruits to his ship, he was always open to hosting visits by guardians from 'supplying' unions. They returned the courtesy by expressing their appreciation for his efforts and TS *Goliath's* activity. In the three years between July 1872 and July 1875, he received letters of fulsome praise and appreciation from visitors from St Pancras, Westminster, Holborn, Stepney, Whitechapel, Woolwich and Marylebone – all of which were acknowledged and recorded in the governors' minutes.[20]

SUCCESSFUL ENDEAVOUR

The training ship also gained a very favourable press from specialist shipping journals. In a lengthy piece on 11 October 1871, the *Shipping and Mercantile Gazette* reported a visit to TS *Goliath* by the good and the great of the poor law and shipping worlds.

In the year since the first recruits took residence, 449 boys, it said, had been accommodated, of whom 16 had already gone into the Royal Navy, with 40 more soon to follow. Thirteen had gained positions within the merchant marine, while 25 had returned to their unions as the rigours of the ship had not suited them. There were 399 boys on board, at the time of writing, 100 short of the maximum permitted number of 500.

The same shipping paper, two and a half years later, gave a glowing account of the success of the ship, and heaped praise on Bourchier for his leadership:

> The work which is carried on in this vessel consists in training pauper lads to become good and efficient seamen, and those who witnessed the way in which the boys went through a number of nautical exercises yesterday were unanimous in their praise of the system employed by the excellent Captain W S Bourchier which produces such effective and happy results.[21]

The *Gazette* gave a detailed insight into the curriculum, life on board and the priorities set for its boys. Some 115 of those recruited had been given instruction in bandsmanship, in addition to training in seamanship. There were four bands on board, as well as 100 singers, and they performed for the guests attending the open day. In addition to seeking placements in the royal and mercantile marines, Bourchier sought employment opportunities for his charges in naval and military bands.

The governors of TS *Goliath* were keen to reward excellence and encourage good behaviour and endeavour. Although, by law, they were unable to pay for prizes from public funds, they sought private donations to pay for recognition of achievement at their annual prize-giving days. Awards were given for seamanship, smartness aloft, the best sail makers, best coxswains of boats, buglers (for the bands) etc. In addition to schoolwork and seamanship training, the boys were expected to be self-sufficient and keep the ship in good order; to this end, effort was recognised and prizes given to the best tailors, shoemakers, carpenters and painters.

Some of the £6,000 refitting costs paid for by the FGSD was accounted for by the construction, in June 1871, of a swimming pool on the ship (60ft x 30ft and up to 6ft 6ins deep). Within three months of its opening, 189 of the boys could swim, compared with just 29 before the pool was constructed. To recognise this, the awards ceremony introduced prizes for the best swimmers.

Social and life skills were commended too. Rewards were given to the best captain of messes; the boys who kept their clothes or band instruments in best order; one for the boy who attended most carefully to the sick and two for the most popular boys on the ship, 'decided by a species of informal and unconscious plebiscite on the part of the boys themselves', as it was described then – or democratically, as we would say today.

The *Gazette* testified to the beneficial effect that life on TS *Goliath* had on the health and stature of its residents: 'School records show that though commonly feeble and stunted in growth when they embark, numbers of them have grown by as much as two inches around the chest.' The *East London Advertiser* concurred as another detailed account of life on board TS *Goliath*, published in 1875, reported that, 'Boys rapidly increased in height and girth after joining the ship. The minimum height for joining the navy was 4'10" and a chest girth of 29" ... this was soon achieved by many.'[22]

The positives were impossible to ignore. Even Edward Tufnell, the schools' inspector who had been so sceptical about the value of *Goliath*, had changed his opinion significantly. He was quoted by *The Clerkenwell News* on 12 Oct 1871, as a convert:

> I have in several late visits examined the school in all its departments, and can conscientiously speak in the highest terms of commendation and of the general arrangements, the efficient way in which the several officers discharge their duties, and, as a necessary consequence, of the satisfactory examination passed by the children both in the intellectual and industrial departments.

A summary of a report by a 'Special Commissioner of the Metropolitan Poor Board' said that on the occasion of his visit there were 468 boys on board, divided into two groups. At any time, half of them were in school and the other half were learning seamanship. They switched halfway through the day – on the half-timer principle that was currently common for older children in board schools.[23]

The ship, according to his account, was 'just like any other' children's workhouse establishment. It had a 'head master and four assistants' on the teaching side – although there were other trainers in seamanship. The lower decks of the ship were fitted as mess rooms. Each boy had a bunk bed and a locker and were all given a bible and a prayer book to be kept in it, when they entered the ship. The boys had to be self-sufficient and were all involved in cooking, washing, cleaning, clothes making and carpentry – keeping the ship in good order: 'In this *Goliath* differs from district and other schools, where a considerable paid staff is maintained for cleaning, washing and other purposes. All the washing is done by all the boys – eight items each – on Monday mornings.'

There were a number of small rescue boats attached to the ship, which set sail every day, with two crew and 20 boys, which provided much of their practical nautical training and experience. On one occasion one was struck by a larger vessel, with all on board the smaller boat surviving. The commissioner contrasted it to a similar event in 1870, when a rescue boat attached to TS *Chichester* was hit and a number of boys drowned. He put the difference down to the excellence of TS *Goliath's* training regime.

He observed: 'It is amusing as well as gratifying to see the lads performing work usually done by adult sailors. They row and steer the boats, bringing goods alongside and haul up sacks of potatoes, flour etc. ... in the most expert and approved manner.'

In other brief observations the report's author noted that discipline on TS *Goliath* was strict, that there was some land attached, upon which gardening was taught, and that there was a 'hospital situated on shore ... the sick list is always very short, the percentage being about one.'

However, while life on board TS *Goliath* was definitely preferable to that in the workhouse school, it was demanding, not just for the boys, but for the staff too. Bourchier was clearly a hard taskmaster. Within a year of the ship's commission, its governors noted that the staff worked 14-hour days, which they felt 'to be an injury in many ways'. This workload, the governors concluded, helped explain 'the great difficulty experienced in obtaining certified teachers.'

They asked Bourchier to lighten the load, as 'it is too much to ask the schoolmaster to teach in the school and then supervise the musical education of 100 boys.' The governors were, however, at pains to show their 'high appreciation of his services'.[24]

Bourchier made it clear that staff were not allowed to leave the ship without his prior permission even in their few hours 'off-duty', and that any authorised shore leave was a 'privilege'.

Bourchier also drove himself hard. In the short five years of TS *Goliath's* operation, he did far more than simply recruit and manage the rapid turnover of 500 boys and 25 staff. He extended the facilities and broadened the opportunities available to those on board.

Within a year of TS *Goliath* becoming operational, he was given 10 days leave to inspect training ships and other institutions in Liverpool and elsewhere, with a view to learning from their good practices. He discovered much, as displayed by initiatives he pursued in his remaining years captaining TS *Goliath* and its successor vessel.

As well as making the case for, and supervising the construction of, the aforementioned swimming pool, he sourced and acquired the brigantine *The Steadfast*, as a tender supply boat to TS *Goliath*. Having acquired it, in October 1871, he negotiated with the local water companies to use it to ferry daily supplies of fresh water to the mother ship.

As captain, he also obtained a long-term lease (14 years at £100 pa) on Sherfield House and its surrounding four acres, in nearby Grays to act as an infirmary and sick bay.

In contrast to life at the FGDS, Bourchier was determined to ensure TS *Goliath* did not become isolated from its local community. A prime example of community engagement came with a fire in Grays in April 1872. Several officers and boys from the ship went to assist the rescue; many damaging their clothing in the attempt. The insurance company, Sun Fire, wrote to Bourchier with a cheque, by way of compensation, adding, 'The fact that the calamity was prevented from assuming a still more serious dimension was mainly attributable to the energy and direction displayed at the time, under your direction.'

Bourchier was successful in promoting TS *Goliath*, by attracting influential visitors and participating in high-profile events, thus ensuring he kept the good name of his project in the public, boards of guardians and opinion-formers' eyes. To celebrate 18 months' operation of the ship, he promoted an event hosted by the Poplar union, to reassure the local ratepayers that they were getting value for money.

A concert, featuring music, song and recitation was held, at which about half of TS *Goliath's* 500 boys participated. Local poor law guardian and wealthy shipping owner, Thomas Scrutton, officiated at the event and 'spoke pointedly of the great and unquestionable financial advantages to the ratepayers, as well as to the nation at large, from placing these lads as trained seamen on shipboard.'[25] The boys stayed in the Poplar workhouse overnight, and left by train for Grays and home the next day.

Six months later, in July 1872, boys from the ship performed a drill in front of the Prince of Wales, and the following month, its second prize-giving ceremony was conducted in the presence of the first and progressive President of the LGB, Right Hon James Stansfeld (1820–1898).[26] The attendees of the ceremony heard that 684 boys had been received on board since the ship was first commissioned and 383 were resident at the time of the event, a third admitted over the previous year.

Of the 300 boys who had been moved on, 101 had been sent to sea, mainly to the Royal Navy. Every boy who had been recruited had been taught how to mend and look after their clothes, the gathering was told, and 250 had learned to swim. 'Capital reports have been received from the Royal Navy for many of the boys sent there, and in some cases their wages were doubled on their second voyage,' the visitors heard.

Yet despite these obvious triumphs, the governors experienced difficulty in keeping TS *Goliath* operating at full capacity because the cost to the unions of training the boys was greater than keeping them elsewhere. Guardians were often reluctant to fund the training and Bourchier had to go on a significant charm offensive to keep the numbers up. Such was the ship's success, however, the government wished to see it extended to a number of northern ports, Stansfeld told the July 1872 prize-giving meeting.

The government had, from the outset, used the MCPLF to subsidise the running costs of TS *Goliath*. Unions, other than the three FGSD partners, were able to send boys for training to the ship at negotiated rates. The core costs were divided between the MCPLF and the three governing unions, with other unions paying marginal sums for their placements. All of which seemed eminently reasonable.

As with the Forest Lane establishment, the financial contributions of the FGSD unions were not based on a flat rate, per boy sent, but the rateable value of each union. Hackney faced the same double jeopardy charge with TS *Goliath* as it did with the Forest Gate school. It was the richest of the three unions, in rateable value terms; but, as the one furthest – literally and metaphorically – from having a naval tradition, it sent the fewest number of boys to the ship.

Bourchier played an effective marketing role in attracting custom from non-FGSD unions. But this only exacerbated Hackney's sense of injustice, as these boys were effectively being subsidised by its ratepayers.

The problem came to a head in the autumn of 1875 when a Hackney guardian wrote to the LGB, outlining his dissatisfaction, complaining that the parish was paying £84 per head per year for its boys, while the City and other London parishes paid only £26, and for some outside London, as little as £10. Why, he asked, did the MCPLF not pick up the whole charge?[27]

The scale of the problem was aired in December that year, when returns to the LGB showed there were boys from 47 separate unions on board; 374 from 20 London unions and 91 from 27 non-metropolitan unions. Fewer than 100 of the 480 boys came from the FGSD unions (41 from Hackney, 36 from Poplar and 22 from Whitechapel). Only nine London unions had no boys on board. St Saviour's had as many as Hackney, and were among another seven that had as many, or more, than Whitechapel. The financial arrangements were clearly unjust and unsustainable.[28]

The *London Evening Standard* outlined Hackney's case on 30 December, documenting its dissatisfaction with the governance and financial arrangements, and its desire to have control of any successor vessel moved from the FGSD to an all-London body.

Bourchier's success in recruiting trainees from a wide range of unions was due to his ability to get positive messages directly to unions who placed boys, and to high-profile publications and influential decision makers.

In April 1874 he received John Storer, the chairman of convocation of the University of London on board the ship. Storer wrote a letter of thanks, stating that: 'When one comes to consider the class of society from which the majority of their boys are chiefly drafted, it is impossible to over-state the importance of the vigorous bodies and bright frames … . My visit was a red-letter day in my educational experience.'[29] Bourchier ensured his remarks were widely disseminated.

On 7 November 1874, the captain/superintendent engineered some very positive coverage in the armed forces press, in a direct appeal to their recruiters to employ TS *Goliath*-trained youngsters, The *Broad Arrow* commented:

> The health and morals of the boys on board *Goliath* continues to be highly satisfactory. The vessel is employed as a means of giving a good education and one entirely removed from all association with pauperism to a certain number of lads drafted from the Forest Gate District School. The school itself is maintained … with the object of separating pauper children from the influences of those necessary but gloomy [workhouse] establishments. *Goliath* receives a certain number of those boys who appear fitted for a seafaring life; but as they are allowed a free choice of a future, many eventually choose a soldier's career.

Just two months later, Wyndham Holgate, Tufnell's recent replacement as inspector of metropolitan poor law schools, reported to the governors that educational standards were on a par with those in other union establishments, and 'there was a good standard of naval education'. He concluded by saying: 'The discipline is admirable, the school work is generally well done and the intelligence of the boys appeared to be thoroughly brought out.'

There was good copy for the training ship in the prestigious *Pall Mall Gazette* seven months later in June 1875. The boys on *Goliath*, its readers were told, 'are kept from contact with pauperism … it is hopefully and reasonably believed that life on board ship does not produce the "torpidity" observed in children brought up in the wards of a workhouse.'

Yet despite all this fulsome praise, Bourchier was, just like the sponsoring FGSD, found wanting in his treatment of the ship's Catholic trainees. Rumblings of discontent from local priests were ignored during the training vessel's early days, so the Catholic community appealed directly to the PLB.

In July 1871, its governors received a letter instructing that the devotional needs of Catholic pupils be addressed. The governors replied that the ship's command was unable to get them to an appropriate church or to find a priest who would serve them on board.

It appears probable that Bourchier and/or his staff applied pressure on the boys 'to convert' to the CofE – as seemed to be the case in Forest Gate – rather than find a 'Catholic solution'. Within two months, the captain told the governors that 15 *Goliath* boys, registered as Catholic, had indicated that they wished to convert to the CofE. In July the following year, he told them a further five were seeking 'conversion', and in 1874, he said 17 more had followed in their footsteps. He was, thus, able to take some of the pressure off himself, as the problem of addressing Catholic needs appeared to be diminishing.

Some means of getting Catholic boys to Catholic services was found by July 1874. But attendance was not made easy for them, whether this was by bullying, vigorous attempts at 'conversion' or simply obstruction, is not clear. By September Bourchier told the governors that 'several Catholic boys' were refusing to attend the Catholic services, and had expressed a desire to attend CofE ones instead. The governors informed the LGB of this but received no response.[30]

Given Bourchier's resourcefulness in finding solutions to the many administrative obstacles he faced while running TS *Goliath*, it seems likely that it was his own prejudices, rather than organisational difficulties, that resulted in the Catholic boys not having their faith needs recognised and respected.

A balance sheet of Bourchier's and TS *Goliath's* achievements in its five years of operation was, nevertheless, overwhelmingly positive. The training ship and its regime improved the health, education and job prospects for its charges. It instilled self-pride, a high degree of self-sufficiency, and thus self-confidence in its trainees. The effort the management expended on the recruitment of boys was essential in ensuring the experiment survived and prospered.

The progressive attitude to community and external relations, and towards improving conditions and facilities on board for the young sailors, was very different from the insulated, sterile conditions in other poor law institutions for the young, notably the FGDS.

The contrast between the culture of the ship and the institution in Forest Gate was evident, but it came at a price. As has been noted, the cost per trainee was higher on the ship than on land, but there were good reasons for this. The ship's staff were better trained and far better paid than those in the district school. TS *Goliath's* staff to pupil ratio was more beneficial. Boys were taught to take pride in their appearance and a responsibility for their own clothes – the quantity of which was more extensive than that provided to Forest Gate's children. And despite the cramped conditions on board, facilities for the pupils were superior. The swimming pool on deck predated one built in Forest Gate by 20 years.

There is not a single reference in any of the considerable volume of publicly available evidence of any abusive staff, unauthorised corporal punishment, medical malfeasance, severe outbreaks of any contagious disease, food poisoning, staff disruption, overcrowding, insanitary conditions, maltreatment of the boys or public concern about the ship during its five years of commission. All of this is in stark contrast to the Forest Gate institution, where a much narrower range of publicly accountable bodies regularly expressed concerns about all of the issues above.

Bourchier worked his trainees and staff hard in pursuit of his goals, but he did not exclude himself from a punishing work schedule. The single, most obvious, failing of the regime was its almost cavalier approach to the devotional needs of its Catholic boys.

External observers praised TS *Goliath* and condemned the district school, but did not conclude, or were unwilling to accept, that differential funding was a factor. The better-resourced establishment produced the better results.

Parsimonious guardians and the government's pursuit of 'less eligibility' did not encourage the better funding of land-based poor law children's establishments.

Which begs the question why did the authorities breach their natural fiscal conservatism to allow the more favourable pay and conditions on TS *Goliath* in the first place – particularly given the scepticism about the initiative by the appropriate schools' inspector? Although Bourchier was a considerable success as superintendent, it was perhaps his better qualification and employment package that enabled his recruitment to make the difference.

Which provokes the second question, if having seen the added value he brought to TS *Goliath*, why did those responsible for the FGDS and its finances not accept the obvious explanation and recruit better candidates to manage the Forest Gate establishment?

Bourchier's successful five-year promotion and management of the ship, and achievement in turning it into an innovative beacon of excellence, was, however, destroyed within an hour.

FATEFUL FIRE

Fire broke out on *Goliath*, at about 8.00 am on 22 December 1875, when there were 480 boys, aged between 11 and 15, on board. There were, in addition 30 adults, including Mrs Bourchier and the couple's two younger daughters.

Oil lamps for illumination were routinely kept alight on the ship overnight and it was the responsibility of one of the boys to collect these, extinguish them and return them to a 'lamp room' each morning, as dawn broke. On the morning of the fire, Robert Lorber, who collected the burning lamps and trimmed their wicks, didn't fully extinguish one. This set light to some oil that lay on the floor and the fire began.

Lorber, a 13-year-old orphan from Westminster, who had been on board for a little under three years, told the inquest that once he became aware the fire was spreading, he took his clothes off to try to smother it, but to little avail.

Fire spread across the main deck immediately; the alarm was called and an orderly evacuation took place. Fortunately, the boys were well prepared – they had fire drills on ship every Friday morning – and were trained to evacuate the ship completely within 30 to 40 minutes. All but 65 boys on board could swim at the time of the incident.

Fire on TS Goliath, December 1875. (Credit: Thurrock Museum)

Water pumps from the *Steadfast* were worked and boys were sent to collect blankets to help extinguish the flames. But the lower deck was soon engulfed and flames drove boys away from the pumps. The fire spread rapidly.

Once it became impossible to control the blaze, Bourchier ordered the boys who could swim to jump overboard, while he and the other officers remained behind to get the non-swimmers into boats. Several boys swam to shore – about 100 yards away – but not all made it; they were impeded by the high, stormy winds that were blowing at the time.

There were normally 14 small boats on board, for evacuation purposes, but only 10 were available that day; the others had been unable to return to the mother ship because of a hurricane the previous night. Boats from HMS *Arethusa* and TS *Chichester* (Shaftesbury's original training ship), as well as other vessels moored nearby, sent small craft to assist with the rescue.

A 13-year-old boy, William Bolton, emerged as a life-saving hero (see

Hero of the *Goliath* Fire, pages 73-74). As the small boats were lowered into the Thames, boys jumped into them and tried to head for the shore as speedily as possible. Bolton intervened to ensure that each left with as many boys as possible, rather than row away half empty. Newspaper reports suggested that his actions meant 100 more boys were accommodated in the small craft, and consequently saved, than would otherwise have been the case.

Within an hour of the alarm, TS *Goliath* was cleared of people. Commander Bourchier, now badly burned, was the last to leave with his family; his wife having jumped 22 feet into the Thames from the deck.[31] Bourchier received widespread acclaim and praise for his role in the evacuation. As he was supervising the departure of the boys, one called Mudkin is alleged to have begged him to leave the ship and save himself. In a phrase that was subsequently associated with him, he replied: 'No, that is not the way of the sea, my lad.'

'William Sutherland Bourchier', as depicted by Lance Calkin (see text). Calkin had never seen Bourchier, so used his father as his model, and TS Exmouth as a representation of TS Goliath (The Graphic December 1898)

Detailed descriptions of the fire were widely reported in the press (although, with more than a little insensitivity; in the same article that covered the fire, the *London Evening Standard* reported that Hackney was disgruntled with its financial contribution to the ship), and verbatim accounts stretching over many dense columns were devoted to coverage of the inquests.

Perhaps the best newspaper account appeared 26 years after the event and was published in the *Grays & Tilbury Gazette*. It anticipated Bourchier's imminent retirement from his next command, TS *Exmouth*, and featured an interview with him reflecting on his life as a training ship commander. It also included a detailed account of the fire by Richard Fenn, who had been the headmaster on board at the time, and one of the ship's earliest recruits.[32]

Fenn had already become the unofficial historian of the event, having written a popular account in a 68-page booklet, published within weeks of the fire in February 1876.[33] It sold 1,000 copies within the first week and was swiftly reprinted. What follows is an account of the aftermath of the fire, drawing on various press reports and Fenn's booklet.

During the evacuation two boys, 10-year-old Joseph Denholme and 13-year-old William McGrath, were washed ashore; their bodies were recovered within two days. They were the subject of an inquest three days later. Denholme was an orphan, placed on TS *Goliath* by the Stepney Union. He had been on the vessel for four to five months, though the inquest was told that he had no friends on board. His body was discovered on the Tilbury side of the Thames, about 600 yards from the ship, by a Grays-based labourer, George Aylett.

McGrath had been on TS *Goliath* for about two years, and was the son of Sophia, a widow in the Westminster workhouse. She told the inquest that she had last seen him alive three weeks before the fire. His body was found by another local labourer, David Bailey, in the mud, some 200 yards from TS *Goliath*, on the Essex bank of the river.

A recently appointed assistant school master, Richard Wheeler – who could not swim – was the only adult to perish in the fire; he drowned aged just 20. He had joined the ship ten days previously, having recently graduated as a teacher from Winchester College. Given his short period of service, he was probably not as familiar with its lay out and the meticulous evacuation procedures and fire drills as most of the boys. Because he couldn't swim, he jumped into one of the small supply boats, but it capsized and Wheeler drowned, while the boys who were able to swim managed to clamber to shore.

Sixteen other boys were reported missing. Two of them (Alfred Smith and

James Dickerson) were found washed up on shore a few days later.[34] The names of the other boys who perished do not appear in Fenn's booklet or any subsequent newspaper or contemporary government records or public accounts of the fire and its victims. This appears to be because the ship's register of boys on board was lost in the fire and it was left to the imperfect memories of survivors to piece together the names of the missing boys.

News of the disaster spread quickly and Bourchier received 63 telegrams of condolence in the hours immediately following the fire. He even received a message from the Queen, who wrote 'to express to yourself, your officers and the boys Her Majesty's great satisfaction at the admirable behaviour of all on board, under very trying circumstances.'[35]

A low-key funeral for the victims took place in February 1876, with no apparent press coverage. They were buried in an unmarked mass grave in Grays Old Cemetery. Assiduous work by local historian John Webb and the Thurrock Local History Society has unearthed the names of 15 of the victims.[36] The only memorial to all the fire's victims is a plaque in Grays Parish Church, paid for by Bourchier and his fellow officers. It reads:

> In appreciative remembrance of Richard Wheeler, assistant school-master and the boys of the training ship *Goliath* who lost their lives through the destruction of the vessel by fire 22nd December 1875. 'In the midst of life we are in death'. This tablet is erected by the captain superintendent and officers.

Memorial to Richard Wheeler, Grays Parish Church. (Photo: Author's Own)

There is a second memorial plaque, to Richard Wheeler alone, which survives in his alma mater, Winchester College.

Harry Leach, the medical officer of the Port of London, wrote to *The Times* the day after the fire and his letter was printed the following day, 24 December 1875:

> It is right that the public should know from independent sources how excellently well this particular ship was administered. Less than 24 hours before the fire broke out I was congratulating him [Bourchier] on the absence of a sick boy and on the fact that there were but five invalids out of a compliment of more than 500 boys.

Emergency accommodation was found for the surviving boys and staff. Ninety boys were billeted in Sherfield House, TS *Goliath's* infirmary, and the FGDS was asked to take as many as possible. It says something of the reputation of the institution that, on hearing of their destination, some of the boys who were due to be sent back there attempted to abscond. They were soon rounded up and despatched, almost like criminals back to jail. The boys not accommodated in either Sherfield House or the FGDS were sent back to their home unions.

The ship's staff were asked to find temporary accommodation for themselves in Grays, and were suitably compensated for the costs by the ship's governors, until a replacement vessel could be commissioned and adapted for their continued employment.[37] They were, in addition, awarded two months' salary and living costs, in recognition of the bravery they showed during the rescue operation.[38]

Bourchier told the inquest: 'In the end, all the boys but the deceased and the missing ones escaped, and I believe that every boy got out of the ship; I did not see the deceased boys in the water.'

The Grays' social establishment contacted the ship's governors, expressing their feelings and indicating that the ship, its crew and boys had a close relationship with the town:

> We have been gratified to see waifs and strays from London, especially the eastern portion of it, improving from day to day, both physically and morally and we have heard with sincere pleasure of the hundreds you have been the means of introducing into Her

Majesty's navy, into the mercantile marine and into various and useful positions ashore.[39]

The Dean of Westminster preached at his annual service for children in Westminster Abbey and remarked that 'the conduct of the boys on board showed how much could be done by careful training.'[40]

Despite this period of mourning and reflection, the embers of *Goliath* had barely been extinguished before the authorities displayed unseemly behaviour. While accepting that the ship was 'beyond all controversy an excellent and useful facility', Hackney guardians were at the door of the LGB within 10 days with their complaints about the excessive financial burden the ship had placed on them and arguing that responsibility for its replacement should rest with the Metropolitan Asylums Board (MAB).

Another unsavoury episode related to the insurance pay-out. The vessel was insured for £14,000. The Admiralty claimed half of that as compensation for the loss of its property and the FGSD claimed the other half on account of their contribution to the ship's refitting costs.

This left unpaid the estimated £1,500 value of the officers' (including the Bourchier family's) clothes and property, and the meagre possessions of the boys. The Corporation of London established an appeal fund to make up that shortfall.[41]

One of the subscribers was Florence Nightingale, who wrote effusively to *The Times* about the effectiveness of TS *Goliath*, praising the ship and its work and stating: 'Every so trained and so de-pauperised boy is a bequest to England worth making.'[42]

The fire captured the public imagination, in a number of ways. The magazine *Punch* recorded the event in a lengthy doggerel poem[43] describing the incident in dramatic and heroic terms:

The Burning of the *Goliath*

(As told an old Salt to a mess mate in Greenwich Hospital.)

A dirty, foggy morning 'twas:
Grays loomed large, close a-lee:
The watch was holy-stoning decks
As white as white could be:
There were five hundred workhouse lads
A training for the sea.

'Goliath' was a giant hulk
Built in the days of yore:
And more than one small David
Upon her books she bore.
No iron in her; knees of oak,
And oak heart the core.

The bell had just struck half-past seven,
As broke the winter's day –
On the main deck 'twas dousing glims
And stowing them away.
Darn that new-fangled paraffin! –
Whale oil's the stuff, I say!

Young Lorber had lamps in charge –
A steady boy, I'm told –
One of 'em burnt his fingers, till
He couldn't keep his hold
Down fell the lamp; along the decks
The blazing oil it rolled.

'Fire!' Beat to quarters! Man the pumps! –
I could cry like a fool
To read how them lads mustered all,
As if for morning school.
In their skylarking at Christmas
They wasn't half as cool.

I've heer'd of Balaclava –
But they were bearded men,
And these were little fellows.
Most 'twix twelve and ten –
Some calls 'em gutter-children –
God bless our gutters. then!

The Capt'n was at his post.
A smile upon his face;
And not one officer or lad

But knew and kept his place,
Though soon was plain as plain could be,
The fire must win the race.

Most of the little chaps could swim;
But. swim or not, they made
And kept their lines as regular
As soldiers on parade.
Bourchier had wife and girls aboard
But by them lads he stayed.

Till when the pump no longer sucked,
Boat-tackles scorched, in-board;
Ship loss! lowering the boats!
The captain gave the word,
'Leap from the ports; swim, them that can;
The rest, trust in the Lord.'

One little chap hung round his neck
A blubb'ring 'burnt you'll be.
Jump over first – and then we'll jump.'
'No, no. my boy,' says he,
'The skipper's last to leave the ship –
That is our way at sea.'

So young and old their duty did.
Like sailors. and like men.
There was Hall and there was Norris,
And Gunton. Tye, and Fenn
Who swore he'd save the women.
And did it there and then.

The captain's wife jumped thirty feet –
Needs must, when Vulcan drives –
Hand over hand—in sailor style –
His daughters saved their lives:
Brave girls you see and well brought up,
The stuff for sailors' wives!

On the tank barge some twenty boys
Had climbed dear life to save;
The flames flared out, the pitched sides
Yawned like a fiery grave;
And some set the cry 'Shore off!' –
Lads will like lads behave.

But Billy Bolton's boyish voice
Was heard – 'I'm the mate in charge;
There's room enough' for plenty more.
Hold there with the barge.
That Billy Bolton may run small
The heart of him looms large.

But I can tell you half the tale
How, when they got ashore.
The kind good women kissed and hugged,
And stript the clothes they wore
To wrap the boys, as mothers will –
Or what is mother for?

There was a little soldier lad,
His shipmates came to see
He's gone and some half-dozen more
And Messer Wheeler, he
Is with them little lads in heaven
All rated there A. B.

As long as England's Workhouse lads
Work up to such good stuff
Britannia still will rule the waves
Though here and there a muff
At Whitehall afloat may make
Old John Bull cut rough.[44]

WILLIAM BOLTON
HERO OF THE *GOLIATH* FIRE

Thirteen-year-old William Bolton emerged as a hero of the TS Goliath fire. According to Bourchier's records,[45] his home union was Westminster and he was just 4ft 5ins tall, with a chest circumference of 26ins, and weighing 67lbs (4½stone or 30kgs) at the time of the fire. He was barely any bigger when he left TS *Exmouth* in 1876.

During the fire, he ensured that the small rescue craft on board were filled with trainees and staff before they left for shore, rather than see the boats depart half empty. His actions were estimated to have saved the lives of 100 of his peers, who might otherwise have drowned, been incinerated by the fire or suffocated by the smoke it emitted.

He featured in the *Punch* poem of the fire ('That Billy Bolton may run small, The heart of him looms large'), and was recognised for his actions, later being described as 'the little hero of the disaster'.[46] He was awarded a Bramley Moor silver medal for bravery, similar to that received by superintendent Bourchier.

In addition, he was presented, in absentia, with a silver watch, as reward from the President of the LGB and a £10 gift from the Maharaja of Burdwan at a ceremony at Mansion House in August 1876. This was obviously a huge sum for the boy. William was unable to collect these awards in person, having left TS *Exmouth* on 7 June 1876 to enlist as an apprentice with Shaw, Saville and Co passenger shipping line. He signed up initially for four years,

Sailing ship Pleiades, *the ship that ran between Britain and the antipodes on which Goliath fire hero, William Bolton, rose to become chief officer.*

with payment of £10 per voyage for round trips to either Australia or New Zealand.

He completed his apprenticeship in June 1880 and visited TS *Exmouth* to inform Bourchier. The following month he qualified as a second mate and was posted to Shaw, Saville's and Co's ship HMS *Pleiades*, which specialised in emigration voyages, and set sail to New Zealand in August.

He remained with the vessel for a number of years and, aged just 20, was promoted to the rank of its chief officer in 1883. He was an annual visitor to Bourchier and TS *Exmouth* until around 1890, and according to his former superintendent, 'He seems to maintain the high character he bore when on the ship.' Contact was lost with Bolton after that year and we have no further details of his subsequent life.

AFTER THE FIRE

A USEFUL MANUFACTURE.

THE "RAW MATERIAL." | "WORKED UP."

["Goliath" Training Ship burnt December 22nd, 1875.

Cartoon from Punch, immediately after the fire (January 1876), illustrating 'before and after' images of the beneficial impact Goliath had on 'street urchins'. (Credit: Mary Evans/Peter Higginbotham collection)

Bourchier was feted for his leadership during the tragedy, and later featured in an almost unheard-of colour supplement in *The Graphic*,[47] and in a poem by the celebrated religious poet Frances Ridley Havergal, which was later set to music.[48] His celebrity was confirmed via a painting by the artist Lance Calkin, also in *The Graphic*, which purported to showed TS *Goliath* in flames, and Mudkin imploring him to save himself. Calkin, it later transpired, had used some artistic licence in his portrayal of Bourchier, whom he had never met. He based the drawing on an image of his own father, George Calkin. He also used TS *Goliath*'s replacement, TS *Exmouth* as the background for the picture.[49] So, the famous painting depicting the fire was created by the artist using neither Bourchier nor *Goliath* as his models!

Bourchier was later awarded the first-class testimonial from the Royal Society for the Protection of Life from Fire for his exertions, and also the Bramley-Moore silver medal of the Liverpool Shipwreck and Humane Society.[50] He was not alone in receiving recognition. The Lord Mayor of London held an event in August 1876 at which he presented 33 framed certificates for bravery to nearly all the officers of TS *Goliath* and the other training ships that lent assistance. The same occasion was used to host one of the strangest events to be inspired by the burning of *Goliath*.

The Maharaja of Burdwan wrote to *The Times* in February 1876 to say he wished to use its good offices to acknowledge and reward the bravery of those involved in the rescue operation. He had silver medals struck for all of the crew, and arranged for 400 purses to be purchased, into each of which was placed 5 shillings. These were to be given to the boys on board TS *Goliath* at the time of the fire, when they eventually left its replacement training ship and began to make their way in life.

The Maharaja, Mahtab Chand Ray Bahadur (1820–1879) was a very pro-British Bengali prince at the time of the Indian Rebellion (imperially known as Mutiny) in 1857. He was a keen supporter of the establishment of the British Raj and the designation of Victoria as the Empress of India the year following the fire. He explained to the press that his gallantry awards were 'to show that heroism, like theirs, has not merely a local name, but is known and appreciated in the most distant parts of the Empire.'[51]

The last substantial press article[52] about *Goliath*, before its demise, provided a simple, uncluttered epitaph:

> Since the ship was established in November 1870, 1,474 boys have been admitted, about 1,000 placed out in various ways and 458 remaining on board ... *Goliath* is unique in its results, as it is in being the only one under the Poor-Law system ... . As regards the management and discipline, we would say that it is strict, yet there is evidently no tyranny.

The Admiralty was keen for the training ship initiative to continue – and for blameless Bourchier to take command – and they quickly moved to offer a replacement vessel. They tried to hand over an inadequate ship with sub-standard sanitary conditions within days of the fire and its aftermath.[53] Although clearly distressed and preoccupied by the fire, Bourchier resisted their offer, claiming it was too old and unfit for purpose, even with a refit.[54] He held out for a more appropriate ship, which he found on an exploratory trip to Plymouth. This turned out to be TS *Exmouth*.[55]

Hackney guardians got their wishes when, on 26 March 1876, the LGB transferred responsibility for this ship's finances and management from FGSD to the Metropolitan Asylums Board (MAB), which had no experience of training ships.

The MAB established a governing committee of 12 to supervise the running of TS *Exmouth*; these were representatives of 12 London boards of guardians, under the chairmanship of Admiral Robertson.[56] Bourchier took command of the vessel in 1876 and remained at the helm until his retirement, aged 78, in January 1902.

During his stewardship some 8,000 lads came under his influence, of whom an estimated 2,600 joined the navy and 1,200 army bands. However, the costs to unions of training their boys on board continued to be greater than keeping them in other forms of institution and training. It remained a problem that Bourchier had to work hard to overcome throughout his time managing the vessel.[57]

On his retirement, Bourchier claimed that TS *Exmouth* had been fitted out exactly as he wanted in order to provide the conditions he felt were necessary for a training ship. He had been able to boast that in his last 10 years commanding TS *Exmouth*, he had 'sent more boys to the navy than all the other training ships together.'[58] He emerged as the outstanding leader and figure in the training-ship movement – in a post-naval retirement career spanning over 30 years. He cut his teeth in this significant poor law training field, as an employee of the FGSD.

Two years after his retirement, a poor law conference was most complimentary about the impact of the vessel, commenting that it was a good way of improving the prospects of poor boys, and that a boy from there, who went into the Royal Navy could, at the age of 40 'secure a pension of £50 for life.'

The Bourchier family, William, wife, Mary and children. (Photo.: courtesy of Bourchier family.)

Bourchier retired to live in Purley, Surrey, where he died, two and a half years later, aged 80 on 18 June 1904.[59] On news of his death, flags on TS *Exmouth* were flown at half mast. He was buried in Grays, near both his wife and his former ship.

Contemporary news reports described a huge funeral procession through the town, attended by members of the MAB and the Grays District Council, together with its fire brigade, as well as 1,200 boys from training ships. 'Houses and shops all along the road to the cemetery had their blinds down.'[60]

His death meant TS *Exmouth's* days as a training ship were numbered and, a year later, it was condemned as unfit for service, to be replaced by another ship bearing the same name. This continued in service until the outbreak of the Second World War.

However, the training ships' initiative had petered out soon after Bourchier's retirement. By 1911, only 453 boys, nationwide were being trained on them – possibly because of their relatively high cost. The future of the project suffered, perhaps, from a lack of the ambition, and Bourchier's relentless drive.[61]

ONWARD JOURNEYS OF SOME *GOLIATH* TRAINEES[62]

Training Ship Exmouth, *the replacement vessel for TS* Goliath *after the fire. Most of Goliath's survivors were accommodated here, from where they launched their future careers.*
(Source: postcard)

Superintedent Bourchier maintained a visitors book on TS *Exmouth*, and recorded details of previous trainees who returned to see him and his colleagues.[63] There are sketchy details of almost 200 ex-*Goliath* boys. Their visits were a testimony to the high regard in which Bourchier was held by his former trainees and his log was an indication of his concern for their longer-term careers and well-being. Extracts of his notes for seven former TS *Goliath* boys are reproduced below. They are not a representative cross section, simply an indicative sample of those records.

Robert Loscombe, home union Camberwell. Discharged from TS *Exmouth* aged 14 on 26 March 1876. He was 4ft 9ins when he entered TS *Goliath* and 5ft 1in when he left TS

Exmouth. His weight increased from 70lbs to 78lbs and his chest circumference had expanded from 26ins to 30ins. On discharge from TS *Exmouth*, he joined HMS *Visitor* where he was to be paid £40 for four years' service, with a £2 gratuity for good performance at the end.

Arthur Jennings, home union St Saviour's. Discharged from TS *Exmouth* on 15 June 1876. On leaving, he joined HMS *Violet*, on a four-year contract, worth £40. His general conduct on board the training vessels was described as being very good, and his seamanship good. He 'served two years and six months at sea and left on account of an accident; right arm amputated at shoulder: subsequent occupation a hawker in Gravesend.'

Walter Myers, home union Stepney. Discharged from TS *Exmouth* on 14 April 1876 aged 14. General conduct and seamanship both described as very good. 'Visited ship August 1879. Doing very well as a lighterman on the river [Thames].'

John King, home union Whitechapel. Discharged from TS *Exmouth*, aged 15 in May 1878. Joined a ship in Whitby on a four-year contract worth £40. 'Visited ship on 18 April 1881. Went to sea for two years then took a situation as a hostler [horse keeper]. April 1882 the mother visited the ship and stated that he had enlisted in the City of London (late 7th) Regiment.'

James Burke, home union Hackney. Discharged from TS *Exmouth*, aged 13 in June 1876. General conduct and seaman-ship both described as very good. 'Returned to the care of his mother. The mother of this boy remained in the workhouse while he was being educated ready for the sea. When she discharged herself, she claimed the boy.'

Samuel Drake, home union Hackney. Discharged from TS *Exmouth*, aged 15 in January 1878. Conduct described as exemplary and as being 'fit for sea'. It continues:

> Sent to shipping office in Limehouse to wait for a ship. 17 August 1879 visited the ship and is employed on shore, but is anxious to go to sea. August 1880 still on shore as a florist. Paid 15/- per week. This

boy was a storage boy and would make an excellent 2nd steward or pantry boy. Was quartermaster of his division when discharged.

John Hay, home union Poplar. Discharged aged 15 from TS *Exmouth* March 1880. Joined 56th Regiment, Portland. In July 1878 had been 'Rated gold lace boy'. His proficiency records on departure indicated very good conduct, good seamanship, moderate schoolwork, very good swimming, and first-class brass and stringed band work. 'Visited ship Dec 80 is being trained as a musician at Kneller Hall [home of the Royal Military School of Music in Richmond]. Extract from a letter received April 1882 "I am now solo horn player and I am getting on very well with my violin. I have a good conduct badge."'

NOTES

[1] Higginbotham, *Children's Homes*, pp. 53-4

[2] *Shipping & Mercantile Gazette*, 11 Oct 1871

[3] NA, MH 27/101

[4] *Essex Standard*, 3 Aug 1875

[5] *ELO*, 28 Aug 1875

[6] *Grays & Tilbury Gazette*, 28 Dec 1901

[7] 1871 Census, RG10 1683

[8] *The Portsmouth Evening News*, 21 Jun 1904, *Army & Navy Gazette*, 25 Jun 1904

[9] *ELO*, 28 Aug 1875

[10] NA, MH27/102

[11] NA, MH27/102

[12] *East London Advertiser (ELA)*, 15 Jun 1872

[13] *Essex Standard*, 3 Aug 1875

[14] *The Clerkenwell News*, 30 Dec 1870

[15] *ELA*, 3 Aug 1875

[16] 1871 Census, RG10 1683

[17] *Times*, 11 Oct 1871

[18] *The Croydon Advertiser*, 24 May 1873

[19] *The Croydon Advertiser*, 31 Jul 1875

[20] LMA, FGSD/016

[21] *Shipping and Mercantile Gazette*, 25 Jul 1873

[22] *ELO*, 28 Aug 1875

[23] Ibid

[24] LMA, FGSD/016

[25] *ELA*, 22 Jan 1872

[26] *ELA*, 10 Aug 1872

[27] *ELO*, 11 Sep 1875

[28] The numbers from each London union in December 1875 were: Hackney, 41; Poplar, 36; Whitechapel, 22; Camberwell, 4; Chelsea, 24; St George's, 30; Greenwich, 12; Islington, 6; Kensington, 6; Lambeth, 3; Lewisham, 33; City of London, 19; Marylebone, 8; St Olave's, 27; St Pancras, 22; St Saviour's, 41; Stepney, 2; Wandsworth, 10; Westminster 28; and Woolwich, 10. The numbers for non-metropolitan unions were: Brentford,

19; Colchester, 2; Croydon 7; Dartford, 4; Edmonton, 3; Eton, 2; Horsham, 8; South Stoneham, 9; Tonbridge, 4; Walton, 2; Dorking, 1; Eccleshall, 1; Bishop's Stortford, 3; Epping, 4; Uxbridge, 2; Hereford, 1; Romney Marsh, 1; Sudbury, 2; West Ashford, 2; Royston, 2; Newbury, 1; Ashford, 1; Biggleswade, 2; Hadfield, 1; Leighton Buzzard, 3. NA, MH 27/104

29   LMA, FGSD/017

30   *LMA, FGSD/016*

31   *Army & Navy Gazette,* 25 Jun 1904, *Tower Hamlets Independent and East End Local Advertiser (THIEELA),* 1 Feb 1902, *East & South Devon Advertiser,* 1 Jan 1876

32   28 Dec 1901

33   R. J. Fenn, *The Burning of the Goliath,* Shaw and Sons 1876

34   *The Essex Herald,* 4 Jan 1876

35   *The Portsmouth Evening News,* 21 Jun 1904

36   The burial records at Thurrock Council record them as Joseph Denholme, aged 10 (discovered 28 Dec 1875); Paul Leonard, 14 (27 Jan 1876); James Dickerson, 15 (1 Jan 1876); Alfred Scarfe, 13 (1 Jan 1876); Alfred Smith, 13, (1 Jan 1876); George Skinner, 14 (27 Jan 1876); William Burrell, 14 (20 Jan 1876); Charles Leggett, 13 (31 Jan 1876); Frederick Cook, 14 (22 Jan 1876); Richard McKay, 14 (31 Jan 1876); Alfred Powney, 15 (25 Jan 1876); William Giddings, 14 (31 Jan 1876); Richard Wheeler, 20 (1 Feb 1876); William McGrath, 14, Clement Harris, age unknown. See also Neal, Wendy, *With Disastrous Consequences – London Disasters 1830–1917,* Hisarlik Press 1992, p. 158

37   *LMA, FGSD/016*

38   *NA, MH27/104*

39   *The Essex Herald,* 4 Jan 1876

40   Ibid

41   *The Essex Herald,* 4 Jan 1876 and *Taunton Courier* 12 Jan 1876

42   *Fenn,* p. 4

43   See *Fenn*

44   *Grays & Tilbury Gazette,* 28 Dec 1901

45   Ibid

46   *Chelmsford Chronicle,* 18 Aug 1876

47   *The Graphic,* 25 Jun 1904

48   *The Portsmouth Evening News,* 21 Jun 1904

49   For more on Calkin, visit www.calkin. co.uk/calkin041b_art.html; Phil Carradice, *Nautical Training Ships – an Illustrated History,* Amberley Press, 2009, p. 148

50   *Hampshire Telegraph,* 25 June 1904

51   *The Staffordshire Sentinel,* 22 Feb 1876

52   ELO, 28 Aug 1875

53   *The Scotsman,* 31 Dec 1875, *The Globe,* 7 Jan 1876

54   *The Morning Post,* 7 Jan 1876

55   *Grays & Tilbury Gazette,* 28 Dec 1901

56   *The Croydon Advertiser,* 8 Apr 1876; *London Evening Standard,* 4 Feb 1876; *Aldershot Military Gazette,* 19 Feb 1876; *Sheffield Daily Telegraph,* 2 Mar 1876

57   *Cheltenham Chronicle,* 25 Nov 1893

58   *Grays & Tilbury Gazette,* 28 Dec 1901

59   *Army & Navy Gazette,* 25 Jun 1904

60   *The Essex Newsman,* 25 Jun 1904

61   Higginbotham, *Children's Homes,* p. 206

62   www.ancestry.com/search/collections/61332/

63   www.ancestry.com/search/collections/61332/

CHAPTER 5

PROGRESS AND PIONEERS

Conditions in the Forest Gate children's workhouse changed little during the first 20 years of its operation – it remained a part of the punitive poor law system and the children's social and emotional needs went unaddressed. However, attitudes towards the care of pauper children elsewhere in Britain were gradually changing to become more child-centric.

Even before the establishment of the FGDS, a number of British social commentators had begun to compare the successful outcomes of the Mettray and Rauhe Haus experiments in France and Germany with the failings of Britain's huge children's workhouses, and were arguing for reform. As a consequence, some more progressive childcare solutions began to emerge.

The reformatory schools' movement, for example, was pioneered in the 1850s. It offered an alternative to prisons for young offenders, and was modelled on Mettray, where institutions were created to provide a family-type environment, based on love, and there was no enforced work.[1]

The Industrial Schools Act of 1857 established institutions for children between the ages of seven and 14, who had been convicted of vagrancy. They were mainly charity-led organisations, and although their regimes were not very different from those at Forest Gate, they tended to offer a much wider range of industrial training, such as blacksmithing, basket and brushmaking and printing, which could result in genuine job opportunities for many of their ex-residents.[2]

One or two smaller charitable organisations began to lay the basis for what later became known as 'cottage homes'. The Home for Little Boys was established in Farningham in Kent in 1865 and the Princess Mary's Home for Little Girls was opened in 1870 in Addlestone in Surrey. These small institutions offered a greater standard of personal and pastoral care to children than was typical in other poor law children's facilities.[3] By the mid 1870s, poor law unions in Liverpool and West Ham (where the FGDS was located) were experimenting with modifications to the system, while more faithful iterations of the scheme were applied in South Wales and Birmingham, and in Kensington and Chelsea in 1880.

The first of the 'big three' national childcare charities was emerging at this time; the Methodists' National Children's Homes was established in Lambeth in 1869. Influenced by the Mettray and Rauhe Haus principles, its homes were run by resident house parents, whom the children referred to as 'mother' and 'father'.[4] The initiative grew, and in 1871 moved to Bethnal Green, the centre of the catchment area for the Forest Gate school. The scheme consisted of a number of single-sex, family-style households, where the range of industrial training embraced plumbing, baking, printing and carpentry. The project eventually grew to accommodate 300 children – hardly an insignificant or fringe development in the East End.

REFORMING GOVERNMENT ZEAL

The 1867 Reform Act radically altered the national political landscape – doubling the size of the electorate in England and Wales from one to two million. The following year came the election of the first modernising Gladstone Liberal government (1868–1874) which transformed the operations of the British army, the civil service and legal and voting systems, by attempting to stamp out nepotism and corruption.

William Forster's Education Act of 1870 was one of the high points of the administration. It introduced a national system of publicly funded education for the first time; extending access to the 50 per cent of English children who previously hadn't been to school. The schools were to be administered by locally elected boards.

Neither the 1870 Act, nor the government's education department – which functioned between 1856 and 1899 – overly concerned themselves with the role or operation of district schools, reinforcing the notion that these were not so much educational facilities as poor law institutions. They continued to operate under the auspices of indirectly selected governors which were supervised by the PLB, rather than by directly elected school boards, governed by the Ministry of Education.

Gladstone's zeal for institutional reform did, however, partially embrace the administration of the poor law, and he used the visionary James Stansfeld (1820–1898), the MP for Halifax, whom he appointed as president of the PLB in 1871, as his agent. Stansfeld was a radical, friend and colleague of Forster and was later described by the historian J. L. Hammond as 'a Victorian champion of sex equality'.[5]

One of his first actions as minister was to sponsor the Local Government Act of 1871, which merged parts of the Home Office and Board of Trade with the PLB, to form the new Local Government Board (LGB). Stansfeld was aware of the criticisms of the way in which poor law institutions treated children, and of some of the progressive initiatives that were emerging outside of the state system. He was sympathetic to anti-barrack school sentiments, and in particular growing criticisms made about the effect they were seen to have on girls and young women.

JANE SENIOR'S BLUEPRINT

Mounting credibility was given by people such as philanthropist Octavia Hill (1838–1912) to the notion that it would be better for girls, in particular, to be brought up in family environments rather than in regimented institutions. These smaller units, they argued, would better equip the girls to become domestic servants – their most likely employment destination – and, equally importantly, good mothers for the benefit of future generations and society.

In 1873, against the advice of his officials, Stansfeld determined to appoint Britain's first woman civil servant to embrace this thinking and conduct a review of the conditions of girls in poor law schools, and their subsequent fates from 'a woman's point of view'[6]. His first choice was Octavia Hill, who passed over the opportunity and recommended her friend Jane Elizabeth (commonly known as Jeanie) Senior (1828–1877) for the job. Jane was a sister of Thomas Hughes, author of *Tom Brown's Schooldays*, which will have given her insight into the brutality of institutional life some middle-class Victorian children faced.

More significantly, perhaps, she was also the daughter-in-law of Nassau Senior, one of the architects of the 1834 Poor Law Reform Act, whose 'less eligibility' principles she strongly decried. The pair also clashed on the

Jane Senior (1828–1877), Britain's first female civil servant, and barrack school reform advocate.

question of poor law separate and district schools. Nassau was a keen supporter, and recommended that every poor law union should have one – a sentiment she firmly rejected.[7]

Jane Senior was very much her own woman, and her 1874 report – published as an appendix to the LGB's annual report – provoked widespread controversy. She criticised barrack schools for being breeding grounds of disease, and for failing to give the children individual attention. She was quite explicit about her priorities, saying, 'Every question of mere administration ought to be subservient to the promotion of the health and vigour of the children.' In a withering attack, she accused the schools of 'failing to provide pauper girls with love, mothering, a sense of joy, individual worth, life skills and intellectual stimulation.'

She said that the massing of girls together in large numbers was corrupting and led to failure, that their physical and moral conditions were not sufficiently catered for, and that the education they experienced was poor.

Senior offered practical solutions, advocating, for example, the Mettray plan and arguing for cottage homes, housing children in households of no more than 20 or 30, in a rural setting which would, she said, offer 'a more home-like character' and provide a 'free and natural mode of life'. She felt these would offer something more akin to a family structure and suggested the older girls should spend a year or two helping to look after the infants, in an 'elder sister' role, in order to develop 'a sense of mothering'. She reported that too many of the children in the existing institutions looked weak and feeble, and called for improvements to their diets.

She felt that the children were too institutionalised in barrack schools and said they ought to have half-yearly excursions to help them acclimatise to the outside world. She also argued that older girls in either barrack schools or cottage homes should be allowed out to do shopping for the institutions, both to break the monotony of life within them, and to gain social and practical experience and build self-confidence for the future.

Her report urged that all the facilities should learn from good practice elsewhere, in particular she praised TS *Goliath* for encouraging boys to become self-reliant and taking responsibility for themselves. She also called for a better system of vocational training, and the separation of 'deserted' and 'casual' children into different groups and classes, in an effort to address the specific needs created by the ins and outs issue.

Senior stressed the importance of breaking down the impersonal nature of large establishments by adding colour and fun to children's lives. She called for paintings to be hung on walls, ornaments to be placed around the homes, poetry and dancing classes to be held and libraries to be introduced, as well as for corporal punishment to be banned.

Her report supported 'boarding out', which started to be referred to as fostering, as an alternative to barrack schools. This had its origins in Scotland, and became more widespread there following the passage of the 1845 Scottish Poor Law Amendment Act, which encouraged the system as a cheaper and better option to institutional childcare.[8] The English PLB commissioned a study of the system in practice in 1870[9] and consequently issued a boarding-out order, permitting English unions to adopt the system under the supervision of care local committees. Dr Barnardo, of whom more later, is reported to have said that 'boarding-out … owes its introduction in England to the indefatigable labours of the late Mrs Nassau Senior.'[10]

Under the scheme, pauper children could be housed in privately run accommodation, certified as fit for purpose. The foster parents were originally to be paid four shillings per week and, in signing up, 'agreed to bring up a child as one of their own, and provide it with proper food, lodging and washing, and endeavour to train it in habits of truthfulness, obedience, personal cleanliness, and industry, as well as suitable domestic and outdoor work.'[11]

The appeal of boarding out to Senior was clear, given her critique of barrack schools. The scheme was widely adopted by English boards of guardians by the 1880s and by the end of the century about half of all unions used it, looking after 8,000 children in total.[12]

Senior's report also advocated the radical step of breaking up large district schools into 'scattered homes', where the children would live under one roof and attend local schools, without stigma.

She was also interested in the after care of girls released from barrack schools, and visited a number of former residents who were now in work. She expressed concerns for their physical and moral well-being and called for the establishment of a body to address them. Two years later she established the Metropolitan Association for Befriending Young Servants (MABYS), specifically to undertake this function. She was supported by Henrietta Barnett, who joined her the following year, and was later to have a significant influence on the FGDS.

Mettray, an influential French establishment, founded in the 1830s for reforming delinquent boys.
(credit: Mary Evans/Peter Higginbotham collection)

Edward Tufnell, London's poor law schools' inspector, whose low opinion of the state and fate of workhouse children has already been noted, attempted, unsuccessfully, to prevent her report from being published; dismissing Senior's observations of barrack schools as 'sentimental follies'.

In one of his last acts as schools' inspector, he told her, 'no fair conclusion could be arrived at by a party of ladies trying to master so complicated a question in a few months.'[13]

Senior's report was a landmark in public policy attitudes to poor law children – advocating that they should be treated as individuals, with respect, and not as mere numbers in a total institution. Her recommendations would go on to help shape public thinking and practice about the unsuitability of barrack schools for the next 30 years.

However, she was forced, through ill-health, to resign from her civil service post in November 1874 and she was not replaced, nationally, by a sympathetic successor. Her resignation came just months after the replacement of her sponsor, James Stansfeld, as president of the LGB, and the board's impetus for reform quickly evaporated.

A recurrent problem of the new department was that poor law administration was both literally and metaphorically its poor relation, and beyond endless tinkering at the edges, little was done to address some of its systemic problems.

Throughout its history, the poor law functions of the department rarely attracted the most dynamic of ministers or innovative civil servants, with the result that it was conservative in approach and largely risk averse. The LGB's supervision lacked drive and ambition; instead it micro-managed poor law unions and their affiliated bodies in unimaginative ways.[14]

As a result, it showed no interest in promoting the progressive approaches to childcare that were being pioneered throughout the country to the poor law bodies it supervised. It offered no leadership and little indication of interest in supporting many of the humane initiatives aimed at improving the conditions and life chances of destitute children. It was happy to simply keep its deficient regimes and establishments in office and power, despite considerable evidence of their shortcomings.

The LGB immersed itself in the relative trivia of determining individual children's diets, staff salaries, personnel appraisals, supervising creed registers, and most of all, keeping an eye on expenditure, down to the very last penny.

So little was it interested in the education of those in the care of poor law bodies, that for over 30 years it resisted attempts to place the 'schools' it had responsibility for under the jurisdiction of educational bodies.

Despite being responsible for literally dozens of 'educational institutions', embracing tens of thousands of children at any one time (see Appendix), it did not consider sponsoring a single one for education in the capital. Instead, it was happy to preside over the creation of London-wide bodies to assist with poor law administration. When it sought a new governing regime for TS *Exmouth*, it placed it under the supervision of the MAB, a body established principally to supervise 'lunatic asylums'.

PROGRESSIVE PRACTICE OUTSIDE THE STATE SYSTEM

Thomas John Barnardo was born in Dublin in 1845 and underwent a conversion to the Plymouth Brethren sect in his late teens. He intended to become a missionary in China, and moved to London in 1866 to train as a doctor at Whitechapel's London Hospital. He lived in nearby Stepney and was moved by the widespread poverty he witnessed, which had been exacerbated by the effects of a cholera outbreak. He refocused his missionary attentions to the young poor of east London.

Barnardo's first significant institutional involvement with poor children was in ragged schools, which aimed to provide an education and often a meal for them. In September 1870, he opened a home for impoverished working lads in Stepney Causeway, which he soon operated under the banner 'No destitute child ever refused admission'. He later set up another ragged school in nearby Copperfield Road (today The Ragged School Museum).

Within two years of Jane Senior's report, Barnardo established his first home for girls, explicitly influenced by her considerations.[15] In 1873, he and his wife – Sara Louise who was known as 'Syrie' – were given a large home in Barkingside, Essex as a wedding gift. They transformed it into a refuge for destitute and homeless east London girls. In 1876 it was redeveloped into his second major innovation for the local young poor – a number of small family-style houses arranged as a girls' village home. Within six months he announced that he had a total of '1,700 boys and girls under my care requiring daily food, education and clothing.' Six months later the figure was 2,149.[16]

The girls' village homes eventually extended to over 60 cottages, housing more than 1,500, who were offered something resembling a reasonable

A VIEW IN THE GIRLS' VILLAGE HOMES,
BARKINGSIDE, ESSEX.

Thomas Barnardo was infamous for his use of staged photography to raise funds. This is an example of the tradition continuing after his death, in the form of a postcard published by Barnardo's in the early twentieth century, presenting an idealised view of the girl's village he established in Barkingside.

domestic life, and were taught skills that would enable them to become live-in servants for middle-class families. The site also included the village's own school, library, hospital, church and laundry.

From the mid-1870s, poor law unions in Bolton, West Derby and West Ham began to adopt tentative experiments with cottage homes, but by using existing buildings and usually with up to 50 residents.[17] The LGB published a survey conducted by F. J. Mouat and Captain J. D. Bowley on cottage homes in its 1878 annual report. The authors, having visited six of them, commented favourably on the practice.[18] The board, however, did little to promote or encourage the adoption of their recommendations.

Barnardo's offer to keep an ever-open front door for the destitute young required a very open exit door, if he were to manage the demand for places. In the 1870s, in his third major childcare experiment, he began sending some children to the expanding new farmlands of Canada. This policy was formalised in 1882, when he established a permanent settlement near Niagara Falls.

By 1888 he had sent 3,733 children, and according, to one biographer, 98 per cent of these had settled successfully.[19] Although there were periodic concerns about this policy and practice, he and his organisation continued to transport up to 1,000 children per year until the start of the First World War (Barnardo, himself, had died in 1905).

Barnardo's fourth significant initiative with east London's young poor was a large-scale application of boarding out. By 1887, the charity was boarding out 330 boys – mainly aged five to nine – with 120 families, usually in rural areas. The foster parents were paid, supervised and required to provide a broadly Christian upbringing for their charges. In 1888 he declared that he was 'deeply convinced that of all methods of training children, none are so advantageous, none so economical and none so successful in every way as boarding-out.'[20] By the end of that year he was able to claim that '500 of our bairns are so placed.'[21] That figure doubled within four years, and by 1896, his organisation was boarding out more children than all of England's poor law unions put together.

The third of the 'big three' children's welfare charities (after Barnardo's and National Children's Homes) was the CofE's Waifs and Strays Society (later The Children's Society), which was founded in 1882, in East Dulwich, South London, to provide accommodation in a family environment for destitute children. It made boarding out a priority, caring for a third of its children via that route, and using CofE clergy to recruit the foster parents.

Meanwhile, the thinking around social policy was progressing elsewhere. In 1889, reformer and commentator Florence Davenport-Hill published a book in which she examined some of the care options for pauper children. In it she raised concerns about the artificial nature of the cottage homes scheme, then regarded as being at the cutting edge of empathetic, childcentric thinking. Although the regime was considerably more progressive than the one in Forest Gate, she saw deficiencies within it, pointing out that:

> Everywhere there was the faint but unmistakable impression of an artificial system; everywhere was the stamp of the poor law, the mark of the pauper. The Cottage Homes and their families were much too large for reality; their studied neatness and affected homeliness did not give the *feeling* of home; for its genuine conditions were wanting.[22]

There was an almost immediate response by the board of guardians in Sheffield where, from 1893, significant steps towards the de-stigmatisation of children were adopted via the isolated or scattered homes initiative.

This approach had been endorsed, in outline, by Jane Senior in 1874, but it was two decades before the concept gained much traction and application within the social care system.

Under the scheme, groups of 15 to 20 children were placed under the care of house parents in homes scattered throughout the city. They attended local schools – with measures taken to prevent the emergence of 'ghetto schools', where there were concentrations of workhouse children. The children wore ordinary clothes and were encouraged to mix with other local children. They were not given 'industrial instruction', which was seen for its true purpose as cheap labour to keep establishments running at the lowest possible cost. The isolated homes model was later adopted by other unions, notably by West Ham in 1913, and was not dissimilar to common local authority care practices almost a century later.

As the following chapters will show, most of those responsible for the FGSD were either oblivious to, or unconcerned about, the benefits almost all the alternatives to their regime could have on young children. They did little to adapt and adopt, and generations of young children suffered as a result..

NOTES

[1] Higginbotham, *Children's Homes*, p. 13

[2] Ibid, pp. 22-25

[3] Ibid, pp. 202-203

[4] Ibid, pp. 92-97

[5] www.civilservant.org.uk; Stansfeld later sacrificed his parliamentary career by supporting Josephine Butler in campaigning against the Contagious Diseases Acts, which stigmatised and criminalised prostitutes – *James Stansfeld* by J. L and B. Hammond, 1932, p. 101

[6] 'Girls in pauper schools', *Third Annual Report of the Local Government Board*, 1873–4

[7] *Ross*, p. 29

[8] Rosemary Steer, *Children in Care: 1834–1929: The Lives of Destitute, Orphaned and Deserted Children*, Pen and Sword, 2020, p. 111

[9] J. J. Henley, *Report to the Poor Law Board on the Boarding-out of Pauper Children in Scotland*, 1870

[10] www.civilservant.org.uk/women-jeanie_senior.html

[11] Higginbotham, *Encyclopaedia*, p. 102

[12] Higginbotham, *Children's Homes*, pp. 81, 221-2

[13] www.civilservant.org.uk/women-jeanie_senior.html

[14] One of the problems of the LGB was the high turnover of ministers in charge. There were 10 presidents between its formation as a ministry and the dissolution of the FGDS in 1897. Although some of them, such as Joseph Chamberlain and Arthur Balfour, were dynamic and high-profile politicians, their stays at the Board were brief and simply stepping stones to higher office. The longest-serving president was Charles Ritchie (serving 1886–1892), who just happened to be the MP for Tower Hamlets, whose constituency contained many children who ended up

in the FGDS. Despite this, and the fact that his term of office spanned some of the FGDS' most difficult years, evidence from *Hansard* suggests he had no interest in the institution. In the six years of his presidency, he made 2,685 appearances at the despatch box in the House of Commons, making speeches, delivering statements or answering questions. Not one of those appearances related to the FGDS, although he did make reference to many other poor law institutions (Sources: *Hansard* and Wikipedia).

[15] See Appendix for details.

[16] T. J. Barnardo, *Three Tracts*, London, 1888

[17] Higginbotham, *Children's Homes*, p.72

[18] *Report on the Home and Cottage System of Training and Education the Children of the Poor*, LGB 1878

[19] J. Wesley Bready, *Dr Barnardo, Physician, Pioneer, Prophet*, Allen and Unwin, 1935, p. 156

[20] T.J. Barnardo (ed), *Night and Day: a Monthly Record of Christian Missions*, Vol 12, London 1888

[21] Ibid

[22] Florence Davenport-Hill, *Children of the State*, 1889, p. 36

CHAPTER 6

IGNORING GOOD PRACTICE

———

Overcrowded conditions prevailed in Forest Gate in the 1870s, even after the establishment of TS *Goliath*, and Hackney's dissatisfaction at the funding arrangements continued. At the same time, bad managerial practices went unchecked. Despite the great successes of TS *Goliath* and some revised thinking at the centre of government, life remained pretty much unchanged. The problems and behaviours at FGDS continued almost unabated.

Newspaper articles about the school were dominated by reports of boards of guardians' meetings and were overwhelmingly concerned with financial matters – getting value for money for ratepayers, the faction of east London which was literate and thus the newspapers' readers – and rarely about the needs or condition of children, how they lived, or their longer-term welfare and prospects. The poor were unlikely to be major subscribers to those papers, and so their requirements were often neglected in the reporting.

There was a single notable exception in one article from the *Hackney and Kingsland Gazette* on 23 October 1872. It is quoted at length because it is the best contemporary description of the physical condition of the institution and the lives of the children within it, and also because its tone gives an indication of the prevailing establishment thoughts on pauper children. It was clearly written from the perspective of the ratepayer, rather than pupil or parent, as its opening sentence made clear:

There are many besetting questions which occur to the heavily taxed ratepayers of Hackney, and amongst them, perhaps that which appeals to the highest degree of sympathy is: What becomes of the outcasts, orphans, and pauper children of this parish?

The writer's attitude was one of pity towards the children, rather than empathy, or a desire to seek justice for their plight. It continues: 'There is not a single individual who would begrudge his mite towards the sustenance of the little helpless ones who need support.' The journalist provided a setting and a vivid description of the institution's buildings, giving insights into its spartan conditions:

In about a half hour's journey by rail from Dalston Junction, the station of Forest Gate may be reached, within a few hundred yards of which there stands, fronting the line upon which we had passed, an extensive range of red brick buildings, faced with white, extremely neat in appearance, but unpretentious in architectural decorations.

The central portion, which constitutes the entrance, has a slightly projecting portico, above which on the first floor, is a bow window, with plain but massive brick mullions, surmounted with neat mouldings, composed chiefly of the same material. This portico of the building rises slightly above the rest, and is crowned with a pyramidal roof.

Right and left from this central entrance proceed ranges of three floors, the windows of which are arched and bounded with white bricks. There is a substantiality, apart from expansiveness, about its general appearance. From the extreme ends and the centre of this frontal line extend other ranges of buildings, of even less ornamental character; and these combined constitute the Forest Gate Schools, within which the pauper children of Hackney are educated.

The main building stands at some distance from the highway, the intervening space being devoted chiefly to grassy plots and flower beds. An iron fencing, panelled in geometric form as though it were intended to be glazed, with pillars of the same material intervening, bounds it by the road.

Passing the entrance-gate we come first upon the porter's lodge, which is likewise appropriated as a reception room for the parents to visit the children. Then proceeding along a broad and carefully kept gravelled walk, between two winding lines of shrubs and flowers, at the extremity of which two arborvitaes lift their heads and stand like sentinels, we reach the entrance of the schools. The walls of which have, as chief decorations, two marble tablets, the one on the right indicating the date of the building, when it opened in 1854 to the Whitechapel board, and the other, which is directly opposite, the date of transfer in 1869, to the united districts of Hackney, Whitechapel and Poplar.

By the ceiling entirely surrounding the hall is a pretty wreath of artificial flowers and foliage in white and green; while suspended beneath are numerous choice engravings, and upon the tables which constitute almost its only furniture, besides, are cases of stuffed pheasants, starlings and other birds.

The left wing and upper frontage is [sic] devoted to the various requirements of the girls, and the right one to similar purposes for the boys. There are school rooms, plainly but completely furnished with desks and suitable appliances, the walls being adorned with pictures of religious subjects, or such as are calculated to impart instruction in geography, natural history and the like.

Each room is heated by either an open fire or stove, which is carefully protected by a substantial guard. To the principal school rooms, special lesson rooms are attached, and for the girls in addition thereto, others for instruction in sewing, mending, and the use of sewing machines. The rooms in the boys' department are simply devoted to the general purposes of education, all extraneous teaching being outside the main building.

Proceeding directly from the hall we come upon a series of rooms devoted respectively to the offices, the dairy, bread room, larder, pantry, servants' hall and kitchen. In the latter are eight steam heated coppers, two of which are devoted to the boiling of milk, while the others are employed in the cooking of meat, vegetables, and puddings. Besides these there are two other large coppers for milk, which are used on special occasions and heated apart for steam. Two large gas ovens are the opposite side of the kitchen and fitted with every convenient appliance. The sculleries, one of which is devoted for the use of the officers, are very completely arranged, and piles of dishes, plates and various other utensils abound on every hand. In one of these there are also placed two other large gas ovens, for the cooking of the officers' food.

We then enter the dining hall. It is dinner time, and a scene presented itself for which we were not prepared. It was a large and lofty room, ornamented with mottoed shields, flags, battle axes, spears, and small festoons of crimson cloth. Near the centre, by one of the side walls, is a plain oaken pulpit and reading desk. For this hall is employed likewise as the chapel. A main aisle passes lengthwise, which is intersected another half way down the room. At the moment we entered there were upon something like narrow dwarfish desks, upwards of eight hundred plates and dinners, already prepared for eight hundred children.

We were asked to stand just on one side of the central crossing, and at a given signal, three out of the four doors were opened. At one extreme end, the school band of the boys struck up a lively air, the boys marching in order up the aisle, while from the opposite end, girls entered and proceeded in similar procession, and the infants, equally well trained, advanced along the side entrance.

In less than two minutes, the eight hundred children were seated in their respective places. The band ceased to play, every instrument was laid upon the floor, and the utmost silence reigned. At a given signal every child arose, and grace was sung in sweet harmony, by these little sons and daughters of poverty. At another signal each one resumed his seat, and the rattle of knives and forks began in real earnest.

Meanwhile, a solemn jackdaw sat perched upon the sash bar of an open window, and immediately the children began their midday meal, his sable majesty descended from his lofty perch, and flew about the room with unmolested delight. This is his daily custom. There are two jackdaws at the school, who in the daytime never quit the children. They are thorough pets, and are favourites alike with all.

The meal concluded, the departure was similar to the entrance, the band playing as they recede, the undying strain and heart stirring melody, *Home, Sweet Home*. The children then proceeded to their respective playgrounds to enjoy their various sports.

Of these playgrounds there are three, each one of which is entirely flagged, and contains a large slate-roofed shed, in which the children disport themselves in rainy weather. There are swings in all, but the boys have in addition thereto, a substantial and complete gymnasium. All alike seemed frolicsome, merry, and happy as little children should be. They were clean and neat, comfortably though humbly clad; and although a superintendent attended each one of the grounds, yet there was evidently no terror inspired thereby.

The children rise daily throughout the year at 5.45 am, attend prayers at 6.45 am and after breakfast go into school at 9 am, where they remain until 12 o'clock, with a quarter hour's recess for play. After dinner they re-enter school at 2 pm where they continue until 5 pm, with another quarter of an hour's respite intervening. At 6 pm supper is served; then they are permitted to play for the remainder of the evening, with the exception of the time devoted to prayers and all are in bed by 8 o'clock. The infants, of course, are exceptional to these general rules.

Given earlier press and governors' reports about the extent of over-crowding in the establishment, and cramped conditions in the dormitories, the account gave what was probably an unduly positive description of the sleeping arrangements and accommodation:

The dormitories are spacious, lofty and well-ventilated rooms, with tiny beds all scrupulously clean, and by each of which is placed a basket for the day's clothing, as it is taken off. The counterpanes for the girls are white, and for the boys, brown, the knots upon which constitute the inscription, 'School District Forest Gate'. The little iron bedsteads are curtain-less, and there is not a vestige of carpeting in the children's rooms. A single light burns feebly through the night, and as a nurse's room adjoins each dormitory, with a little window opening, therein, she can look up on the little sleepers and immediately attend in case of any emergency.

Similarly, some of the public health and hygiene issues the institution regularly faced were glossed over in a rather upbeat account of the toilet facilities:

The lavatories and baths are of the most complete description. In one room there are 45 basins set into and hinged on a long slate table, with most ingenious arrangements for letting the water both on and off, and above each basin is a long roller towel. There are also two extensive plunging baths through which the elder children must pass twice a week, while the younger receive complete ablutions under less pretentious arrangements.

The Infirmary is a building separated entirely and some distance from the schools, and out of nearly 850 children there are but 36 afflicted, and of those, except the constitutionally diseased, there is not at present a serious case, while it affords us utmost pleasure to record that during the last five months there has not been a single infectious patient, or a case death. The infectious wards are separated from the Infirmary, and are now, happily, tenantless.

The author proceeded to address the question posed at the beginning of the article: 'What becomes of the outcasts, orphans, and pauper children of this parish?' Unsurprisingly, he highlighted the 'industrial' training the youngsters received and focused on the preparation the girls received for future employment as domestic servants. As far as the boys were concerned, the journalist described the vocational training they received in some detail, but did not refer to any of them gaining jobs in these trades. The only future employment mentioned was the armed forces.

This suggests that the skills taught in the establishment were imparted to enable it to be run as cheaply as possible with the boys working to keep it operational, rather than offering them practical training in work-related areas. The fact that the boys were later placed in the army and navy indicates that they were being groomed for a home from home; from one disciplined institution to another. Hardly surprising, when ex-army personnel were invariably appointed to manage the institution.

Children leaving at 14 were too young to make their own way in the world; domestic service provided a home for the girl leavers and the armed forces for the boy pupils. Indeed, the 1885 LGB annual report showed that fewer than two per cent of girls who left district schools for work over the previous 11 years had entered an occupation other than domestic service.

The article continued:

Eighty boys are trained industrially in tailoring and shoemaking, twenty in each department being engaged during alternate days in each department, the remainder of their time being occupied in education. Then there are the carpenters' and engineers' shops fitted with lathes and supplied with tools by which they may in after life be enabled to follow as skilled artisans the respective trades they choose to adopt.

The girls are trained to house, laundry, needle work, and so thoroughly is the system carried out, that the whole work of the schools is performed by the children, with the exception of the making of new boots.

During the past two years 95 girls have been sent to service, and 96 boys have either joined the army or navy, or have enlisted in the bands of various regiments.

Attention was given to the decent but not ostentatious accommodation which the resident staff occupied:

> The officers' apartments, including those of the Master and Matron, Chaplain, and Surgeon, are furnished with neatness, in fact there is no extravagance in any part of the building; not even in the board room, whose chief adornment consists of a ground-plan of the schools, and photographs of the ship, and the boys in training upon *Goliath*.

The period of quarantine and isolation experienced by newcomers to the establishment was also mentioned:

> Every child upon entering undergoes a fortnight's probation in the reception wards, which are also apart from the general school. This is done as a matter of precaution to ensure healthiness and prevent both infection and contagion.

The writer concluded, satisfied with what he had seen:

> Moral, social, religious, and training, are alike enforced, and the little waifs of Hackney, when they leave the schools, are fully fitted to enter upon the grand duties of maturer life. Strict order and discipline are enforced under the judicious superintendence

of Mr. and Mrs. Barnett [James and Elizabeth], for without these essentials, no general good result would follow, and we left the Forest Gate Schools, firmly impressed with the belief, that not only is no cruelty practised, but that the poor children of Hackney are under mild supervision, and properly cared for.

A year later the LGB sent a questionnaire to the superintendents of all district schools about their condition. What follows is a summary of the FGSD's response.[1]

The establishment and its grounds, the reply stated, occupied 12 acres. As far as newcomers were concerned, the Hackney and Whitechapel guardians certified that they were in good health before leaving their workhouses. Only in Poplar did the medical officer examine his union's children before certifying their good health. The institution had a probation ward that could accommodate 50, who were kept there until there was room in the main buildings. If there were excess demand, the overflow of children would be accommodated in the infirmary.

Once resident, the children were examined monthly by the medical officer and the results were reported to the governors. All children were examined for cleanliness each morning before breakfast and twice per week, after baths.

The boys wore the same clothes all year round, while girls wore gingham frocks in the summer and stuff frocks and petticoats in winter. Body linen was changed twice per week. Children only had one pair of footwear each, which was changed when it became wet.

Children aged two to nine slept in double beds and the older children had single beds. The mattresses were made of flock – or straw in the case of children who still wet themselves – and the bed sheets were changed weekly.

Personal washing took place in large lavatories with fixed basins. The pupils did not have their own towels; roller towels were used to dry themselves, which were changed twice daily. Pupils had baths twice weekly, but without soap. The water closets (which were open) were deemed to be in a satisfactory state; the sewerage from them was disposed of via the main drain. 'It used to be used on the land, but that was objected to.'

The playground was flagged, and the children were taken outside the establishment once a week, sometimes to visit nearby Wanstead Flats. The boys had four hours a week drill – two hours each on Wednesday and Saturday afternoons. The girls did not receive equivalent exercise.

The questionnaire sought details of the 'industrial' work undertaken by the children. The response confirmed that in practice, 'industrial work' was more about keeping the establishment functioning with as few staff as possible, than it was in teaching children skills. It listed the occupations followed:

> Boys: tailors, 38; shoemakers, 36; gardeners, 22; carpenters, 6; engineers, 6; cleaning lavatories, 6; carrying coal, 6; office, 1. Girls: dormitories, 68; housework, 52; kitchen, 20; laundry, 16; hall, 18. There are 75 boys in the band, divided into two bands [for which they received six hours practice per week, in preparation for them gaining positions in the army as bands boys]. All boys are employed in some class of the above work. There are 14 girls in the needle room who do no other industrial work; but the girls employed in the dormitories, housework and hall, go to the needle room, where their other work is done. The girls in the laundry and kitchen go to a sewing class twice a week.

A typical school day for the children is considered in the next chapter. After school supper was taken between 6.00 pm and 6.30 pm, although the working day for most did not end there. Children under 10 retired to dormitories at 7.00 pm and the older girls were expected to work in the needle room between 7.00 pm and 8.30 pm on Tuesdays and Thursdays. The older boys had singing lessons between those hours on Mondays, Wednesdays and Fridays. On the days the children weren't occupied with these tasks, they were expected to clean shoes, knives and forks etc. between 7.30 pm and 8.15 pm. The older children retired to their dormitories at 8.45 pm. On Sundays all the children rose, took their meals, and were required to attend divine services at times directed by the governors.

The above paints a dispassionate picture of life in the institution in the early 1870s, although it did not mention chronic overcrowding. Nor did the account address some of its long-standing cultural deficiencies relating to cruelty, lack of nurturing, inept management, anti-Catholicism, and the intertwined problems of unhealthy living areas and cramped conditions.

In contrast, PLB records at this time described a number of cases of severe corporal punishment. James Galloway, a recently appointed teacher, was found guilty of beating three boys in the summer of 1870.[2] The first, Frederick Veal had 'one mass of severe bruises and wales on his arms and every portion of his body, to his hips and of such a character that the punishment must have been most severe.'

Second was William Lovell, who was 'Terribly waled over his arms, shoulders and back. This lad was punished with his coat off.' And finally, John Carney, who was described as being 'Much bruised, was knocked down in the playground by Mr Galloway and there are distinct marks of his knuckles in two places on the boy's side.'

Galloway was eventually dismissed, after a governors' inquiry during which he maintained he did not know the rules in relation to corporal punishment.

In May 1873, disciplinary hearings were heard against another teacher, John Henry Trowell. He had previously been cautioned for inflicting inappropriate corporal punishment and he was initially suspended for his second offence. He was sacked on 23 May, with the dismissal confirmed by the PLB.[3] Interestingly, the chaplain, the Rev Poole, condemned Trowell's brutality, not so much for its harshness but because the actions were 'calculated to incite mutiny at the school.'

Ill-discipline and poor management continued, when three junior members of staff were sacked because 'a spirit of insubordination has recently been exhibited by some of the servants at Forest Gate schools to the superintendent and matron.'[4]

Although we do not have contemporaneous statements from the FGDS teachers about their attitude to their pupils, on 4 June 1870, William Imeson, headmaster of the former Central London District School, now Hanwell District School, gave a flavour of his view, which may have typified those held in Forest Gate. He was quoted in a letter to *The Times* saying the children in his care were:

> The dregs of the population. They arrive here in various stages of squalor and disease; all of them are more or less debased; their intellectual capabilities are of the lowest order; their moral sense is stifled or inactive through suspicion and obstinacy. Many of them inherit the hoarse indistinct utterance of the London costermonger … . Their natural bias is to run the course of their fathers in ignorance and it may be in crime. With a strangely marked precocity, they are ignorant to a degree that can scarcely be overrated.[5]

The ill-treatment of Catholics re-emerged as a significant issue in the FGDS in 1871, when local Catholic clergy complained to the governors and PLB that their children weren't having their religious needs met. The governors were dismissive, claiming that it was a matter of little importance and that in any case, many one-time Catholic pupils had converted to 'the established church'.

There was an escalation in the Catholic response, which secured a significant intervention by Britain's leading Catholic cleric, Henry Manning, the Archbishop of Westminster. He wrote to the LGB in April 1873, complaining that 'The provisions made for the education of Catholic children in the Forest Gate District Schools were not only not productive of advantage to the children, but even injurious to them.'

There were 110 Catholic children there, but the governors only permitted a Catholic priest access once per week. The archbishop said that this was unlawful.

The institution, Manning claimed, made it particularly difficult for the infants to attend a Catholic church and did not provide daily religious tuition for Catholic pupils, as it did for CofE pupils. This was made worse, he said, because there were no Catholic teachers and, therefore, nobody in authority to whom Catholic children could turn for spiritual support and guidance.

Manning wanted the establishment to appoint a resident Catholic chaplain, to be supported by a Catholic matron, who would cater for the religious and spiritual needs of their under sevens.[6]

The matter rumbled on and by February 1875 an uneasy compromise was struck with the governors agreeing to permit Catholic priests to visit every Monday. It also made arrangements for some of the older pupils to attend church services in Stratford, as long as they had a chaperone. By October, 59 Catholic children – a little more than half those on the creed register – were receiving one hour of appropriate religious tuition per week.

The establishment, however, remained largely unsympathetic to the plight of Catholics and in December 1875 told the LGB that more of their children had 'decided' to change their faith from Catholicism to CofE.[7] In an effort to appease the Catholic hierarchy and prevent undue pressure and manipulation of Catholic youngsters, the LGB said they wished to investigate every application made by children for a change of creed designation.

This was little more than window dressing. The LGB had scant interest in intervening in individual cases, and ended up applying a rather crude formula to the notifications. Applications for children under the age of 14 to 'switch' creeds were routinely rejected on the grounds that the children were too young to make informed judgements, while those on behalf of the over-14s were accepted, without question.

The level of LGB disinterest was highlighted in March 1878 in correspondence about a young girl, referred to as 'the Jewess'.[8] She was Rebecca Warzberg, who the governors said had been found destitute on the streets of Whitechapel in 1870, aged four. She had been classified in the institution's creed register at the time as Catholic (the most frequently used non-CofE option), but in 1878, aged 13, was fully aware of her heritage and wished to have her creed classification altered to Jewish, with the full support of the governors. The LGB rejected the application on the grounds that she was too young to make that decision.

Overcrowded accommodation, unhealthy conditions and a casual approach to safety continued to have seriously detrimental effects on the health of the children, at the same time as TS *Goliath* was winning praise and plaudits for its approach.

In March 1871, for example, the PLB received a report that two unsupervised girls, aged four and six, had died from drinking carbolic acid from an unattended glass, which had been carelessly left out by a porter who planned to use it to clean water closets later that day. He was merely given a verbal warning by the governors for his negligence.[9]

Public health issues were problematic from the outset, and Thomas Vallance, the establishment's medical officer, was at the centre of most of them. As early as June 1871, the governors expressed their concern to the PLB about his inadequate response to an outbreak of ringworm.

But it was his approach to ophthalmia that caused greatest dissatisfaction, locally and nationally. It was an eye disease – similar to a severe case of conjunctivitis – first identified in 'pauper schools' in 1841, which could result in permanently damaged eyes and even loss of sight. It became the bane of many children's residential establishments in Victorian Britain. Rates varied between institutions and over time, but it could affect up to 30 per cent of children during any bout. Poor diet and foul air – exacerbated by the prevalence of open soil bucket toilets in overcrowded dormitories – were the main causes. Sharing towels for washing was clearly an unrecognised contributory factor.

There were 40 cases at the FGDS when it first opened and the disease plagued the school throughout its entire existence. Vallance always displayed a casual attitude towards ophthalmia, which invariably worsened the contagion. In the early 1870s, an outbreak nationwide lead the LGB to reduce the maximum permitted capacity in all children's workhouses. As a result, Forest Gate's was capped at 650, thus increasing the pressure to find additional accommodation for excess pupils.

Following an inspection of the establishment in June 1874, the LGB noted the prevalence of unhealthy sanitary conditions:

> The water supply and drainage of the establishment generally requires attention. In particular, the drains near the kitchen and offices were observed to give off a well-marked sewage odour and appear to require a very thorough examination.

A follow-up visit by the LGB's medical officer, Dr Bridges, found a high incidence of ophthalmia. He reported that only 133 of the children had healthy eyelids; 463 had slight symptoms of the disease and 237 had a fully developed condition. Vallance challenged the figures and set in train an argument between the two medics that spanned a decade.

Bridges recommended 200 children be transferred to spare capacity in Shoreditch's institution in Brentwood, which had recently expanded its capacity for 900, although only 650 places were occupied. In compliance, the Forest Gate governors transferred 200 of their children, at a cost of seven shillings per week per child, to Brentwood.

The LGB's ophthalmia concerns returned in 1877, when Vallance's claim that there were only 16 cases in the institution was challenged by Bridges, who insisted 74 children were affected.[10] Although the condition was contagious, Vallance said he didn't believe contaminated children should be kept in isolation, because of the 'evil moral effects and loss of their education'. He also maintained that Bridges had been duped by a number of boys who feigned the condition and 'are playing tricks with their eyes in order to get into the infirmary.'

Bridges would not be silenced, and reported the following in strong terms to his employers, the LGB:

> I regret to say that I found a greater amount of ophthalmia among the children than I have on previous occasions ... . I cannot say that I was very favourably impressed with the conditions in the boys' department ... . The lavatories and privies were in bad

order. The basins had in many cases dirty water and soap suds left in them. There were large puddles of water on the floor in the privies in the yard. The dormitories were far from tidy ... in a slovenly condition ... . I found evidence of an unhappy state of feeling among some of the principal officers ... I am convinced that without greater harmony than exists at present, there cannot be good administration.[11]

The following year the LGB expressed deep concern at the establishment's dreadful annual death rate; it was running at 19 per 1,000 pupils per year (38 children had died in the institution between 1875 and 1877), compared with a rate of only 13 per 1,000 of the whole population of Whitechapel.[12] The board said that not enough was being done to isolate children with infectious diseases.

Vallance dismissed their concerns and blamed the children for being 'very trivial and 'unco-operative'. He said that he was not in favour of isolating the infected children, instead prescribing that they should be given more green vegetables, with their meals having 'some vinegar poured over them'.

In 1879, the LGB expressed concern over the incidence of whooping cough and felt that 'the unusual number of fatal cases may be attributable to over-crowding in the infants' department.'

In 1882, the governors sought the LGB's approval to appoint a medically qualified person to examine 'differences of opinion between the medical officer of Forest Gate District Schools and the medical officers of the Whitechapel and Poplar unions' on the state of the children's health. The LGB agreed, commenting that Dr Bridges felt that Vallance operated a 'careless and slovenly mode of administration'.[13]

Bridges cited that there were no bed cards in the infirmary with details of the patients' illnesses, nor were nurses given written prescriptions for medicines and that important and necessary medicines were often missing from the infirmary's stock. He said that Vallance had been slack in his approach to the vaccinations of the children, concluding that 'I cannot doubt that a systematic revaccination of all the children [against smallpox] would result in a large number of successful cases.'

Despite these criticisms of Vallance by their own medical officer, and the wealth of evidence of his multi-tasking and moonlighting, the LGB refused the governors' request to sack him, and his bad medical practice continued unimpeded.

Meanwhile, the question of excess demand for places had turned from an overcrowding issue to a displacement one. As a result of the relocation of 200 youngsters to Brentwood in 1875, and the redeployment of 83 FGDS charges from TS *Goliath* to the former hospital in Grays, more than a quarter of the district's pupils were now located outside Forest Gate.

In February 1876, the FGDS had more than 900 children under its jurisdiction, spread between three establishments, some distances apart: Forest Gate, Brentwood and Grays:

Union[14]	Forest Gate	Brentwood	Grays	Total
Hackney	210	54	20	284
Poplar	216	76	32	324
Whitechapel	212	54	31	297
Total	**638**	**184**	**83**	**905**

This displacement led to a revived consideration of building an extension to Forest Gate, at a cost of £20,000, to accommodate the outplacements locally.

Wyndham Holgate, the recently appointed inspector of metropolitan poor law schools, favoured the proposal, and saw it as an ideal opportunity to erect a purpose-built infants facility catering for the 220 under-sevens. The FGSD governors bought some land adjacent to the existing establishment with a view to extending it.

However, Poplar's guardians vetoed the new construction proposal, calling instead for the three-union district to be dissolved. Hackney responded by negotiating with Shoreditch about transferring its 284 pupils to Brentwood and converting its separate school into a district school, controlled by the two geographically adjacent unions.[15]

The LGB mediated the arrangements and Whitechapel and Poplar agreed to pay Hackney £4,820 to buy it out of the FGSD; Poplar, £3,010 and Whitechapel £1,810.[16] The FGSD switched from being a three-union district to a two-union project, and funding formulae and governing arrangements were amended accordingly.

NOTES

1 LMA, *FGSD governors' 1873/4 Annual Report*
2 NA, MH27/102
3 NA, MH27/103
4 Ibid
5 Letter from John R Collins, 4 Jun 1870
6 NA, MH27/103
7 NA, MH27/104
8 NA, MH27/106
9 NA, MH27/103
10 Ibid
11 Ibid
12 To put these appalling figures into perspective, the current death rate for children aged one to 17 in London is 12.2 per 100,000. The figure at the FGDS in the mid-1870s was 150 times higher.
13 NA, MH27/106
14 LMA, FGSD 001
15 Ibid
16 *ELA* 24 Aug 1878

CHAPTER 7

POOR APPOINTMENTS

═══════

The decade after Hackney left the FGSD was perhaps the most stable in its 50-year history. At a national level, the LGB had bedded itself in as the government watchdog, and following Stansfeld's lead and Jane Senior's report, was responsive to minor incremental reform within children's workhouses. Its overall approach, however, was characterised by caution, frugality and an unquestioning adherence to the status quo. It failed to deal adequately with the very obvious failure of the FGDS.

The guardians of Whitechapel and Poplar co-operated in the administration of the establishment and there was no significant movement by either board to leave the district or extend its membership. There was a gradual improvement in the conditions experienced by the pupils throughout the decade – many inspired by the work of Henrietta Barnett, of which more later. The journey was not, however, unremittingly positive.

This, then, is a convenient place to present something of a snapshot of life in the institution's history, its influencers, staff and pupils and the conditions they experienced.

The building was laid out in four blocks. The main building had three floors and housed four schoolrooms, two recreation rooms, a dining hall, kitchen, sewing and needlework rooms and 18 dormitories. There were another five dormitories in the infants' block, which also had two school rooms and two day rooms. The third block, an infirmary (still standing to the left of and set back from the main block, facing from Forest Lane) had six wards to cater for up to 36 children. The fourth building, a probation or reception lodge (most of which still stands at the entrance to Forest Lane Park) took 36 youngsters during their quarantine period.[1]

The establishment was run by a board of governors, the majority of whom were representatives from the boards of guardians of the constituent unions. They were all unpaid part-timers and typically wealthy local ratepayers who were usually more concerned with keeping the rates down than looking after the interests of the children.

They did not experience the kind of stringent lifestyle they imposed on their charges. They chose, instead, to travel in style to meetings at the institution and eat lavishly while there, for which they were surcharged by government auditors in December 1895. Their justification: 'We've been doing it since 1869.'[2]

The guardian-appointed governors were supplemented by a number of ex-officio members, nominated by the LGB, to broaden the experience of the group. Henrietta Barnett was the most prominent of these, serving for 20 years (1876–1896). She was the first woman 'manager' appointed nationally, and the only female governor of the FGSD throughout its history.

The three highest paid officers of the establishment were the clerk to the governors, its medical officer and the chaplain. Unlike the majority of staff, they were non-resident, although they had accommodation on site. They were from the ranks of what at the time would have been considered the professional middle class (unlike teachers); and each prospered by taking multiple paid jobs inside and outside the institution.

Typically, the clerk was also the secretary of one of the constituent boards of guardians, and he would have taken a salary from both posts. As one governors' clerk retired, he was replaced by another, from a different board, on an almost Buggins' turn rotation.

Perhaps the most famous of them was William Vallance (FGSD clerk 1887–1892). He was a significant and controversial figure in poor law administration. On his appointment as secretary to the Whitechapel board in 1868, he declared himself to be a fierce opponent of outdoor relief, and encouraged its guardians to send all successful applicants for poor relief to the workhouse.[3]

His attitude, according to one of his obituaries[4] made him 'the best abused man in England' and provoked riots in Whitechapel that the police had to break up. In later life, he became a noted speaker on poor law reform and a witness to government and parliamentary enquiries – invariably encouraging the same hard line be taken towards poor law claimants.

His tough stance in defending the public purse did not prevent him from simultaneously acting as secretary to the Whitechapel guardians, registrar of births, marriages and deaths for the district and, additionally, becoming clerk to the Forest Gate governors, for which he was paid £200 per year. He became a wealthy man by administering the poor law. Having started from humble beginnings, when he died in 1909, he left an estate valued at almost £11,000 (£1,300,000 today).[5]

On his retirement from Whitechapel, the London County Council (LCC) made an exception to its rule, and named a road after a living person, creating Vallance Road in Bethnal Green. It had been previously known as Charles Road, was the location of the Whitechapel workhouse and is better known today as the former home of the Kray brothers.

The second significant 'professional' on the payroll was the medical officer. Thomas Vallance was from Stratford and, having been appointed medical officer to the Whitechapel establishment in 1866, simply transferred over to the district, aged 40, on its foundation the following year. He held the post for a further 15 controversial years. Despite sharing an uncommon surname, he was not closely related to William.

In addition to his local private medical practice, Thomas was employed by three separate poor law organisations simultaneously. He was appointed medical officer to the West Ham workhouse (786 inmates) in 1867, receiving a salary of £200; the same year as he took the post of medical officer to the FGSD, with 857 children on a similar stipend. He also became medical officer to the West Ham children's workhouse (330 children), with a salary of £80 in May 1881, without relinquishing either of the other posts.[6]

The three publicly funded posts were to give him an annual income of £480, to supplement his earnings from private practice. Clearly he could not be in more than one place at once, and, as will become clear, his patients in each institution suffered as a result.

The third of the trio of well-paid professionals was the chaplain. Samuel Poole held the post from 1854 until his death in 1891 and was for many years its highest paid officer, on a salary rising to £220. He also had paid jobs as chaplain to Tower Hamlets Cemetery and to Trinity Almshouses for much of the time.[7] It will come as no surprise that the FGDS' governors frequently complained about his absence from the site. He was succeeded by the Rev Henderson Burnside, vicar of nearby St Saviour's Church. It didn't take long before the governors were complaining about his poor attendance – less than 25 per cent of what was expected – because they believed he spent too much time on other duties. He was asked to consider his position, and agreed to resign in 1893.[8]

DYSFUNCTIONAL MANAGEMENT

There were 47 adults (36 female and 11 male) resident in the buildings on the night of the 1881 census and all except the superintendent's wife were staff. The resident adult to child ratio was 1: 13 during most of the week.

The onsite staff comprised superintendent and the matron, together with teaching, nursing and domestic staff. James Barnett, 61, was the district school's first superintendent, having previously managed the Whitechapel separate school. He was ex-Royal Artillery, and had been given a fifty per cent pay rise – to £180 per annum – to head the district school. His wife Elizabeth was the matron, receiving £70. The couple retired on the grounds of ill-health in 1873, on generous pensions of £135 and £65 a year respectively, determined by the FGSD and ratified by the PLB.

They were replaced on the cheap. Low pay was certainly an issue in recruiting the superintendents, which probably accounted for the poor quality of the appointees. They were typically paid less than the three outside professionals, despite the fact they lived on site all the time, while each of the others had at least two additional jobs.

The new chief, Joseph Epton Hardwick, was paid just £150 pa, and his matron wife, Rachel, £60 – £5 less than the pension that her predecessor had been awarded. They had previously been master and 'wife' of a workhouse elsewhere, but proved to be a disaster in Forest Lane.

Within four years there were complaints from Whitechapel's guardians, the chaplain and other staff about the 'Failure of the superintendent and matron to have generally inspired confidence in the officers and servants during the whole of their administration ... resignation of about 80 persons ... while they have had 25 per cent more officers and servants proportionately than their predecessors.'[9] The governors told the LGB that 'the superintendent and matron do not possess the tact, management and respect of the officers and children which an institution of this kind demands.'

Despite the severity of this criticism, the LGB persuaded the governors not to sack the Hardwicks. The couple were eventually persuaded to resign, in November 1877, following a report of an unauthorised beating of 28 pupils. The fact that they were not sacked meant they were free to be employed by other poor law establishments, despite their obvious unsuitability and incompetence. The LGB really was woeful in protecting the inmates of workhouse institutions from unsuitable staff.

For the first 50 years of its existence, none of the institution's superintendents had either an education or care career background. It wasn't until the twentieth century that an educationalist was appointed to be in charge.

Albert Augustus Pollard replaced Hardwick as superintendent five months later. His was obviously a controversial choice, only being given the job, subject to a three-month probation period, by a six to five majority of the appointments committee. He was a 38-year-old widower from Hackney, with eight years military service, but no relevant education, childcare or poor law administration experience.

Within six months of his confirmation, he married, and the governors used his changed marital status to seek his resignation, with which he complied, reputation and reference intact, in May 1879.

The governors tried to appoint a replacement three months later and offered the job to John Rayment. He quickly turned them down having heard about the state of the institution from a previous post-holder.

The matron, Harriet Perfect, was given an 'acting up' allowance of £12 for effectively being in charge of the establishment through the periods of vacancy during the merry-go-round of superintendents. It was the only time the institution was led by a woman, and apparently nothing untoward occurred.[10] Henrietta Barnett was later to quip, however, that her surname was a poor indicator of her attitude and behaviour towards the children.

In desperation, the governors looked within and appointed 47-year-old Charles Duncan, who had been the institution's teacher of military music since 1869. He was another ex-military man, married and living in Gurney Road, Stratford. He was permitted to take his wife with him to live in the married quarters. He was a cheap option, tripling his salary as bandmaster, from £50 to £150, the same as the district school's first superintendent, a decade earlier, and less than half of what Bourchier received when commanding TS *Goliath*. He offered continuity and stability, but had no real managerial experience, which became apparent as poor staff relationships and discipline continued on his watch. He held the post for 16 years, and was an uninspired appointment.

Within six months he mishandled the case of Miss Mary Coleman, and was bailed out by the governors. Coleman had been assistant head of the infants' school, but wasn't promoted to its top position when it became vacant. She responded by becoming disruptive; bullying her subordinate staff and ignoring unauthorised punishments of her young charges. All five of her staff resigned in protest and the governors had to step in, persuade the teachers to withdraw their resignations and suggest Coleman get a job elsewhere because of her 'violent discourteous manner'. They needed the support of LGB to secure her resignation the following month. Another inappropriate staff member left with a clean CV, free to work elsewhere within the poor law system.[11]

BADLY PAID, POOR CALIBRE TEACHERS

The teaching staff at the newly established district school consisted of three masters, paid £120, £65 and £45 pa, and three equivalent mistresses, paid £75, £35 and £30. No equal pay here – the women receiving between 40 per cent and 50 per cent less than their male equivalents. There were, in addition, three needlework teachers, paid £30, £24 and £14 14s, and two infant teachers, paid £40 and £21 pa. The institution opened with around 860 pupils, giving it an initial teacher to pupil ratio of 1:78.

All but one of the teachers were unmarried; with two widowed. Most were very young, particularly the men and the infant teachers. The average age of the four schoolmasters was 24; the three schoolmistresses 35 and the two infant mistresses 25. The teacher to pupil ratio on the night of the census was 1:46.

There were five onsite nurses. The rest of the resident adults were support staff, of which there were three yardsmen (general site labourers), one porter/groundsman, one apprentice mason, five laundresses, one portress, three attendants, four housemaids, one cook, one scullery maid, one pantry maid, three infant attendants, one boys' attendant and one girls' attendant.

Six of the live-in staff were under the age of 20. There were, in addition, eight industrial trainers who lived outside the complex, not included as resident on census night, and classified as day visitors. The superintendent was from Wiltshire and only six of the remaining adults on site were from outside the home counties (one from Ireland and three from Somerset).

There were 648 pupils at the institution on census night, 269 of whom (42 per cent) were female and 379 (58 per cent) male. Infants and children aged up to seven comprised 128 pupils (20 per cent). Among them were three children who were just two years old; 18 who were three; 33 who were four years old and 38 aged five. It was not until the 1889 Education Act that the minimum age for admission to children's workhouses was raised to three.

The median age of the pupils on census night was 10 years and two months. Although the establishment was often referred to an 'an industrial school', it is difficult to envisage that useful 'industrial training' could have been imparted to a 10 year old. The institution was in reality little more than a children's workhouse.

Post-holders regularly appealed to the LGB for pay rises, via the institution's governors; but they were routinely refused on the grounds that they were already paid as much as their opposite numbers in other metropolitan district schools.

It was a frequent complaint that the teachers were not given parity of esteem or status with teachers in state elementary schools. Consequently, they were usually inadequately or barely qualified. One cleric, writing in 1882, characterised the problem surrounding teachers in children's work-houses[12]in general:

> It yet remains true that workhouse school teachers are, taken as a whole, of a distinctly lower grade, educationally speaking, than teachers of elementary schools; their certificates do not rank so high; their qualifications have never been so thoroughly tested; their knowledge of men and books is not so wise. Trained teachers from our colleges are as rare in workhouse schools as blackberries in May; it is said that only failures answer the advertisements of guardians.

Each teacher was expected to spend around 18 hours per week in the classroom. As residential staff they were also required to undertake a large number of child-minding tasks during non-class contact time. The 1886 job description of a needlework teacher illustrated this. In addition to a very detailed list of teaching duties, she was required to:

> Assist in bathing girls, inspecting their skins and heads for disease, be present at all bathing times. Assist in maintaining order in dining hall at all meal times. Teach children how to use cutlery. Be responsible for ensuring the needle room is kept tidy by the girls given responsibility for it. Be in recreation rooms or grounds every third evening to ensure order, and ensure prayers are said

and girls put to bed in an orderly way. Teach girls good habits: neatness, good timekeeping, cleanliness etc.[13]

Staffing difficulties in the infants' department were also exacerbated by low pay and in July 1886 the governors wrote to the LGB seeking to raise their salaries, because of rapid staff turnover. Over the previous 12 months 12 individuals had occupied the four assistant posts, which resulted in disruption, lack of continuity and inconvenience. The governors explained their difficulty in finding suitable candidates 'who are willing to discharge the onerous and at times unpleasant duties for the salary'. Reluctantly, the LGB sanctioned a small pay increase.[14]

Given the level of additional responsibilities, it is no wonder the institution had difficulties in attracting competent and qualified staff, particularly as it offered nothing by way of enhancing their CVs. In order to get a teachers' proficiency certificate for work in board schools, applicants required two years' satisfactory probation in a school. Service in poor law schools, however, did not qualify for this purpose until 1890.[15]

This was because it did not come under the aegis of the education department. Even though there had been a central government education department since before its inception, it was the responsibility initially of the PLB and latterly the LGB.

One consequence of this was that it was exempt from various 'half-timer' school regulations in the 1880s, which greatly reduced the industrial training of youngsters until the age of 13. Poor law schools' youngsters under that age did not get the full school day's education that their opposite numbers did in elementary schools.

This point was addressed directly in a conference on district schools held in Shoreditch in 1889. It called for children's workhouses – with a total of 30,000 pupils and 780 staff – to be placed directly under the control of the education department because their syllabus was too restricted. Having district schools placed under the supervision of the LGB was, it was argued, 'visiting the sins of the fathers on the children'.

Mr Cook of the FGSD (the owner of the large local employer, the East London Soap Works) said it had difficulties recruiting suitable teachers because they were treated as subordinates to other officers in the establishment and that 'Guardians and managers would find they were asking too much of their teachers in requiring them to live on the premises and of taking up a good deal of menial work out of the schoolroom way.'[16]

Responding to a government inquiry, in 1897, the FGSD admitted its teachers were poorly qualified and the standard of education was below that in elementary schools. They accepted the fact that the two statements were probably related.[17]

Only two of its six masters were fully trained at that time and only one of its female teachers was certified by the Department of Education. The governors demanded that the same qualifications should be sought from barrack-school teachers as they were in elementary schools. They felt the FGSD should have come under the government supervision of the education department rather than the LGB.

The unsatisfactory conditions for teachers continued until 1907 when the first educationalist superintendent of what was by then Poplar's school, William Dean (BA), condemned them in his evidence to the Poor Law Royal Commission:

> Unfortunately, from an educational point of view, the Poor Law child is only just beginning to get his chance. Till quite recently educational development had passed him by ... and he has too often fallen into the hands of teachers too ill-qualified to obtain posts in elementary schools.[18]

Dean said the salaries paid to teachers in poor law schools were appreciably lower than those paid in other state schools, which in turn explained the poor quality of candidates they were forced to employ. If that were true in 1907, it certainly was so 30 years earlier.

NON-TEACHING STAFF

As well as the teaching staff, there were the industrial trainers who lived outside the institution and were day visitors. Children aged 10 and over were allocated a 'trade' by either the superintendent or matron, and spent four hours on alternate days, away from school work, receiving training. The trades and the annual salaries paid to these staff members in 1896 were military music – £60; carpentry – £54; tailoring – £52; shoemaking – £45; military drill – £40; engineering – £20; laundry work – £20; and needlework – £16.[19] There were, at various times, also trainer gardeners.

The list provokes a number of observations. Firstly, those who taught the traditional 'women's' skills of needlework and laundry were, like their female teacher colleagues, paid considerably less than those who taught the 'men's' trades. Only a quarter as much, in the cases of the needleworkers compared with the military musicians. More surprising, perhaps, is that the engineering trainers were so poorly rewarded, probably because the reality of what was being taught were handyman-type tasks, rather than sophisticated engineering skills.

Secondly, military subjects such as music and drill featured prominently. This was because district schools tried to place their leavers in the army and were encouraged to do so, with army units willing to employ semi-trained and non-family-dependant youngsters as bandsmen or raw recruits.

Indeed, in the early 1870s, Edward Tufnell, the London poor law schools' inspector, provided the war office with the names of around 300 boys each year that he recommended for employment as army bandsmen.[20] The 1882 LGB annual report provided details of 508 boys from London poor law schools who left to find work, and 408 of them were identified as joining either the army or the navy.

Finally, with the exception of the military trainers, all the others taught trades to help the institution remain as self-sufficient as possible, and thus keep the overhead running costs to a minimum. So, the tailor trainer taught pupils to make and mend the children's uniforms, as did the shoemaker trainer and with their shoes. The needleworkers taught the manufacture of linen goods (sheets, towels) and shirts and blouses for institutional consumption. The engineering and carpentry trainers were expected to produce general handymen, who would fix equipment that became broken. When employed, the gardener trainers acted as supervisors of children who cultivated up to eight acres used for growing fruit and vegetables for the establishment's consumption.

Most of the ancillary workers lived on site, on pitiful salaries, complemented by their board, lodging and laundry. There was a huge turnover reflecting long hours, poor pay and conditions and weak management.

The poor quality of the training provided was highlighted in the LGB's 1876 annual report, which said quite explicitly that good tradesmen preferred to give jobs to boys who had *not* been partially trained in children's workhouse, as they had to unlearn much of what they had been taught. Wyndham Holgate, the London schools' inspector commented that such boys would only attract the lowest wages in over-staffed trades and soon be back in the workhouse. Despite this shocking observation, little was done to improve industrial training for a quarter of a century because the governors were more interested in getting free labour to keep running costs down than offering adequate job training that would offer their charges a way out of poverty.

Governors' reports listed, in considerable detail, the output of the trainees in each of the taught disciplines: down to the last pillow sewn, door mended and shoe repaired, for example:

It is astonishing the amount of work the little ones do in the course of a year. For instance, in the tailor's shop, some 194 articles of clothing were made and over 15,000 repaired. The carpenter's shop was kept busy throughout the year in effecting minor repairs and alterations to the school's buildings, in the needle room no less than 4,799 articles were made and 77,450 repaired.[21]

There was no published syllabus for the apprentices, or organised training regime for the children.

DAILY ROUTINE

Day-to-day routine and conditions for the children could best be described as dull and tedious. This reflected the poor law's philosophical paradox, of treating them according to 'less eligibility' principles, while allegedly offering them a route out of pauperism. The practice was to uncaringly occupy them in as miserable a way as possible, until they were deemed old enough to fend for themselves, be moved on to other institutions or to the households of unknown people, to act as their domestic servants.

As we have noted, on entering the establishment, children had their heads shaved (as a de-lousing and anti-ringworm precaution) and their clothes taken away and replaced by a uniform. Unlike the boys on TS *Goliath*, however, they were not issued with their own clothes – with a subsequent need to take care of them – but were given items from the laundry, whenever their existing ones were deemed dirty, on a basis of taking which ever fitted best.

The boys wore dark brown knickerbocker suits, brown cloth cloaks, dark blue knitted socks, white collars and fawn woolen cloaks. Girls were dressed in blue serge frocks and white pinafores, brown leather belts, dark blue knitted stockings, brown cloth cloaks and black straw hats.[22]

The dreary diet, which was prescribed by the LGB, was not, however, dissimilar to that experienced by the boys on TS *Goliath*. A slight enhancement was adopted in June 1881, when fish was introduced, once a week, at the behest of the LGB. Two months later, however, the FGDS superintendent was reprimanded by the governors for diverting the fish from the children's plates to his own and those of the staff. [23]

The classroom timetable was equally monotonous with classes of more than 70 being common. An analysis of the week's timetable for girls in 1878, indicated an overwhelming concentration on the three 'Rs'.[24] The six-day, Monday to Saturday timetable, as approved by the LGB, for standard grades one to six was:

> **9.00 – 9.45 am:** mental arithmetic and tables (on alternate days, children aged 10 and over, undertook industrial training between 9.00 am and 11.00 am, when they joined the other pupils in the establishment until 2.00 pm. They then had a further two hours of industrial training).
> **9.45 – 10.30 am:** reading (grades five and six – composition)
> **10.30 – 10.45 am:** break
> **10.45 – 11.30 am:** writing (grades five and six – composition)
> **11.30 am – 12.15 pm:** Mon – Thurs, scripture; Fri, singing
> **12.15 – 12.45 pm:** dinner
> **12.45 – 1.15 pm:** recreation
> **1.15 – 1.55 pm:** washing and preparing for afternoon school
> **2.00 – 2.45 pm:** word building and spelling
> **2.45 – 3.15 pm:** reading, writing and arithmetic
> **3.15 – 3.30 pm:** break
> **3.30 – 4.00 pm:** geography (Mon and Thurs), letter writing (Tues and Fri), half day (Weds and Sat)
> **4.00 – 4.30 pm:** recitation (Mon and Fri); needlework (Tues and Thurs), half day (Weds and Sat)
> **4.30 – 5.00 pm:** singing Mon and Fri and needlework Tues

The only exceptions to the three Rs in the timetable were scripture and needlework, each for four periods per week, and geography and singing, each of which was allocated two periods. There was no attention to science, the arts, history or physical education – although some organised exercise activity took place outside of school hours.

The boys' timetables were broadly similar, but without the needlework, which was replaced by drawing and elementary science. One variation in the English section of the boys' curriculum was the appearance of dictation, presumably in preparation for secretarial-type work, which was almost exclusively a male preserve at the time. Another was that they had two hours of drill on Wednesday and Saturday afternoons, probably in preparation for future employment in the armed forces.

The infants had play, 'maypole', natural history, knitting and 'kindergarten' built into their timetable, as well as two periods of religion per day.

As far as religious education and observance were concerned, all children took prayers every morning, over breakfast, between 7.00 am and 7.30 am (three and a half hours per week), and half an hour over dinner, between 6.00 and 6.30 pm each (another three and a half hours). In addition, there were three hours of church services each Sunday (an hour in the morning, another in the afternoon and an hour of Sunday school). There was also a one-hour religious service each Thursday evening and three hours of religious instruction built into the school timetable each week.

In total, pupils under seven had 16 hours of CofE based religious instruction and participation per week, while those over seven had 14, which was as much as they spent on non-religious school work.

Over the years, improvements were made to the fabric and conditions of the institution but the issue of insufficient accommodation was not addressed and nor were other historically poor features, such as woeful attention to health and inadequate staffing appointments.

In response to LGB suggestions about improving children's access to fresh air, £115 was spent in March 1880 to convert part of the establishment's gardens into a play area.

In November that year, a school inspection report noted that:

> Much is here done to improve the dining hall and school rooms and infirmary wards by fixtures and screens, which give a light and cheerful look to the school and must have a beneficial effect on the children in teaching them to copy the surroundings within which they now live with their future homes.[25]

Four months later a new receiving ward, designed to ease overcrowding, was built at a cost of £4,450. The following year £160 was spent on better bathing facilities. In 1887, the institution also purchased its first ambulance.

However, none of these advances was introduced as a direct initiative of the governors, who were seemingly content to turn a blind eye to the children's living conditions: each came in response to directives from the LGB.

NOTES

1. Neal, p. 158
2. NA, MH27/110
3. *ELA*, 10 Sep 1892
4. *ELO*, 14 Aug 1909
5. Ibid
6. NA, MH27/106
7. NA, MH27/105
8. LMA, *Minutes FGSD* May 1893
9. NA, *MH27/105*
10. NA, MH27/106
11. Ibid
12. Rev J. Wood, *Transactions of the National Association for the Promotion of the Social Sciences*, 1882, p. 341
13. NA, MH27/107
14. NA, MH27/106
15. LMA, *FGSD Governors 1888/9 Annual Report*
16. *Shoreditch Observer*, 1 Jun 1889
17. *Criticism of the Report of the Departmental Committee*, King and Son, Westminster, 1897
18. Tower Hamlets Archives, LC 7999: Poor Law Royal Commission, 1907, evidence of William B. Dean BA
19. NA, MH27/110
20. Ross, p. 306
21. *THIEELA*, 18 Jul 1896
22. Neal, p. 159
23. NA, MH27/106
24. Ibid
25. Ibid

CHAPTER 8

ENTER HENRIETTA BARNETT

One of the more progressive steps taken in the governance of the FGDS was the appointment, by the LGB in May 1874, of Samuel Barnett as an ex-officio governor. Barnett, the vicar of St Jude's Whitechapel, quickly saw how inhumanely the children, particularly the girls, were treated. Just as Stansfeld had appointed Jane Senior to make recommendations to improve the conditions for girls in barrack schools the previous year, Barnett sought a similar solution in Forest Gate.

Within six months of his appointment, he lobbied the LGB for his wife, Henrietta, to join him there. He said that she was 'a clever and energetic woman', who should be appointed 'to have a particular oversight on the position of girls' in the establishment. In her unpublished autobiography, she said she considered her role was to 'brighten the lives of the crowded-together, unloved children.'[1]

Henrietta Octavia West Barnett (née Rowlands) was born to wealthy parents in Clapham on 4 May 1851. After a privileged but socially conscious childhood and education, she met Samuel and married him in 1873. The couple shared a reforming zeal, sometimes later described as 'practical socialism'[2] or 'scientific charity'.[3]

Motivated by idealism and a desire to improve social conditions for the poorest, the couple left a comfortable ecclesiastical parish in a middle-class community and moved to St Jude's in Whitechapel, which the Bishop of London at the time described as 'The worst parish in my diocese, inhabited largely by criminals.' Henrietta was only 22 when they arrived.[4]

Henrietta Barnett (1851–1936) (Credit: Toynbee Hall)

Britain's first female poor law guardian, Martha Crawford Merrington, was appointed in Kensington in 1875 and Henrietta swiftly followed her when she was placed on the Whitechapel board by the LGB later that year.[5]

She was also the first woman governor of a district school – the FGSD – when she appointed an ex-officio member by the LGB in 1876, a position she held, as its only female, for 20 years.

Henrietta was appalled at what she saw in Forest Gate. According to her biographer, Micky Watkins, she reported that:

> The children were dressed in a uniform, and no-one had his or her own clothes. They wore any that happened to fit as they were handed out on the day of the weekly change … . Silence reigned at meal times. The regulation weight of food was handed out to each child according to its age, but regardless of its size.

The hours out of school were not play hours. The girls scrubbed vast areas, I had almost said acres of boarded rooms, but they were not even allowed to do it together. Each child was placed a few yards off the other.

The children were not called by their names. Each was commonly addressed as 'child'. They had no toys, no library, no Sunday school, no places in which to keep personal possessions, no playing fields, no night garments, no prizes, no flowers, no pets, no pictures on the wall, no pleasures in music, no opportunities for seeing the world outside the school walls.[6]

The pictures of children featured on the cover of this book, and below, are from a volume of her memoirs and show institutionalised, emaciated, emotionless youngsters, heads shaven and dressed in unattractive garb.[7] At first glance they resemble some of the shocking photos of children that were taken in Nazi concentration camps in the 1940s.

According to Henrietta's autobiography, she set herself a target to 'gradually persuade Matron Perfect to call children by their Christian names, rather than "child" as she was in the habit of doing.'

'Killing individuality by too much discipline' – Henrietta Barnett's caption to this photograph of FGDS children in her 1935 book Matters that Matter

She soon realised she could not effect much change as a lone voice within the governing body, so she co-operated with others – outside – to establish organisations that could assist to improve the lives of the children.

Working with Jane Senior, she developed the Metropolitan Association for the Befriending of Young Servants (MABYS), as an after-care service for the girl leavers. It aimed to prevent young working-class girls who were leaving children's workhouses from becoming prostitutes, criminals, alcoholics or being abused by their employers. MABYS visited the leavers annually at their workplace until they were 21, and offered candid and often frank assessments of their progress to them and the institution's governors, with recommendations for appropriate corrective action, for the benefit of the young women (see Life in Service, Post FGDS, see pp 177-9). The organisation was able to rescue young women from the clutches of abusive households and place them elsewhere.

Barnett persuaded the FGSD to use MABYS, which soon visited over 100 of its former girls each year, providing them with a degree of support they had not received before.[8] In 1877, while on holiday in Devon, Barnett conceived the idea of Country Cottages for Children – to provide a break and give East End children some exposure to the outside world. This soon morphed into the Children's Country Holiday Fund (CCHF) which was set up 'to introduce the children to warbling birds, flowers, the sky and animals.'[9]

She sought a high-profile patron, and recruited Queen Victoria's youngest child, Princess Beatrice. On 13 May 1881, national newspaper *The Daily News* was able to report that: 'A new departure had been made by the managers of the Forest Gate District Schools, which received pauper children, who under the auspices of the society sent twenty of the most delicate children for a fortnight to cottages in Sussex.'

Another Barnett-led innovation was to take some of the older girls from Forest Gate and train them in housekeeping skills in a home she and her husband had acquired in Hampstead. Here, she was taking her lead from schools' inspector Wyndham Holgate's contribution to the 1879–80 LGB annual report describing 'training' for girls in district schools, in which he observed:

> Owing to the size of many of the buildings and the number of children collected in them, the three chief occupations of scrubbing, washing and mending become absolute drudgery (and result

in) a perfunctory rather than a satisfactory performance of the work and arouse the worst point in the girls' characters, the sullen, obstinate and careless spirit peculiar to them.

The Barnett housekeeping scheme was an important initiative, because although the governors claimed they provided domestic service training for girls in Forest Gate, the reality was using free child labour to work on an industrial scale. Preparing 50lbs of meat in the kitchens, or laundering clothes for hundreds of children was hardly appropriate experience for attending to the domestic needs of a middle-class family.

At Hampstead she said they 'learned to cook, sew, to wash, to wait on tables and the biggest lesson of all, to love.'[10] Barnett later claimed, with some exaggeration, that 'for many years I took every pauper girl as she reached fourteen as an under-servant into our little Rest House in Hampstead.'[11]

The *East London Observer* was quick to recognise her achievements: 'Mrs Barnett evidently ... has established a home and obtained the certificate of the Local Government Board for ... the purpose of removing girls from workhouse schools, at the age of say fourteen, and training them in the duties necessary to qualify them for service in a family.'

The paper readily acknowledged the benefits the opportunity offered the girls:

> This home will be conducted not on the institution principle, but in the same way as any ordinary house, with the cooking, cleaning, and other domestic operations carried out in the way common amongst private families. This of itself will be an advantage to the girls, but the greater one still will be that the few months spent on probation in such a house may suffice to rub off the indescribable, but apparent something, which attaches to a girl coming straight from a pauper school.[12]

With this practical success under her belt, Barnett was able to persuade the governors to set aside space in Forest Lane for the same purpose. The institution received permission from the LGB to allow its older girls to live in separate apartments on the premises, with kitchen and laundry facilities. They then spent two weeks as cooks, two as parlour maids and two as general servants, under supervision of the training mistress. They were also given money by the establishment to buy and cook food for themselves.

The school's inspector was so impressed that he suggested the scheme be extended to give the girls money to buy materials to make their own clothes.[13] This was a hitherto unheard of degree of trust and empowerment of the pupils, built on the back of Henrietta Barnett's initiatives.

Other progressive initiatives included banning corporal punishment of girls and establishing a lending library at the institution, with books bought and chosen by her. Later she encouraged a friend to go in once a week to run it. She saw this as 'the thin end of the wedge' in getting visitors admitted to the establishment.[14]

Indeed, in an endeavour to broaden the children's horizons, she encouraged friends to visit the children which 'hitherto had been entirely shut off from the outside world.' She also 'introduced musical entertainments, including such simple pleasures as musical chairs, to add a cultural and entertainment element to the children's experience.'[15]

In 1883, a rare acknowledgement of the positive impact Barnett's gender had on the institution appeared in the *East London Observer* when it opined: 'If all ladies used the "little brief authority" so judiciously as does this lady manager, boards of guardians might welcome them with open arms – metaphorically speaking, of course – but that has to be risked.'

Over the years, however, it was more widely recognised. 'On the job' training emerged as a success, as reported in governors' annual reports.[16] There was also progress in enriching the lives of the children through wider social contact. The 1888 annual report noted that a special train had been hired, at a cost of £70, to take 517 pupils for a day trip to Clacton, funded by a collection held among the governors and local guardians. The excursion was repeated in 1891, this time paid for by public subscription.

In 1893, 558 children and 42 staff went once more to Clacton, to celebrate the Duke of York's wedding. In order to pay for the outing, the governors arranged for an exhibition of the children's work to be displayed at Stratford Town Hall, along with demonstrations of gymnastics and a concert by the band boys, at a charge of between sixpence and one shilling.[17] The children marched through Clacton during the trip, accompanied by a band, spent some time on beach, where they ran races on cliffs, used the swings and were 'entertained by a phonograph'. Superintendent Duncan described the event in governors' minutes as 'a red-letter day in their life's history'.[18]

The 1892 governors' report recorded that 'Mrs Barnett offered holidays for 15 ailing girls at a home in Broughton Sands.' The following year the

CCHF wrote to the governors offering children two weeks' holiday in the countryside at a charge of 12 shillings for the fortnight. In 1894, 50 'physically weaker' children were given a country holiday and the governors were pleased to record that they were 'generally in a better state when they got home.'

Colour and culture were brought into the life of the youngsters at a very low cost. The 1890 report announced that 'under a London-wide scheme, we agreed to purchase pictures to put on walls, to brighten them up. The first payment of £6.17/11d was made.'

The unsatisfactory parental visiting rights was addressed, finally, in 1892. Until then, they were only permitted access on the second Tuesday of alternate months. Unsurprisingly, the 400 or so relatives who usually took advantage proved an unmanageably large number for the institution to handle. The governors agreed to ease matters by allowing parents access twice weekly in future.

'Lined up for the dreary outdoor exercise' – Henrietta Barnett's caption to this photograph of FGDS children in her 1935 book Matters that Matter.

External gestures of kindness began to impact on the establishment. From the late 1880s, the editor of the Christian publication *The Truth* sent a box of toys and a sixpenny piece for each child every Christmas. Sunday schools, run by local residents, started at about this time and the 1895 governors' report recognised that they did 'much to relieve the monotony of their [the children's] lives.' In addition to church services, local residents began to provide 'accompanied walks of Wanstead Flats and Epping Forest', managed the library and introduced new books to it.

Nevertheless, after years of gradual reform, it became clear to Barnett that the changes she had managed to force through did not address, fundamentally, the central problem that barrack schools created. It was the system and not the practice that required addressing.

As she wrote in her biography of her husband Samuel: 'Slowly, very slowly, the conviction grew that, though the school as a school, was excellent, the system was wrong. The keynote of character development is love, and that was missing. No one can love 600 children, each one of whom needs the comfort and the stimulation of personally rendered affection.'[19]

NELLIE DOWELL
FROM RAGS TO ASSOCIATION WITH RICHES

Nellie Dowell was born in Whitechapel in 1876, to a 'respectable' working-class family. When her father, a seafarer, died in 1881, the family descended into poverty and moved to Poplar. Her mother passed Nellie and her siblings to the local guardians. They initially boarded them out in Leighton Buzzard, but in 1883 she and her sister were transferred to the FGDS and her brother, William, to TS *Exmouth*, where he was a success and later became a naval officer. Nellie's later close associate, and probable lover, Muriel Lester, described her introduction to the institution:

> Nellie caused some trouble among the attendants and even had to be taken to the matron during the first month of her stay ... an awful and terrifying thing for the inmates of any institution. This was because she had passionately resisted the hair-cutter, when it came to her turn to be cropped .... She had been terrified by the big scissors wielded over her head by

a strange person. A strange sense of outrage filled her as she saw herself shorn of her curls.

Cook's East London Soap Works in Bow, where Nellie worked for a while before suffering bouts of ill-health. The company's chairman, Edward Cook, had been a governor of the FGDS for many years.

According to her mother, Nellie was taught 'a rude form of religion by people who did not even pretend to believe it themselves.' Nellie's sister, Alice, was sent to Henrietta Barnett's cottage to learn the finer points of domestic service (see the account of A. D. Life in Service text box, p. 179). Nellie left the FGDS in November 1888 and secured a job in a local match factory with R. Bell and Co. Following a strike at the company in 1893, of which there are no records of Nellie's participation, the firm looked to establish production outposts in the empire and elsewhere in Europe. They sent Nellie to work at a factory they founded in New Zealand in 1900 for three years and in 1907 to another, in Sweden, where she remained until 1909.

She left the match industry soon after her return from Sweden and took a job at Cook's East London Soap Works, (see p. 118)whose owner had been a long-time Poplar guardian and sometime chair of the FGSD. She soon became ill, suffering two bouts of rheumatic fever and found herself unable to work in the factory, which dragged her further into poverty.

During her second bout of fever, she suffered delirium and was transferred to the 'Lunatic ward of Whitechapel Infirmary'. It seems likely that poverty and the chemicals she had worked with had contributed to her illnesses and the medication she received for them may have induced the delirium.

Sometime between 1903 and 1909 she met Muriel Lester, daughter of a wealthy Leytonstone shipwright, who had moved to the East End as a middle-class philanthropist. Surviving correspondence indicates they had a very close relationship for the remainder of Nellie's short life. Both suffered protracted bouts of illness during which time they cared for each other.

In 1915, the couple founded Kingsley Hall in a former Baptist church in Bow (named after Muriel's recently deceased brother), which they described as a 'people's house', located about two miles from the FGDS. In it they sought to 'set up the Kingdom of Heaven at Bow' and it became an outpost of pacifism (difficult when surrounded by First World War jingoism), feminism and socialism. It had a Montessori-type nursery, school for civics and scripture and provided a restaurant for working women, under the auspices of the London Society for Women's Suffrage. George Lansbury was its biggest supporter locally, and it seems probable that he and Nellie swapped stories about life at the FGDS.

Bad health continued to affect Nellie and she died at home, in Bow, on 31 January 1923. Muriel pursued her radical work in the East End and for a while was a Poplar councillor, replacing Minnie Lansbury, George's daughter-in-law, following her premature death in 1922, after imprisonment for the part she played in the Poplar rates revolt. Kingsley Hall had its finest hour when it provided accommodation for Mohandas Gandhi when he came to London in 1931 to argue the cause of Indian independence.

(*Thanks to Seth Koven, whose book* The Match Girl and the Heiress *provides the basis for this section.*)

NOTES

1   LMA/4063/006, *Henrietta Barnett: Be-friending the Friendless, Her Autobiographical Memoirs*, ch. 5

2   www.spartacus-educational.com

3   Seth Koven, *The Matchgirl and the Heiress*, Princetown University Press, 2014, p. 50

4   Alan Palmer, *The East End – Four Centuries of London Life*, John Murray, 1989, p. 81

5   Higginbotham, *Encyclopaedia*, p. 120

6   Micky Watkins, *Henrietta Barnett in Whitechapel: Her First Fifty Years*, 2005, p. 55

7   Henrietta Barnett, *Matters that Matter*, John Murray, 1933, pp. 168, 186

8   LMA, FGSD Governors' annual reports from 1878

9   Barnett, *Autobiography*

10   Ibid

11   Barnett *Matters*, p. 151

12   *ELO*, 14 May 1881

13   LMA, *FGSD Governors' 1888/9 Annual Report*

14   Watkins, p. 55

15   Barnett, *Autobiography*

16   LMA, *FGSD Governors' 1888 Annual Report*

17   *Stratford Express*, 16 Sep 1893

18   LMA, *FGSD Governors' 1893 Annual Report*

19   Henrietta Barnett, *Canon Barnett, His Life Work and Friends*, Vol 1, Boston, 1921, p. 682

Out of Sight, Out of Mind

CHAPTER 9

FIRE, POISON AND DISEASE

Despite Henrietta Barnett's best efforts, the failures of the previous decade – neglectful management and sub-standard health care – exploded in the 1890s. Their negative impact was then magnified by two dramatic tragedies that attracted national attention and notoriety.

Ill-discipline among the staff in Forest Gate continued and Charles Duncan's behaviour was found wanting. In July 1888 a teacher, Frederick Perry, was suspended and subsequently dismissed for giving two pupils, Henry Williams and Arthur Board, black eyes 'for speaking out of turn'. Both the 32-year-old head teacher, Joseph Salmon, and Duncan knew about the punishment, but took no action against Perry, nor did they record it in the incident book.

The governors discovered the violence by chance, launched an enquiry and relieved Perry of his duties. They also reprimanded Duncan and Salmon for knowing about, but failing to record the inappropriate punishment. Duncan apologised, citing forgetfulness, an excuse he gave the authority for many of his failings. The governors recorded their displeasure at the pair, noting that they 'had seriously failed in their duty to the board in with-holding from it a matter of such grave importance',[1] but took no disciplinary action against either.

This, however, seemed to have provoked a wake-up call. There followed a few years of innovation and significant educational progress. In 1888, for example, the governors proposed introducing mixed-sex classes, which was receiving consideration by the LGB, when the matter was overtaken by other events in the establishment.

Educational performance improved considerably. The inspector of schools gave the establishment a good annual report in 1894, noting that examination results had been notably better over the previous decade. School leavers were assessed in reading, writing and arithmetic before departing. In 1882, 70 per cent of boys passed all three subjects in their leaving exams, this figure rose to 89 per cent a decade later, and for girls the improvement was greater, rising from a 69 per cent to a 90 per cent pass rate.

Some familiar problems, however, remained unaddressed. Medical Officer Vallance's war of words with the LGB continued. In May 1888 Dr Bridges wrote complaining of Vallance's 'culpable neglect', with particular reference to his treatment of children with ophthalmia. He stated, 'I don't think that more than 35 infants [out of about 140] were ophthalmicly-free' and said that the washing arrangements for the children required improvement.

He stressed that Vallance had repeatedly been advised to 'isolate victims since 1874 ... you have continued to regard such cases as of little importance .... [the levels of sickness] ... are largely due to your neglect.' Bridges also condemned the medical officer's tendency to leave the treatment of the disease to the nurses, without his personal supervision. The governors responded saying that they 'concur with your board that there has been grave negligence on the part of the medical officer [Vallance].' [2]

Eight months later the governors wrote to the LGB stating that they 'are and have long been dissatisfied with his [Vallance's] conduct in the matter of treatment of children suffering from diseases of the eye ... . There has been gross negligence.'[3]

The governors examined Vallance's attendance records over the previous 12 months and discovered he had been present on average less than 90 minutes a day because of his other commitments; on some occasions even sending his son – a medical student – to deputise. They sought the LGB's permission to sack him.

The LGB, in what was now becoming a familiar pattern, was weak and would not concur. Instead, it wrote to Vallance suggesting that he may have taken on too many jobs and asked him to review his overall work load with the possibility of reducing it. Vallance responded by seeking – and receiving – praiseworthy testimonials from West Ham's Board of Guardians for the jobs he performed for them. He sought, but did not receive, similar reassurances from the FGSD. Seeing the writing on the wall, he chose to resign as its medical officer in 1889, without a stain on his CV, so that he could continue with his lucrative appointments with West Ham and in private practice.

Had the LGB permitted his sacking from the FGSD, his tenure in West Ham would have been put in jeopardy. It was an opportunity missed, as revealed in a libel action a decade later. John Joseph Terrett, a butcher, was the secretary of the Plaistow Radical and Democratic Association and in the later 1890s he became a West Ham councillor and member of the visiting committee of the West Ham workhouse. That committee had questions about the health and care of some of the boys in the workhouse and they were passed, by the master, for medical officer, Vallance's, response.

Terrett saw that Vallance had submitted notes to the workhouse master which were not meant for the committee's eyes. One 12-year-old boy, Bowers, had some years previously received a wound to his head, which had healed. The visitors had asked whether he should have been provided with some protection of the wound. Vallance, in his notes, agreed, but said that it could be 'no use to him, as he would need a new one every week.' Another 15-year-old boy, Sullivan, had been blind in one eye since infancy; the committee asked whether he would have benefitted from a visit to an ophthalmic hospital. Vallance's notes said it would be a waste of time, that nothing could be done for the eye, and that he would 'take his eye out, at my leisure.' None of this was disputed by Vallance during an eventual court case.

The visiting committee was horrified and referred the matter to the guardians, who called upon Vallance to resign. A borough election was imminent. Terrett campaigned vigorously on the case, parading banners which said 'The Board has asked the monster to resign' and: 'Prevent the re-appointment of the brute.'

Vallance responded by suing Terrett for libel, and in yet another example of whistleblowers paying the price, Terrett was found culpable and told to pay £150 in damages, with legal costs of £63, a sum he did not have. Not to be deterred, Vallance bankrupted Terrett for his troubles. It was the bankruptcy proceedings which revealed that, as noted previously, Vallance was in receipt of annual salaries totalling £1,200 from the public purse, as in addition to his roles as medical officer to both West Ham's workhouse and its associated children's institution, he was also the borough's registrar of births deaths and marriages.

This man had been medical officer for the Forest Lane establishment for 23 years. Despite overwhelming evidence of his incompetence and multi-tasking, the LGB permitted his tenure to continue in West Ham, unblemished, causing unnecessary misery to many, and probable death to some, of his future patients.

Vallance may have destroyed Terrett financially and, because of the bankruptcy, effectively barred him from public office, but he did not silence him politically. J. J. Terrett re-emerged as a prominent supporter of the Plaistow Land-Grabbers – a group of direct-action anti-unemployment activists a few years later.[4] As for Vallance, although he was not removed from office by West Ham's guardians, they did at least ask him to resign. He retired, quietly, soon after, aged 73, on a pension sanctioned by them.[5]

FOREST GATE FIRE

Following the fire on TS *Goliath*, the LGB had been active in encouraging better attention to fire-prevention measures in all workhouse institutions. It sent copies of its 1882 report *Dangers from Fires in Workhouses*, and a follow-up report, for consideration and implementation. The governors responded by erecting two additional staircases, as fire escapes, in September 1882 and November 1886.[6]

They were not sufficient, however, to prevent a fire at the establishment in the early hours of New Year's Day 1890 that killed 26 pupils.[7]

Accounts of this fire, and the subsequent inquest – including dramatic line drawings and illustrations – occupied acres of national newsprint over the following weeks. Memorials to the dead survive to this day.

A lengthy, unsensational and detailed account of the tragedy appeared in the following week's *Stratford Express,* stating that: 'On Tuesday mid-night [the Forest Gate institution buildings] were the scene of a fearful calamity – unprecedented in the history of West Ham.'

The fire, which broke out in the three-storey boys' building, was discovered by the 36-year-old wardrobe mistress, Julia Bloomfield. It had started in the needlework room on the ground floor from sparks from a stove pipe which had recently been cleaned. This ignited children's clothes that were awaiting repair. It soon spread to the dormitories on the two upper floors, in which 84 boys were asleep.

Superintendent Duncan called the fire brigade, stationed in Forest Gate,[8] and started to work the fire hydrant, which was located in the establishment's grounds. Ladders were raised to the upper storey windows, to allow the boys to escape. Twenty-five lads, however, became trapped and suffocated. The dormitory doors had been locked from the outside, so potential escape routes were restricted.

These drawings are from the Illustrated London News of 11 January 1890, showing the fire. The top image is a general view of the FGDS. The boys' dormitories which were affected are to the left of the main block. In front of them is the maypole, which featured prominently in the exercises that the infants undertook. The building in this distance on the left was the school's hospital block, which was converted into nurses' accommodation in the twentieth century, when the main buildings were turned into a hospital. The bottom two images are artists' impressions of the dormitories engulfed by smoke.

The dead children were carried from the dormitories, via the ladders, to the surrounding grounds, and according to the *Stratford Express*, were

> wrapped in blankets, with the faces only exposed, and a glance at the features was enough to show that in 25 of the 26 cases deaths was due purely to suffocation; the expressions upon the faces are in most cases those of children 'caught in sleep'. One poor bairn lay face on hand, others had the mouth open indicating the sound sleep of childhood, while scarcely upon one of those cold, upturned faces was there a feature distorted by agony. The body

which is burned is reduced almost to a cinder, and its identification will be a matter of great difficulty.

Neighbours of the institution helped with the rescue and a number of heroes emerged from the event, who were later recognised for their valour and bravery. Public sympathy was widespread and the governors received messages of condolence from Queen Victoria, the Lord Mayor of London and King Leopold of Belgium, among others.[9]

In summary, 26 boys were killed, all but one from suffocation; 18 were from Poplar, five from Whitechapel, two from Croydon and one from Mile End. There were two brothers, 10-year-old Augustus Flowers, and his nine-year-old sibling Theophilus, from Poplar, whose corpses were identified by a third brother in the institution. Five of the dead were seven; three were eight; seven were nine; five were 10 ; one was 11 and three were 12.

A service, attended by 2,000 people, was conducted at St James' Church, which was adjacent to FGDS, on Sunday, 5 January. The funeral took place the following day, at West Ham cemetery, immediately to the back of the grounds, attended by 10,000 people.[10]

Unlike the position after the fire on TS *Goliath,* when a fund was established by the Lord Mayor of London to provide assistance to compensate fire victims and staff for their property losses, there was no public appeal to support the families of the deceased; indeed an attempt to establish such a fund was obstructed by the FGDS governors.[11]

A red polished granite memorial to the dead, which survives today, was erected in the cemetery in June 1890, paid for by the governors and staff from their own pockets, at a cost of £36. The inscription reads: 'In memory of the 26 boys who unhappily lost their lives by the disastrous fire which occurred at the establishment, Forest Lane, West Ham 1st January 1890. Erected as an expression of sympathy with the bereaved relatives, by the managers and staff of the Forest Gate District School.' There was also a flat stone bearing the name of each child and the monument is surrounded by a stone kerb and railing, which is now missing.[12]

The inquest was held within days and the court's verdict was, effectively, 'accidental death'. The jury found the fire was caused by the imperfect way in which the chimneys had been swept, but did not assign culpable negligence to anybody. Soot, they found, was pushed through a flue into a disused fireplace, where it had caught fire. The fire spread to the board, with which the fireplace was blocked up.

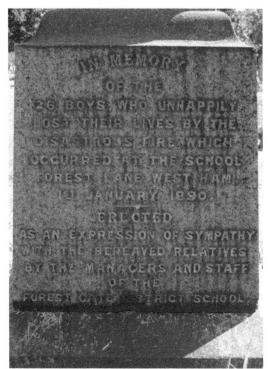

The memorial obelisk to the victims of the 1890 fire, survives in West Ham Cemetery. (Photo: Author's Own)

The jury was at pains to praise officials and others who aided the rescue of the boys from the fire.[13] It, however, added six riders to its 'accidental death' verdict, by way of recommendations for the future. Chief among them was that they 'strongly condemned the practice of locking doors of dormitories at night.' Although, as the senior officer, Charles Duncan was clearly responsible for this dangerous practice, he was not admonished by name, nor was there a call for action to be taken against him. As later became clear, Duncan was an acquaintance of the coroner and this may have accounted for his surprisingly lenient treatment.

The jury recommended a number of fire-prevention measures to be adopted and that a watchman should be appointed to patrol the wards at night. The governors complied within days, and paid him 24 shillings per week.

The coroner also insisted that candles were too dangerous to be used for illumination in dormitories and that the superintendent should have the direct contact details of local fire brigades.

The governors agreed to hold regular fire drills for the Forest Lane site and wanted them to be inspected regularly by 'a competent person' at least four times per year. Chief Superintendent Edward Smith, who commanded the firemen at the tragedy, agreed to do it for four guineas per year. However, his employers, West Ham Council, would not sanction the payment, so the inspections did not take place. Nor would they pay for the installation of a fire alarm with a direct link to the local fire station, on cost grounds, and FGSD governors would not sanction the payment either. The governors wanted school officers who conducted the fire drills to be compensated at the rate of two shillings per drill. The LGB refused to authorise the funding. This parsimony in the aftermath of a fire that killed 26 children is indicative of the low esteem with which the institution's occupants were held by authority.[14]

Artist's impression of relatives of the victims of the fire at the inquest. (Source: The Graphic, January 1890)

Eventually, the coroner called for an official inspection of all similar poor law buildings nationwide, and the execution of necessary structural alterations. Within two months, the LGB put the recommendations into a binding circular and sent it to all boards of guardians.[15]

On 10 April 1890, The Royal Society for the Protection of Life from Fire made a number of presentations for bravery to those who were regarded as the heroes of the event. Some were given monetary rewards and medals, others illuminated testimonials and others certificates – presumably in the descending order of perceived valour:

> **Silver medal**: Thomas Jones Oakley [iron moulder of Tower Hamlets Road – a neighbour of the establishment], plus £5; Charles Hipkins [12-year-old pupil – see p. 153], plus three guineas, Henry Elliott [yardman, staff of whom more later], plus three guineas and George Hare [assistant yardman, staff, aged 22] plus three guineas.
>
> **Illuminated testimonial**: Miss Maria Julia Bloomfield [wardrobe mistress], plus three guineas; Charles Duncan and Herbert John Roe [a watchmaker and resident of the adjacent Tower Hamlets Road].
>
> **Certificate**: Miss Laura Terry [head sewing mistress], plus one guinea; Mrs Eliza Roe [wife of Herbert – see above] plus one guinea; John Malcolm [a neighbour of the institution], plus one guinea; Walter Edmond Crisp [a pocket-book maker and resident of Tower Hamlets Road], plus one guinea; Frederick William Roe [son of the Roes] plus one guinea and John Blagdon [police constable], plus one guinea.

Duncan received an illustrated testimonial for his role, despite being negligent in permitting the dormitory doors to be locked from the outside.

Henrietta Barnett later blamed the management of the establishment for the deaths. She believed the number of fatalites was significantly increased as a result of 'the children being locked up in the night wards [the officers out celebrating New Year's Eve]' and added that locking dormitories from the outside was not a common occurrence in barrack schools.[16] Her criticism was blunter in a later collection of essays she edited: 'the officers had gone out in larger numbers than they should have done, and locked the children in the dormitories.'[17]

LOOKING FOR ALTERNATIVE MODELS

Despite the refusal to spend money on many recommended life-saving fire-precautions measures, some steps were taken to improve the health and well-being of the children following the fire. Immediately prior to it, the governors had spent £780 on a 40ft by 29ft swimming pool (possibly one of the few lessons accepted from TS *Goliath*). Post fire, this was commandeered as storage accommodation until the building damage was addressed. It opened as a functioning pool for the children in 1893. In April 1891, new lavatories were installed in the boys' dormitories affected by the fire, at a cost of £100 and a new iron fire escape was built, costing £578.[18]

These improvements, however, did not address all of the main public health deficiencies. Three years later a report on drainage highlighted problems of 'foul latrines' in the reception ward, which were clearly not conducive to the children's good health.[19]

Later that year, an initiative was launched to reduce the likelihood of sick children even getting to the reception ward. The FGDS's new medical officer, 27 year-old George Bell from Leytonstone, expressed concern at the number of unwell children being sent from the Poplar workhouse. He secured the right to visit that institution once a fortnight, to screen would-be recruits to Forest Lane, and prevent those with diseases from being sent. He 'rejected' 25 children in the first six months. However, the initiative was soon aborted.

The FGSD took its first tentative step towards exploring options for replacing their own establishment set-up with something more appropriate in 1889, after a number of its governors visited other children's poor law institutions. Among them was St Pancras' new establishment in Leavesden. The following year, the governors accepted that the Forest Gate buildings were no longer fit for purpose. They considered selling the site, which was becoming increasingly valuable in the rapidly growing suburb of Forest Gate as potential residential land, and building a new facility elsewhere. They established a working party to examine replacing it with a new cottage homes facility, and visited three reasonably local examples of the scheme in practice.[20]

Firstly, they went to the Barnardo's Garden Village in Barkingside, which by now consisted of 48 dedicated cottages, each accommodating 16 girls. The committee agreed the project was more homely and informal than Forest Lane; it had overcome the ins and outs problem, had a much more attentive medical officer and was successful in boarding out some of its charges.[21]

Secondly, they inspected Shoreditch's cottages in Hornchurch, where 12 houses accommodated up to 30 children each, all located within a 72-acre setting. Each home was run by house parents and they concluded, 'It is impossible to speak in terms of too great praise of the excellence of these homes.'

The governors' last stop was the Bethnal Green institution in Leytonstone – about three miles from Forest Gate, built in 1880. It was a modification of the cottage homes system, where siblings were kept together, and older girls were encouraged to 'mother' younger pupils. It was more cheerful than its counterpart in Forest Gate and ophthalmia was almost unknown there.

The investigating committee's conclusions were dramatic. They suggested cashing in on the 'augmented value of the land at Forest Gate' – calculated at around £20,000 – which would enable them to acquire around 20 acres, at about £100 per acre, if they moved further out from London.

Finally, they concluded that they were 'of opinion that the Home system is better calculated to de-pauperise the children than ... the existing school of the district.'

The governors received the report, effectively recommending the sale of the premises and the relocation of the institution elsewhere. But before they could give proper consideration to its content, the establishment was struck by another calamity – brought on by further negligence and corruption.

FOOD POISONING OUTBREAK

On Friday, 23 June 1893, 60 children at FGDS suffered an attack of severe vomiting and diarrhoea. They were attended to by Dr Bell, but his response was at best dilatory. He was called at 9.00 am, principally to examine 14-year-old Edwin Puttrick, who was suffering most. When Bell arrived, over three hours later, he spent a total of 65 minutes examining and prescribing for the 60 patients and did not revisit the establishment for a further 24 hours.

Puttrick died in the meantime, but Bell did not return to examine him or any of the increasing number of affected pupils for six hours after being notified of the death.[22] Other children fell ill and by Monday there were 132 cases of food poisoning. Anna Fish, who was 13, died on Tuesday, 27 June, having displayed symptoms over the weekend.[23] The LGB's Dr Stephenson conducted the post-mortems on the dead children.

An inquest was swiftly convened, and conducted by the same coroner, Charles Lewis, who heard the inquest on the fire. His behaviour was thoroughly unprofessional, displaying a lack of impartiality and possible collusion with Duncan. He stated, on the record: 'I have known you, Mr Duncan, so long that I am perfectly certain you have the interests of the children at heart.'[24] This clear conflict of interest between his duty to undertake an independent inquiry and his association with one of the principal actors in the case undoubtedly impacted on the guidance given to the jury and the very lenient stance taken towards Duncan in his summing up.

With hindsight, it seems possible that most of the relevant FGDS staff felt bullied and certainly frightened at the prospect of giving evidence at the inquest and closed ranks behind their superintendent, expressing innocence and surprise about the causes of the outbreak of the poisoning.

Dr Stephenson was called to give evidence and concluded that the deaths were most likely caused by contaminated meat. Duncan said there had been nothing untoward in the food the children had eaten in the 48 hours prior to the outbreak. On the Tuesday, he reported, their diet consisted of milk and water, bread and butter for breakfast, soup for dinner, bread, milk and water for supper.[25] He then quite blatantly lied, when he told the inquest:

> The meat from which the soup consumed last Thursday was made was brought in on Tuesday last and consisted of 14 stone of salted meat. I had it cooked at once and it was eaten the next day. The soup was made from the stock arising from the meat.[26]

One of the cooks, however, broke ranks when she told the inquest that when she put the soup on, 'The salt beef did not look so nice, so red, so usual. It looked blackish, and she thought that was because not enough saltpetre was used. She tasted the soup and it was sweet.'[27] Henry Elliott, a 53-year-old yardsman and decorated hero of the 1890 fire, gave further incriminating evidence that shocked the inquest.

He said his wife had told him that she had passed through the dining room on the Saturday, and when she returned, had said to him: 'Go into the dining hall and look at the meat, it is being cut up and is running away with maggots.' He went, and told the inquest that in the gravy bowl on the cutting board he saw 'raw maggots. The dining maids were there and remarked that the food did not look very nice.'

Duncan was recalled to the witness box and denied the allegations emphatically. Interestingly, when describing the dead child Puttrick, he did not refer to him as a pupil, scholar, student, child on any other school-related term, but as an 'inmate'. The jury concluded that the children had died of ptomaine poisoning, and, possibly swayed by coroner Lewis' words and demeanour, 'placed on record their confidence in Mr Duncan.'[28]

Duncan seemed to have been exonerated and, with a swagger, blamed the press for causing distress. He summoned a journalist from the *Stratford Express* to his office and admonished him for the paper's 'sensationalist' headline, which read 'Forest Gate District School – Supposed Wholesale Poisoning – 132 Children Affected'. Duncan claimed it caused great distress to parents, saying:

> The unnecessary suffering that announcement has caused, you can have no idea of. Poor women have dragged themselves, I don't know how far, and with scarcely anything to cover them, to know of harm that came to their children.[29]

The journalist responded by stating that the newspaper had only provided verbatim accounts of the inquest proceedings, but ended the interview by apologising for any inconvenience caused.

The case was more complicated, however, and both the governors and the LGB wanted a full inquiry into the events surrounding the poisoning. They suspended Elliott for his outburst at the inquest, while they held their own investigation.

Henry Elliott and his wife, Mary, had been at FGDS since 1876, having previously worked at another industrial school in Chelmsford. He was a caretaker/yardsman and she, a 'reception ward assistant' in Forest Lane. Within two years of his appointment, Henry was given an additional job of teaching the boys to swim, and was paid 1s 6d for every success. He had also been recognised and rewarded as a hero, rescuing boys from the trapped dormitory on the night of the fire.[30] The couple received regular pay rises and were given positive staff appraisals, until the food poisoning outbreak.

Elliott stuck to his maggots story during the inquiry and when called as a witness, said that about 600 children had been fed on the day of the outbreak of food poisoning and that he had seen 'between 60 and 70 maggots, quite white, and about half an inch in length. Some of them wandered around, while others crawled into the gravy of the meat.' He repeated his evidence that the maids were witnesses, even though they later disputed it. The scandal, he said, was a matter of common conversation among the officers there.[31]

Elliott, who was living in Fulham after his suspension from the institution, employed solicitors to threaten to sue the governors for libel over statements they had made about him during the inquiry – quite an extraordinary move for a working-class man at the time.[32] From where he found the funds was never made public, although it almost certainly came from the Barnetts, as will become clear later.

Having succumbed to Duncan's pressure over its coverage of the inquest, the *Stratford Express* weighed in on his behalf to try to discredit Elliott and get him sacked. It commented that the FGDS' 'managers will now have to consider whether they ought to retain him in their service.'[33]

The LGB's schools' inspector, Hadley, studied the FGDS' Provision Receipts and Commission Account Book to try to get to the bottom of the issue; how the switching of the meat had occurred and why infected meat had been used. He concluded that the books' records 'represented a web of lies, or at least very gross and irreconcilable inaccuracies.'[34]

The report, in January 1894, was critical of Duncan and slack management at the institution. It highlighted:

- The lack of urgency on Duncan's part in calling the medical officer to attend the outbreak.
- The lack of urgency shown by the medical officer during the early stages of the outbreak.
- The meat procurement procedures at the establishment.
- Duncan's record keeping and handling of meat within the premises, suggesting that fraud or theft may have been at play.

The report implied that either Duncan had ordered the substitution of good meat with leftover meat from a previous day's staff meal, or the staff had done this without his sanction. There was no direct reference to the fate of the 52lbs of fresh meat that should have been used for the children's meal, or subsequent consideration of whether this was part of a corrupt relationship between Duncan and the suppliers.

Although critical of Duncan and Dr Bell, in what was by now a familiar pattern of behaviour, the inquiry did not recommend action be taken against either. It concluded that although Elliott may have exaggerated about what he saw in relation to maggots, 'those [allegations] made in regard to the provisions are not altogether without foundation. Moreover, it is not clear that he has not been activated in the matter by a misdirected zeal for the interests of the children.'[35]

Nonetheless, the report recommended that 'Mr Elliott's services in connection with the school should cease.' He left in May 1894[36] and his wife Mary, who had played almost no part in the entire proceedings, departed two months later.

In summary, there was a massive closing of ranks behind authority at the establishment, with no action recommended, or taken, against either the negligent medical officer or the culpable superintendent. The whistleblower, however, was dismissed for his troubles.

The food poisoning incident and probable bullying by Duncan to get staff to toe his line at the inquest had repercussions on morale and staff attitudes. Between August and December 1893, at least 14 of the institution's 74 employees left its service. Some Whitechapel guardians, possibly spurred on by Henrietta Barnett, were critical of the stance taken by the FGDS' governors during the inquest and accused them of acting 'flippantly with a matter of such gravity'.[37]

Henrietta Barnett's response to the incident addressed some of the injustices. In her biography of her husband, she wrote that Duncan was culpable of switching bad food for good, and effectively put the blame at his door for the deaths and suffering.[38]

She also took the sacked Henry Elliott under her wing, where he made a brief appearance in her unpublished autobiography. In it she described him as an 'odd man', who was dismissed for 'his bravery in speaking out'. She says that she and her husband took him into their Hampstead cottage, from where she was busy planning the development of Hampstead Garden Suburb, where he lived happily as one of the household. It was from that base that Elliott was to have one final dramatic impact on Duncan's future and the fate of the Forest Lane establishment, as will become apparent later.

One of Elliott's mottos, Henrietta reported, was 'Fear not to sow because of the birds', which was framed in the cottage drawing room. One day, she said, he walked away from the cottage, alone, knowing he was ill and would not recover, and left a note which said, 'I think it will be sad for little Missy if I die with you, so I am off.'[39] Little Missy was the Barnett's adopted daughter, Dorothy. Husband Samuel was concerned enough about Elliott's fate that he went looking for him, 'and the Canon tended him through his dying days.'

Henry Elliott evidently made a lasting impression on Henrietta Barnett, as his motto featured, unattributed, on the title page of her biography of Samuel. She described Elliott, in a footnote in the same book, as the man 'brave enough to tell the truth' and reflected that 'the perplexity of the simple man, because doing his duty to the children had resulted in his downfall, was pathetic.'[40]

During the latter stages of her governorship, Henrietta Barnett suffered from poor health and was a rare attendee at FGSD meetings, being only present at seven of the 79 held between 1893 and 1896.[41] Despite this, she continued to play an active part in trying to improve conditions there. She was a frequent visitor and continued her civilising agenda, with her promotion of MABYS, country holidays for the children, library activities, external visits by children, offering domestic service training in Hampstead for some of the girls and so on. She ceased to be a governor in 1896, when the position of ex-officio governors was abolished for district schools.

It was, however, during these latter stages of her governorship that she made her greatest impact in shaping the direction and fate of the FGDS.

CHARLES HIPKINS
HERO OF THE 1890 FGDS FIRE

Charles George Hipkins (1877-1918), photographed in 1915 as he enlisted for service in First World War. One of the medals he is displaying is for his role in the 1890 fire. The medal's inscription was 'To Charles Hipkins for services at Forest Gate School, Stratford. 1st January 1890.' (Family photo courtesy of Paul Norton)

Charles Hipkins was born in Poplar in 1877. His father, Joseph, died when he was 10 years old and the family fell into destitution and entered Poplar workhouse. Charles was sent to FGDS. According to his testimony at the inquest of the 1890 fire, he was the monitor in dormitory nine, and his job was to count the boys each night, to ensure they were in bed. During the night of the fire he woke, discovered smoke in the room and, when he found the door to the dormitory locked from the outside, opened the room's windows to let the smoke escape. He roused the boys and, using a ladder propped next to the adjacent dormitory, ensured they escaped to safety.[42]

In April 1890, the Royal Society for the Protection of Life from Fire awarded Charles a silver medal and three guineas for his bravery – the highest award given to the heroes of the fire. This would have been riches beyond his wildest dreams – the equivalent to two or three months' salary for some of the FGDS' nurses and teachers.

Charles left Forest Gate within months of the fire and, by 1891, had become a houseboy, or young servant, at the 'Brigade Institution', Ebury Street, St George's Square, Westminster. He later worked as a coachman. Aged 17, he joined the Army Service Corps, becoming a driver in the 5th Battalion East Surrey Queen's Regiment. In 1900, he was posted to serve in the second Boer War, in which he fought for two years and was awarded the South African campaign medal. After that war, he re-entered civvy street as a house painter, but voluntarily re-enlisted in September 1915 – at the age of 38 – 'for the duration of the war'.

A surviving photograph shows him in the East Surrey's uniform displaying his South African campaign medal and Forest Gate Silver bravery medal – despite the fact it was over a quarter of a century since the latter had been awarded.

Charles was injured in 1917 and died of his wound six months later. His widow, Edith, wore black from the time of his death until her own in 1965, mentioning neither the war, nor her husband's injuries, during those 48 years.[43]

NOTES

1   NA, MH27/107

2   Ibid

3   NA, MH27/108

4   www.e7-nowandthen.org/2018/09/a-nod-at-our-neighbours-4-plaistow-land.html

5   *Manchester Evening News*, 30 Jan 1899

6   Ibid

7   Augustus Flowers, 10 and Theophilus Flowers, 9 of 1 Laura Cottages, Millwall; John Jones, 7 of 4 Island Street, Brunswick Road, Poplar; John Taylor, 7 of 3 Amiel Street, Bromley; Michael Vassum, 8, whose mother was in Whitechapel Workhouse; Frederick Smith, 9 of 50 Church Street, Whitechapel; Edward Kilburn, 9, whose mother was in Poplar Workhouse; John Joyce, 10 of 61 Apperion Road, Bow; Richard Page, 7 of 45 Vanne Street, Bromley; James Potts, 10 of 4 Newham Buildings, Pelham Street, Whitechapel; William Hume, 9, of 52 Railway Street, Bromley; Frank Chalk, 7, of Whitechapel; Herbert Russell, 10, whose mother was in Croydon Workhouse; James Rolfe, 8 of 61 Milton Road, Bow; Thomas North, 12, of Poplar Union; Walter Searle, 9, an orphan from Poplar; Charles Biddick, 12 of 4 Medway Road, Mile End; Frederick Scott, 7 of 9 Oliver's Court, Bow Road; Henry Sowerbutts, 10, whose mother was in Poplar Workhouse; Gilbert Allison, 10 of 3 Charles Street, Millwall; Thomas Hughes, 11, whose father was in Poplar Workhouse; William Dawson, 7, whose mother was in Bow Infirmary; Frederick Wigmore, 8, whose mother was in Croydon Workhouse; William Sillitoe, 9, whose father was in Whitechapel Infirmary; Arthur Pigeon, 9, of 31 Burdett Road, Bow; Albert Smith, 12 of 14 Mansfield Road, Millwall.

8   For the organisation of the local fire brigade at the time, see Peter Williams – *West Ham and its Fire Brigade – An Illustrated History, 1800–1965*, E. B. Books (2019)

9   Neal, p. 167

10 *Barking, East Ham and Ilford Advertiser, Upton Park and Dagenham Gazette*, 11 Jan 1890

11 Neal, p. 168

12 *Essex Newsroom,* 28 Jun 1890

13 *Southend Standard and Weekly Advertiser,* 23 Jan 1890

14 Neal, p. 170

15 NA, MH27/108

16 Barnett *Autobiography,* p. 26

17 Barnett, *Matters,* p. 154

18 LMA, *FGSD Governors' 1890 Annual Report*

19 LMA, *FGSD Governors' 1893 Annual Report*

20 Ibid

21 See Appendix

22 A rare insight into the desperate family backgrounds of some of the children in Forest Lane was given at the inquest, when Puttrick's mother gave evidence confirming the dead boy as her son. In her statement she said that Edwin entered the school following the death of her husband who 'died in January 1890 from inflammation of the kidneys … I have had six children. Two only are still alive. One child was drowned, one died of consumption of the bowels and one from strunnous glands [a nineteenth-century term sometimes used for tuberculosis]. My husband was a labourer, and 33 years of age when he died.' *Stratford Express,* 1 Jul 1893

23 *St James' Gazette,* 30 Jun 1893

24 Neal, p. 180

25 Ibid

26 *Stratford Express,* 1 Jul 1893

27 LMA, FGSD/042

28 *Sheffield Evening Telegraph,* 11 Aug 1893

29 *Stratford Express,* 1 July 1893

30 LMA, FGSD/042

31 *Illustrated Police News,* 30 Sep 1893

32 LMA, FGSD/014

33 *Stratford Express,* 17 Aug 1893

34 Neal, p. 176

35 LMA, FGSD/014

36 LMA, FGSD/042

37 Neal, p. 177

38 Barnett, *Canon* p. 684

39 Barnett, *Autobiography*

40 Barnett, *Canon,* p. 684

[41]   NA, MH27/110

[42]   NA, MH27/108

[43]   www.e7-nowandthen.org/2018/01/a-
       survivors-tale-1889-forest-gate.html, and
       private correspondence with Paul Norton,
       one of his great, great grandsons, to whom
       much thanks are owed for permission to
       use the family photographs.

CHAPTER 10

A DAMNING REPORT

Czar Alexander II of Russia was returning to the Winter Palace in St Petersburg on the afternoon of 13 March 1881, having attended a military tattoo, when he was ambushed and assassinated. The drama sparked a series of events which were to impact on the future of the FGDS.

One of the conspirators was Hesya Helfman, a Jewish revolutionary who died later that year in childbirth. Her religion triggered a rise of anti-Semitic sentiment in Russia, and provoked anti-Jewish riots, particularly in the southern parts of the country. The following year, the new czar, Alexander III, introduced a series of restrictions on the movements and actions of the country's Jewish community, which provoked a further three years of pogroms resulting in the large-scale emigration of Jews, primarily to the United States.

Many of them could not afford the fare to New York, and instead sought London as a place of refuge because journey costs were lower. They disembarked in London's docks, located within Whitechapel, and their impact was sudden and dramatic.

Whitechapel's population had remained fairly stable, at around 68,000 in the years leading up to the mid-1880s.[1] The area was also beginning to experience a considerable amount of slum clearance, much of it inspired by the Barnetts. The slums were replaced by housing aimed at 'the deserving poor', who were unlikely to call upon the services of the workhouse or its children's institution.

Czar Alexander II of Russia (1818–1881). In a clear case of the law of unintended consequences, his assassination in 1881 had a direct bearing on Jewish immigration to London and the USA and played a key role in sealing the fate of the FGDS.

Walter Besant's *All Sorts and Conditions of Men*, published in 1882, provided a fictional social analysis of the East End, in three volumes, without a single reference to Jewish people.[2] A huge and unprecedented change in the area's demographics, however, occurred over the following half decade. In 1887, Charles Booth recorded around 28,790 Jewish people in Whitechapel and he felt confident in asserting that 'The newcomers have gradually replaced the English population in whole districts, which were formerly outside the Jewish quarter. Formerly in Whitechapel, Commercial Street roughly divided the Jewish haunts.' [3]

The Jewish community was remarkably self-reliant and rejected direct, public poor law support. The Jewish Board of Guardians (later the Jewish Welfare Board) had been founded in 1859 to assist poor members of the community. Its principal source of funds was the United Synagogue – a confederation of London synagogues.[4]

These guardians sought to establish institutions such as soup kitchens and schools, to provide support to their community. On 2 March 1888, *The Jewish Chronicle* quoted a letter from William Vallance, in his capacity as clerk to the Whitechapel guardians, stating that the superintendent of the workhouse's casual wards told him that during the 'whole time that he has been in his present office a dozen Jews have been admitted to the Wards, that is nearly 17 years, and it is certainly more than twelve months since the last Jew was received.'

The following month the *Jewish Chronicle* commented on the Jews Free School (JFS) – then based in Whitechapel – and said that, 'The work is clearly educational; and the Free School does the bulk of it. Of the 3,000 children within its walls the great majority enter it practically as foreigners.' A decade later this number had risen to 4,300 – making it the largest school in the country.[5] Put simply, by the late 1880s, the JFS catered for the needs of 3,000 Whitechapel youngsters whose parents would not be seeking the guardians' support to send them to Forest Gate. This impacted on the institution's roll.

The number of children Whitechapel sent began to decline towards the end of the decade, and for almost the first time in its history there were no complaints of overcrowding at the FGDS. To compensate, the governors sought to recruit pupils from beyond east London. In 1885 they took about 25 children from each of Croydon and Wandsworth and, because the North Surrey District children's institution had to close temporarily, brought in about 40 from Lewisham.[6] The following year, a small number of children from St Pancras and Paddington were also relocated to Forest Lane.

HENRIETTA BARNETT'S TWIN-HEADED RESPONSE

Reckless behaviour and uncaring attitudes continued at Forest Gate, even after the fire and food poisoning episodes. Charles Duncan felt exonerated and no change was the order of the day. Within six months of the food poisoning tragedy, Henry Elliott's complaints about unfit food being served were revisited. The governors received a letter, complaining that 'weevils had been found in the bread supplied from the [Poplar] workhouse bakery to the school. The baker was called in, and said ... every care was taken in the manufacture of the bread. He was urged to use greater care to prevent the recurrence of the complaints.' [7] Six months later, the drill master, William Berry, was dismissed for brutality towards the children.[8]

The national press had covered both the fire and the poisoning in some detail, and the institution was beginning to register in the minds of the newspaper-reading public in an unflattering way. On 3 May 1894, around the time of Berry's dismissal, *The Westminster Gazette* provided a nuanced and thoughtful overview of the situation in Forest Gate, in a piece entitled

'The Evils of Pauper Schools'. Returning to the poisoning, it was blunt and stated that the FGDS' 'accounts have been seriously and continuously confused, that the children have been cheated ... that waste meat has been substituted for good meat and bread pudding for soup.'

The article continued in a critical vein, drawing attention to the scandals of ophthalmia and the fire. It also attacked the ins and outs process, whereby 'children of that miserable casual class flit like shadows in and out of the workhouse.'

It was well researched, reporting that, 'Of the children at Forest Gate, about 300 are permanent and about 550 go in and out during the year.' The feature concluded that, as far as the 'permanents' were concerned, 'The best system would probably be to place them in small cottage-homes in groups of ten or twelve, under a competent woman, with careful supervision.'

Meanwhile, cases of ophthalmia, diphtheria and scarlet fever continued at alarming rates. On 20 March 1896, the *London Daily News* reported that, as a result, 'strong efforts will be made to close the establishment and build another one further in the country.'

The less than dynamic medical officer, Dr Bell, declared himself to be 'at his wits end to cope with ill health' later the same year, according to his annual report. Having expressed unease about the number of typhoid and diphtheria cases in Forest Lane, he stated that he had seen 514 other children during the year, of whom 113 caused concern: 'Of these 70 were defective in physical development, 7 presented abnormal nerve signs, 21 showed signs of low nutrition, 39 were mentally dull and 27 were afflicted with eye diseases.'[9]

A perfect storm was brewing. The Forest Lane institution had suffered the fire and food poisoning outbreak within three years – both of which reflected badly on the management. The familiar problems of poor health care and undisciplined staff continued, apparently unaddressed. The establishment was beginning to attract adverse press attention and acquire national notoriety. Its buildings were ageing and ceasing to be fit for purpose, at the same time as the land on which they were built was increasing rapidly in value. The demographics of Whitechapel were changing to such an extent that its demand for the FGDS was reducing. And, finally, more compassionate methods of childcare were being pioneered elsewhere in the country, and some of the FGSD governors were sympathetic to their intentions.

Henrietta Barnett was deeply affected by the twin tragedies of fire and food poisoning and critical of the establishment's uncaring culture and the negligence of its superintendent. She seized on public concern to initiate a twin-headed response.

Firstly, she exploited family connections to initiate a campaign in the *British Medical Journal* (*BMJ*) to highlight the health hazards of 'barrack schools'. This produced an attentive and concerned public audience. Then she lobbied to establish and participate in a national inquiry into the state of London's poor law schools. Its report was so damning and coupled with the impact of the *BMJ*'s campaign, the closure of barrack schools became almost inevitable. Decision makers were influenced and the establishments replaced.

The editor of the *BMJ* was Ernest Abraham Hart (1835–1898), a medical journalist who edited the publication from 1867 until his death.[10] He also just happened to be Henrietta Barnett's brother-in-law. Spurred on by her, he picked up the baton of public scrutiny of the FGDS.

Barnett was proud to acknowledge their joint roles: 'Led by my brother-in-law, Mr Ernest Hart, a vigorous demand ... arose for an enquiry [sic] into all pauper schools ... Mr Hart, who poured out facts and figures and conclusively proved that the State was injuring the children it was supporting.'[11]

Under Barnett's prompting, Hart took on the food poisoning case and agitated for a national inquiry into the general health conditions of London's poor law schools.

The *BMJ*'s campaign was impressive, eye-catching and influential. The following extracts give an indication of its relentless, cumulative impact:

26 May 1894, *'The Forest Gate Scandal and Its Moral'*

This provided a summary of the LGB inquiry and conclusions, condemned the management of the institution and blamed it for the food poisoning, stating, 'No one can believe for a moment that the matters brought to light by the Local Government Board Enquiry were accidental and unprecedented abuses. What was accidental was the discovery of the abuse.'

21 September 1895, *'The Forest Gate District Schools'*

The article extended the scope of its attack on barrack schools and focused on their lack of attention to the overall health of the children. Hart observed that, 'On entering one of these large institutions the children are neither weighed or measured.' Which meant, he said, that there were no data to indicate the physical progress made by the children.

The LGB, he maintained, should insist on this for the future, in order to measure the effectiveness of the institutions' impact on their children's health. He asserted that there was no proper exercise regime and that games in the grounds were dull. This meant that 'The children rarely walk beyond the institution's boundaries, and when they do, the large numbers necessitate semi-military marching at a pace suitable for the youngest and feeblest and therefore inexpressively weary to the elder and stronger.'

11 January 1896, *'Sickness in Pauper Schools'*

Hart attacked the whole culture of barrack schools and their lack of attention to the health of their charges:

> If such schools must exist, the public owe it to themselves to see that they are managed by persons capable of understanding the rudimentary rules of public health and courageous enough to face and acknowledge the mistakes of a system which was originated more than 50 years ago and has been abundantly proved a failure both for the children and for the ratepayers.

In early 1896, there was a serious outbreak of scarlet fever. The *BMJ* reported on this and used it as further evidence to support the closure of barrack schools.

21 March 1896, *'Infectious Diseases in Pauper Schools'*

Hart reported that 170 children from the FGDS had suffered from scarlet fever over the previous six months. Accepting that responsible steps, such as clothes burning, had been taken to stop the spread he nonetheless concluded that because there were over 500 children in close proximity, controlling the disease was very difficult. The article concluded by calling for an end to the barrack school system, as this was the only way to prevent the recurrence of similar epidemics.

12 September 1896, *'The Evils of Pauper Schools on Sending Children Away for 2 Weeks, While Cleaning Done'*

Hart reported that, in response to outbreaks of diphtheria and scarlet fever six months previously, the FGSD had taken the unusual (and expensive) step of closing the establishment for two weeks. The buildings and grounds had been subjected to what would now be considered a deep clean, to decontaminate them. The displaced children had been sent to the country, on the advice of the medical officer, and 'boarded out' in foster homes. The operation was managed by the CCHF, that Henrietta Barnett had established.[12]

Hart was withering in his conclusion:

> What irony! to make workable the unholy wieldy system of aggregation, resort has to be had to boarding-out. The children should, by their appearance, on return from their residence in country labourers cottages, exhibit the great benefit of the freer happier life of even a fortnight amid natural surroundings, and there can be little doubt that there will be some difficulty with insubordination before the 550 small mortals can again be reduced to the machine-like obedience necessary to the sterile, monotonous existence of the aggravated life.

Barnett and Hart were successful in persuading the LGB to establish a Departmental Inquiry into System of the Maintenance and Education in Metropolitan Poor Law Schools, to examine conditions in all of London's barrack schools.

The committee was chaired by Anthony Mundella (1825–1897) and Barnett was the first woman to be appointed to such a government inquiry.[13] Mundella was a radical Liberal MP whose background and interests showed him to be ideally qualified, although he was regarded as being difficult. He had been a minister of education in an earlier Gladstone government and was responsible for the 1880 Education Act, which made schooling compulsory in the UK.

During his ministerial career he furthered the cause of technical education and improved the system of school inspection – including appointing the first women inspectors. He widened the inspectorate's brief to incorporate concern for the health and mental well-being of pupils and established the first nationwide system for providing free school meals to poor pupils. He was also largely responsible for ensuring the passage of The Prevention of Cruelty to, and Protection of, Children Act 1889 – popularly known as The Children's Charter.

Hugely talented and widely respected, Mundella resigned from state office following the financial failure of one of his previous businesses. Chairing this committee on London's poor law schools was one of his last public acts before his death in 1897. The committee, which met 50 times, saw 73 witnesses and asked over 17,000 questions, published its report in two volumes in 1896. Only two of the witnesses were former or current inmates or staff members: Henry Elliott and Will Crooks (1852–1921). The latter became a governor of the Forest Gate institution, and, like Barnett, appeared before the committee not to praise district schools, but to bury them. He condemned them as having insufficient and poorly trained staff, and called for them to be replaced by more caring institutions.

One of the witnesses was Maria Poole, secretary to MABYS. In some pseudo-scientific tosh, she tried to characterise the nature of the girls attending the institutions reviewed by the committee in a document entitled *Special Failings of the Girls by Poor Law Union*. She described the girls coming from Poplar as 'Dirty, untruthful, frequently dishonest and fond of change.'[14]

A perhaps more nuanced view of conditions for girls in district schools was offered by social reformer Florence Davenport-Hill, who condemned the 'training' the girls undertook, complaining that 'Children, little things of 10 or 11 years of age, scrubbing the vast corridors and great dormitories' and 'preparing vegetables wholesale by the bushel' did nothing to make them ready for life as a house maid.[15]

The Mundella inquiry gave Henry Elliott, hero of the fire and food poisoning whistleblower, the platform for his finest hour. He gave evidence to, and was given respect by, the committee. He was represented by Mr B. Costello, a barrister and chairman of the LCC's local government committee. For a second time Elliott had legal assistance, which was most unusual for a poor, unemployed, working-class man. In all probability the fees were paid by the Barnett family.

Costello maintained that the LGB's inquiry into the food poisoning had been 'very unsatisfactory' and that the children called as witnesses had been anxious and nervous:

> The superintendent of such a school has such supreme autocratic power in his hands that it must be excessively difficult to find out grave irregularities. It seemed to me quite obvious that it was very unlikely that any officer, or still more unlikely that any child, would be willing to give evidence.

The barrister concluded that the governors' faith in Duncan had been 'almost sublime'. He added: 'I think they believed a great deal too implicitly that nothing could be wrong in the institution.'

One of the committee members, the Rt Hon John Gorst, analysed events surrounding the food poisoning incident and his conclusions appear in the appendix of the Mundella Report. They are an indictment of the FGDS governors and the LGB, and they exonerated Elliott. Gorst condemned the LGB report because it was 'an inquiry into Elliott's veracity only. No inquiry as to how the children came to be poisoned had ever been made by either the managers or the Local Government Board.'

Henrietta Barnett, giving evidence to the committee, reflected on her own experience with FGDS and said that she had trained 135 of its girls under her own roof, because she felt that under the barrack school system, the girls 'have been trained too much by machinery and too little by mothering.'

Barnett called Ernest Hart to give evidence and add weight to their case. He duly obliged, condemning the state to the children's health in the institutions, while declaring 'ophthalmia is practically a barrack-school disease'.

Hart used the committee's proceedings as an opportunity to question Elliott about bed-wetting in Forest Lane, which he said could be an indicator of stress and neglect. Elliott said he had kept a log of such incidents, which showed that in a 12-month period there had been 5,000 episodes in the boys' section alone. He contrasted this with his own experience of running the reception ward, where he said that not one child in 100 wet the bed. He concluded that the difference was accounted for by the lack of attention children received in the main buildings of the establishment.[16]

Mundella's report concurred with the evidence of the FGDS-related witnesses. It accepted Hart's evidence about the relationship between ophthalmia and children's workhouses, as well as Barnett's evidence, declaring that 'the children go untaught' and that 'the effect upon the after-career of the girls is often disastrous'. And in reply to Crooks' submission, it concluded: 'we regard the treatment of the children as cruel in itself and more likely to contaminate them than even a prison.'

The 180-page report unambiguously condemned barrack schools because they were seen to be breeding grounds for contagious diseases, such as ophthalmia, and they fostered emotional deprivation, a lack of social stimulation and care and attention to individuals. It recommended they be replaced with either scattered homes or the boarding out of pupils. It proposed the establishment of a central government authority to have overall responsibility for all pauper children. These findings, complemented by a recent Education Act, called for supervision of the establishments to be transferred from the LGB to the education department, as reformers had been seeking for many years.[17]

The report's central aim was to ensure that, in future, poor law children would benefit from a more natural life, in closer association with the wider community. It wished to see the children emancipated from an association with pauperism. It had a wide-ranging and dramatic impact on, among others, the press, barrack schools, the heavily criticised LGB, Henrietta Barnett and the FGSD itself.

The Times praised its recommendation to transfer supervision of poor law schools to the education department, because it was entirely 'separated from the association and traditions of pauperism. This aim may or may not be realised, but it must be kept in view if we are not to train a whole class of hereditary and professional paupers.'

Although exclusively concerned with district schools in London, Mundella received widespread, detailed and favourable coverage in the country's regional press, as this extract for the *Derby Evening Telegraph* on 7 September 1896, illustrates:

> It would be manifestly unfair to compare schools under the poor law with board and voluntary schools, because while children in the latter remain at school for five, six or seven years, attending regularly day after day, those in the former may be on and off the books for the same number of years, and yet their whole school life may not exceed 12 months. There can be no question that this 'in and out' system, as it is called, is most injurious to the future welfare of the children in that it precludes all possibility of affecting any permanent improvement in their conditions and every effort should be made to provide a remedy for such a state of things.

Nevertheless, the majority of FGSD's governors did not wish to go down without a fight. In August 1896 they produced a lengthy and detailed response to some of the criticisms. Their arguments were weak and read as if they scarcely believed their defence themselves. [18]

They chose to highlight initiatives that Barnett – who by now was hostile to the very existence of barrack schools – had pioneered, as evidence of the great benefits FGDS brought to the children's lives. These included the fact some of the girls were now trained in domestic service outside of institutional premises, others now had holidays, courtesy of the countryside homes initiative, and all the pupils now benefited from regular trips outside the establishment.

They blamed others, notably the LGB, for many of the accepted failures of barrack schools such as their shortcomings in educational standards and overcrowding. They concluded by saying they were willing to change, had no objection to the establishment of cottage homes and would develop their after-care responsibilities for boys until the age of 16 and girls until at least 18.

They accepted that no new barrack schools were likely to be built, but they felt, on balance, that there were no good grounds for shutting down the FGDS itself.

The 20 or so children's workhouses in London were also stung by the hostility of the Mundella Report and responded by publishing a critique of it in 1897, as well as commissioning two barristers to produce a more considered response, which was published the following March. That publication *Our London Poor Law Schools*[19] provided a snapshot of conditions in the 20 metropolitan establishments and addressed issues such as their legal and financial positions, as well as a short discourse on the problems of ophthalmia. Neither publication provided a convincing defence of barrack schools, although the latter report provided useful comparative information on the state of the establishments it surveyed.[20]

The FGDS did not emerge well from the comparative data. It was one of the oldest and much of its fabric required updating. More significantly, it was clear that its culture, the children's living conditions, and in particular their social and emotional needs, failed to match modern thinking about childcare.

The LGB responded to the criticism and accepted the inevitable. Its president, Henry Chaplin, told parliament on 1 February 1897 that his department would not sanction the construction of any more barrack schools, or the expansion of any of the existing ones, saying, 'Much objection has been made to the massing together in one institution of great numbers of children and we fully concur with this objection.'[21]

He also launched an inquiry into the physical conditions of the two oldest London children's workhouses – the now almost 50-year-old South Metropolitan District School, and the FGDS. Following the review, in 1897, he closed the South Metropolitan school. As will become clear, the Poplar board of guardians felt somewhat aggrieved at the way the LGB dealt with the Forest Gate inquiry.

WHITECHAPEL WANTS OUT

Poplar's circumstances were by now very different from Whitechapel's. Its population was expanding rapidly and, by 1887, was almost three times that of Whitechapel's with more than 180,000 people.[22] The London Docks and the shipbuilding industry were situated within its boundaries and both were seasonal and employed large numbers of casual labourers. It was also home to the Bryant & May match factory that employed the poorly paid and badly treated match women and girls, whose 1888 strike gained national prominence.

All of these workplaces employed people who, in bad times, would have sought refuge in the workhouse, with their children being transported to Forest Gate. By the mid-1890s, Poplar alone had more children than the FGDS could accommodate, and some had to remain in its main workhouse until space became available in Forest Lane.

The FGDS' 1894–5 annual report illustrated the problem. Of the 700 on the roll, 600 were from Poplar, whose union also had 137 in its workhouse waiting to be moved to Forest Lane. Although Whitechapel had only 14 per cent of the pupils, it contributed 37 per cent to its costs, and the disparity was widening by the year. In 1884, Whitechapel had 182 pupils (34 per cent) and Poplar 358 (66 per cent). A decade later the numbers were 85 (13 per cent) and 583 (87 per cent).

Poplar's board and its governors in Forest Gate initially wanted to build an extension to accommodate their excess numbers. Unsurprisingly, Whitechapel disagreed, as it would have been required to contribute 37 per cent to the cost of buildings they did not need. William Vallance, in his role as clerk to Whitechapel's guardians, wrote to FGDS' governors objecting to the extension, and called for a re-apportionment of costs between the unions to reflect the usage made by each. This was disingenuous, as he knew from his time as clerk to Forest Lane's governors that it was not a matter under their control, as he was later reminded.

Whitechapel was now in the same position as Hackney, when it left the district. It had the fewest pupils and was paying the greatest proportion of the costs. Its number of pupils was almost the same as that of Poplar's awaiting accommodation. A simple solution beckoned; if Whitechapel left, Poplar would become the sole controller and the institution would be able to accommodate its demand for places. Whitechapel could, meanwhile, seek alternative provision for its youngsters, partially paid for by Poplar buying them out of their share of Forest Lane.

To put pressure on Poplar, in December 1895 Whitechapel announced that it could accommodate all of its children elsewhere within three to four weeks if the district were dissolved. In that case, Poplar said it would not retain the existing establishment, but would sell the grounds and move to more suitable accommodation elsewhere.[23] By now, nobody wanted the FGDS. Whitechapel wanted out, and had found an exit route, Poplar wanted to sell the site and move elsewhere, and following the Mundella Report, the government was losing interest.

The LGB had already made it clear that there would be no further major building work on any barrack school, so 'sell and relocate' would be their only likely formal response. All that was required was for Whitechapel to find accommodation for its dwindling number of pupils and for the terms of the separation to be agreed. In June 1897, following negotiations mediated by the LGB, the Forest Gate site was valued at £42,000.[24] Based on the contributions-to-costs formula, Poplar would receive £26,500 and Whitechapel £15,500, if it were sold at its valuation price. Alternatively, Poplar could buy Whitechapel out. Poplar chose the latter.

To buy Whitechapel out, Poplar borrowed the £15,500 required from the recently established London County Council (LCC). Whitechapel used this money for its new accommodation in Grays 'on condition that it [Poplar] would make equitable arrangements for the reception and maintenance of the Whitechapel children until the cottage-homes that the board proposed to erect for them were ready.' For its part, Poplar requested that the disso-lution be brought forward from the originally agreed 31 December 1897 to 2 October 'in order that the changes may occur during the school year.'[25]

And so it was, without great fanfare the *Tower Hamlets Independent and East End Local Advertiser* announced on 25 September, that:

> From Saturday next the Forest Gate District Schools will cease to exist .... Perhaps few public buildings have had a more unfortunate experience that the Forest Gate Schools. The terrible fire some winters back in which many of the little ones were burnt to death or injured, the succession of fever and diphtheria epidemics, to

say nothing of a scandal or two thrown in, make a history the reverse of pleasant.

It was only once the terms of the separation were agreed that the LGB-commissioned report into the FGDS site was shared with the two boards of guardians. It said that if Poplar decided to remain on the site, it would have to build more playrooms, washing facilities and two more infirmaries, extensive building works that the LGB had already indicated it would not sanction. Poplar felt aggrieved, believing they had been deceived into purchasing a badly damaged asset. On 4 December, the *Tower Hamlets Independent and East End Local Advertiser* recorded their guardians' anger, stating they had:

> Come to the conclusion that they have been unfairly treated. Undoubtedly, if this report had been known before the dissolution took place, very different terms would have been arranged between the two parishes. One thing that strikes everyone as peculiar is that Dr Stephenson's report dates back to 9 March, whereas sanction of the Local Government Board to purchase the schools was dated 26th June. One naturally wonders whether Whitechapel has been, in this instance, distinctly favoured by the Local Government Board, and if so, why?

BARNETT REFLECTS

Henrietta Barnett claimed that, within a year of its publication, 13 of Mundella's recommendations had been adopted by the LGB. However, the most important was fudged. The proposal to switch responsibility for poor law schools from the LGB to the education department did not take place until 1904, as the two departments squabbled over the terms of the transfer. The move in itself, however, did not get rid of barrack and similar institutional schools; because in 1907, only a third of the 50,000 children living in poor law institutions attended public elementary schools.[26]

Twenty-five years after the publication of the Mundella Report, she was still as angry, saying it 'Showed up all the criminal self-satisfaction of the guardians and the still more wicked indifference of the LGB, to evils of which it knew' existed within the institutions.[27] Speaking from her own very bitter experience and frustration at the FGDS, Barnett felt that the report 'Brought out the injustice of the department [LGB] acting as judge, jury and accused when scandals arose, which were often due to the negligence of their own officers and inspectors.'

The report coincided with the end of her governorship of the FGDS, the government having abolished the role of ex-officio governors of children's workhouses in the 1894 Local Government Act.

But she did not abandon the plight of those left in barrack schools. In 1896, she helped establish the State Children's Association, to help obtain the dissolution of large district-type schools, so that children could be brought up by families, in order 'to obtain individual treatment for the children under the guardianship of the state.' She attracted the good and the great to be sponsors and encouraged them to act as a pressure group. It reported regularly to parliament and was only wound up a little after her death, in 1936.

In addition to her relationship with the State Children's Association, Barnett busied herself with other reforms. With husband Samuel, she helped create the Whitechapel Gallery in 1897 and seven years later was active in an altogether different pursuit. She acquired the land on which to establish Hampstead Garden Suburb, and became pre-occupied with its planning and development. Two years later she established what was to become the Henrietta Barnett Girls School, in the area.

Samuel died in 1913 and she drifted into semi-retirement, concentrating on writing, much of which was reflective of the couple's social and reforming achievements, including her contribution to the FGSD.

Barnett's impact on the FGDS can be assessed in her own words, via extracts from two of her books, which were published a fourteen years apart. At first glance the accounts seem almost contradictory. The earlier one, in an almost self-congratulatory tone, celebrated how her reforms had enriched the lives of the children and the latter condemned the very existence of the barrack schools she sought to see closed.

In summary, she commented that you could make life more bearable inside the institutions with minor changes and pleasing touches, but at the end of the day they deprived the children of basic rights, such as care, individual attention and love. Thus, they had no place in a civilised society.

Her 1919 biography of Samuel stated that 'many and important changes had been brought about' under her stewardship in Forest Gate, and portrayed them in a rose-tinted manner:

The children romped in playing fields, dug and delved in little gardens, talked busily at meals, wore night garments, owned three sets of day apparel; possessed toys, large ones, such as rocking horses, swings, bats and dolls houses, to be played with in common; small treasures, such as dolls, puzzle books and boxes, which now had personally owned 'lockers' ... . The children swam and were drilled, walked out, or gambolled in the yards, all with ... the enjoyment of the new life so gladly accepted. Prizes were offered and won, and a library was voluntarily worked by ladies 'out of doors', to use the pauper expression.

Bare rooms had been decorated with pictures, and high hope was to be read through many a motto on coloured, washed walls. Flowers grew in the windows, cats kittened in the laundry, canaries sang amid the whirr of the patent centrifugal wringer. Concerts and entertainments were given almost weekly by staff, or ladies and gentlemen, with power to cause pleasure. Each girl was called by her Christian pre-fix. Each boy by his sire's name. On Sunday afternoon the great hall was turned into a busy Sunday school, when children came into contact with good hearts and gentle influences; and as enough teachers volunteered to allow of the classes being small, each child, anyway for that one afternoon, got the individual notice that everyone craves for. A savings' bank was started, and pennies were both saved and spent when the managers thought well to have a treat and the happy hundreds spent long days by the sea. Kindergarten and its 'gifts' brought interest and variety into the infants' school.

At meal times a happy buzz arose from amid the long tables, and such interest as the conversation provided did something to make the coarse food more appetising. Individual tastes were consulted, at least as far as quantity was concerned, for the children were given less to begin with, and encouraged to ask for more.

Recreation rooms were provided for both boys and girls, and the long winter evenings were anything but dreary, for when the school was done and work over, the children gathered in the brilliantly lit, hot-pipe-heated rooms, and played draughts, bagatelle, lotto or tiddly winks.[28]

Having read this eulogy, one is tempted to ask why she was so determined to see the end of barrack schools in general and the FGDS, in particular. Fourteen years later, she painted a diametrically opposite picture of the institution. Out had gone the warm cosy glow of contentment, in came the anger that had encouraged her brother-in-law to write, influentially, about the tyranny of barrack schools, and the determination she applied to get the departmental inquiry established, with herself in the driving seat.

The sentimental author had been replaced by the hardened, analytical social reformer who pondered on the oppressive nature of the institution. These thoughts appeared in a collection of essays on aspects of her life, published in 1933. Her analysis was of the overall impact of the establishment, rather than some of the minor reforms and softening touches she had encouraged.

In this statement she was unsentimental and clear that 'Large organisations, like Barrack Schools spread disease and dull initiative.' She continued:

> There is a daily monotony and lack of stimulation. Everything is done for the children in Barrack Schools. Too high a turn-over of children, and new ones bring bad habits and attitudes with them, because vigorous discipline is essential, routine is unavoidable and the children lack individual attention — even though many staff would wish to give it. Children in the schools soon develop a stigma ....
>
> The whole life of a child ... is too much like that of a convent or prison, for fear of contagion the children can be allowed little contact with the outside world and never the free interchange enjoyed by those whom chance meetings bring pleasure, interest and variety; for fear of disorder no sudden variety can be introduced – a glimpse of fine weather between showers cannot be taken advantage of for exercise – a short spell of warm or cold cannot be met by changed clothing – the life of the institution has to be elaborately organised and any unexpected variation could upset the machine. But the children who are brought up in such dead artificial surroundings are ill-prepared to fit into a world where growth and change are universal laws.[29]

LOCALLY INVISIBLE

As the district school curtain closed on Forest Gate in 1897, it is worth reflecting on the impact it had had on its locality over the previous 40 years. The answer is surprisingly little, other than the drama surrounding the 1890 fire and 1893 poisoning.

Although over 40,000 children had crossed the threshold since its opening, and it was by far the largest collection of buildings in Forest Gate, little was known or understood about the institution in the area. This is illustrated by the lack of recognition it received in local publications. The old English homily that 'children should be seen, but not heard' was taken a step further with regard to the FGDS – where, apparently, the children were neither seen, nor heard by most neighbours.

The first privately published history of what is now Newham, *History of the Parishes of East and West Ham*,[30] appeared in 1888 and was partial and patchy. It did not make a single reference to the establishment, despite having accommodated up to 10 per cent of Forest Gate's population when it first opened. The omission is the stranger because the book's authors each had direct Forest Gate connections, living in the area and with close ties to Samuel Gurney on whose land the institution was built. Katharine Fry was his niece and Gustav Pagenstecher was a family retainer who did much to administer his estate after his death.[31]

The institution's main local newspaper for most of its lifetime was the *Stratford Express*. Yet it paid almost no attention to it other than the fire and food poisoning episodes. There was little or no acknowledgement of its opening, it becoming a district school, Hackney's departure, the inquiry or the proposal of Whitechapel to leave the district.

A more local publication, the *Forest Gate Weekly News* (*FGWN*), appeared between 1896 and 1900 and ran to almost 200 editions. The FGDS received less coverage in its pages than the local chrysanthemum society. It published just one significant article and referred to it, in passing, on only three or four other occasions; one of those erroneously describing it as a boys' school.[32]

By way of contrast, the *FGWN* published four lengthy articles about the Barnardo's village, in Barkingside, which was five miles away.

An explanation for the lack of coverage appears in the 2,200-word *FGWN* article, in which the author stated: 'I recognised from the first that it was not strictly speaking, a local institution that I was visiting, but if it had been one maintained strictly by and for Forest Gate inhabitants, I could not have been accorded a better reception.'[33]

The piece provided an epitaph on the FGSD, and was rather sentimental (with references to 'a few little chaps' and 'cheerful little folk'), inspired, in part, by Charles Dickens' *A Christmas Carol.* It provided an account of life in the festive season entitled 'A world within a world: my visits to the Forest Gate District Schools.'

The opening sentence illustrated how little known the institution was within its home community: 'There may be readers who would like to know exactly what purpose the Forest Gate District Schools serve, by whom and when they were erected, and by whom they are maintained.' The journalist was blunt and accurate in his assessment, describing the buildings as 'simply workhouse schools carried on, for reasons of convenience, away from the workhouse.'

The article emphasised its detachment from the area: 'Most Forest Gate residents are familiar with the large building in Forest Lane. But probably few of such residents are aware of the extent of the complementary buildings which stand to the west and rear of the main block, or of the "world within a world" which is living out its life.'

The writer said he had to make three trips to take in the scale of the operation, adding that, 'The place is altogether too vast to be grasped or understood at a visit.'

Patterns of daily life were described and the writer was struck by the discipline of the children, particularly around meal times:

> At last a gong sounded … . Every child rose … . The gong sounded again, and now five hundred pairs of hands were reverently folded. A third time the gong sounded; the notes of a harmonium were also heard; and grace was strongly and clearly chanted by all the children, many of whom closed their eyes and moved their heads as if greatly enjoying.

The lack of material possessions or treats was highlighted by the description of their Christmas gifts, which showed 'how much difference every one-pennyworth of fruit administered once in twelve months may make, in a pauper child's life.'

The ins and outs question was addressed simply and in a patronising way, without considering its impact on the children:

> A man tires of the battle of life and goes into the Poplar or the
> Whitechapel Workhouse, taking his children with him. The latter
> are sent to Forest Gate. The man tires of workhouse routine and
> desires to try the battle of life once more. His children are sent
> to meet him and from the workhouse gates they emerge together.

A skeletal history of the institution was offered, with details of dates
of the foundation, establishment of the district, departure of Hackney and
'whispers' about Whitechapel's future relationship, together with the names
of some prominent governors. These did not include Henrietta Barnett,
who, one suspects, Charles Duncan – the journalist's guide – would not
have been keen to promote.

Apart from a single reference to 'the deplorably fatal fire of several years
ago', there was no reference of any incident affecting the children – good
or bad – in its entire history.

Instead, the journalist was steered towards the fact that 'spotless cleanliness is the absolute rule of the place and no deviation there from is, under
any circumstances, permitted.' This was safe territory for the management
to emphasise, in a way that health, well-being and educational standards
were not. The journalist observed:

> As Mr. Duncan passes round he occasionally stoops and draws his
> finger across some portion of the polished flooring but fails to
> bring away with it any trace of dust. His daily pilgrimage through
> all rooms is a matter of some hours and the irregularity that escapes
> his eye must be of microscopical dimensions.

The article detailed the way the children were used to keep costs to a
minimum: 'the dolls' houses themselves and some of the forms and desks
are the handiwork of boys in the carpenters' shop ... . Near at hand are the
boot makers' and tailors' shops where all the repairing for the Institution is
done by the boys.' He recognised that the children were used as free labour,
rather than being provided with useful job skills: 'the vast proportion passes
out into the world utterly untrained in any sort of handicraft. Education is
undoubtedly a good thing, but wage-earning power is surely better.'

The nearest the journalist came to engage in the national debate around
the future of barrack schools was batted away by Duncan:

I asked a question of Mr. Duncan which, he says, almost every visitor asks. It was whether the massing of children together does not lead to hurtful moral results. His reply was interesting and instructive. 'In all my experience here, the matter has not once arisen. I believe these children to be perfectly innocent and that there is even less likelihood of mutual contamination than in a large public school where children of the better classes congregate.'

So, as the debate raged nationally about the future of barrack schools, the benefits of cottage or scattered homes and the conditions of the children, the people of Forest Gate, relying solely on the local press, would not have known the role its own institution had in shaping this thinking, and how it led to the eventual closure of all barrack schools.

LIFE IN SERVICE, POST FGDS

Maria Poole was the secretary of MABYS who, from the early 1880s, provided annual progress reports on the working situation of over 100 former FGDS girls to its governors. MABYS provided an after-care service to the young women until they reached the age of 21 and the governors published her, often very caustic, comments in their annual reports. They give a brief insight into the post-FGDS life of some of the female leavers.

The summaries below are selected from the 1888 and 1890 reports – picked at random (bar A. D. 1888, below) for illustrative purposes. Maria Poole identified the young women by their initials and their home union in her reports.

1888
A. S. *(Whitechapel)*, aged 20. Time in school seven years and one month. *Report* – Very satisfactory. *Particulars* – Living in Denning Road, Hampstead in the same place with her sister,

Mary, having done well in the last place for about three years. Will not report back again. Unlikely to emigrate at present. Over age [for further visits from MABYS].

A Victorian maid of all works - occupational destination for the great majority of girl leavers from the FGDS.

S. R. *(Poplar)*, aged 20. Time in school seven and a half years. *Report* – Fairly satisfactory. *Particulars* – Left her place in March, but has been since May in another, which she seems likely to keep. Over age.

R. G. *(Whitechapel)*, aged 20. Time in school five years. *Report* – Satisfactory. *Particulars* – Has considerably improved and is staying in the same place. Is now over age.

R. P. *(Whitechapel)*, aged 20. Time in school eight years. *Report* – Satisfactory. *Particulars* – Doing well, keeping her place, but a difficult girl to deal with.

E. S. *(Poplar)*, aged 14. Time in school six years. *Report* – Satisfactory. *Particulars* – Doing very well in her place and looks clean and happy.

A. D. *(Poplar)*, aged 15. Time in school four and a half years. *Report* – Very satisfactory. *Particulars* – Sent to service from Mrs. Barnett's Cottage Home. A dear little girl. [Seth Koven identified this young woman as being Nellie Dowell's sister – see page 133 for details.]

1890

A. T. *(Poplar)*, aged 20. Time in school six years and five months. *Report* – With relations. *Particulars* – Did well in service, but now living at home with her mother. Over age.

E. S. *(Poplar)*, aged 14. Time in school five years. *Report* – Satisfactory. *Particulars* – A nice quiet girl, but very ignorant. So far doing well in her first place.

H. M. *(Poplar)*, aged 14. Time in school one year. *Report* – Unsatisfactory. *Particulars* – Has just left her first place, only stayed three weeks; most impudent and dishonest. Now placed again and it is hoped will do better.

1890 summary of former girls visited: Returned to schools, 1; Satisfactory, 65; Fair, 20; Unsatisfactory, 13; Bad, 4; In homes, 5; Emigrated, 1; Married, 0; Dead, 1; Unfit for service, 1; Visits refused, 1; Lost sight of, 4; Returned to relations, 4. **Total 120.**

NOTES

1. William J. Fishman, *East End 1888*, Hanbury, 2001, p. 44

2. Alan Palmer, *The East End – Four Centuries of London Life*, John Murray, 1989, p. 106

3. Fishman, p. 131

4. Jerry White, *Rothschild Buildings: Life in an East End Tenement Block 1887–1920*, Pimlico, 2003, pp. 16-17

5. Palmer, p. 107

6. NA, MH27/107

7. *ELO*, 21 Oct 1893

8. NA, MH9/22

9. *THIEELA*, 18 Jul 1896

10. *Oxford Dictionary of National Biography*

11. Barnett, *Canon* pp. 684-5

12. NA, MH27/110

13. www.hbschool.org.uk/360/about-us/history-of-the-school

14. *Mundella Report, Vol 2 of evidence*, p. 150

15. Steer, p. 72

16. Hart, p. 182

17. *Derby Evening Telegraph*, 7 Sep 1896. The Royal Commission on Industrial Schools, 1882 and the Cross Committee, 1888 had previously called for this, but to no avail.

18. NA, MH27/110

19. Walter Mornington and Frederick Lampard, *Our London Poor Law Schools: Comprising Descriptive Sketches of the Schools*, Eyre and Spottiswood, London 1898

20. This forms the basis of much of the Appendix

21. *Hansard*, 1 Feb 1897

22. Fishman, p. 44

23. NA, MH27/110

24. NA, MH27/111

25. *THIEELA*, 28 Aug 1897

26. Ross, p. 47

27. Barnett, *Canon*, p. 682

28. Barnett, *Canon*, pp. 680-682

29. Barnett, *Matters*, p. 190

30. Katharine Fry and Gustav Pagenstecher – *History of the Parishes of East and West Ham*, privately published, 1888

31. www.e7-nowandthen.org/2017/04/the-most-interesting-personality-in.html

32. *FGWN*, 24 Jul 1896

33. *FGWN*, 1 Jan 1897

CHAPTER 11

WORKING-CLASS REFORMERS

The FGSD was dissolved in October 1897, with Whitechapel's departure, and the institution returned to the status of a 'separate' school, controlled directly by Poplar guardians. Over the previous 43 years it had been Whitechapel's separate school for 14 (1854–68); a district school controlled by three poor law unions for nine (1868–77); controlled by two boards for 20 (1877–1897), before reverting to its original status, under the auspices of a different union, in 1897.

Its culture was outdated and inappropriate, according to the Mundella Report and contemporary social policy thinking, and its buildings had ceased to be fit for purpose concluded the 1897 LGB survey. It was doomed.

Whitechapel, having taken Poplar's money for its share of the site, used it to build cottage homes for its children in Grays – close to the location of TS *Goliath's* former mooring. Its guardians had heeded Barnett's messages. Their intentions were to 'ensure a responsible control [of the youngsters] and at the same time that everyday life of the children should, as far as possible correspond to that of other children of the working class .... with each home under the control of a lady superintendent.'[1] In her husband's biography, Henrietta Barnett noted that 'Canon Barnett took the deepest interest in the planning, execution and staffing of them.'[2]

Meanwhile, Poplar had to make the best of a bad inheritance. It didn't take long before it was reminded of the scale of the problems. The institution was struck by an outbreak of ringworm in January 1898, which was exacerbated by the cramped conditions.

As Whitechapel's Henrietta Barnett was bowing out of governorship of the FGSD, she was passed through the door by two towering figures from Poplar – Will Crooks and George Lansbury – who were to play as significant roles as her in reforming the institution under Poplar control.

The two were elected to Poplar's Board of Guardians, together, in 1893 and rapidly became acquainted with, and appalled by, what they saw in Forest Gate. The establishment reminded Crooks of boyhood traumas, and instilled deep impressions on both of them, which helped shape some of their future political activity. It spurred them to become tireless reformers and committed opponents of barrack schools and other poor law institutions.

WILL CROOKS

Will Crooks MP (1852-1921) (Photo: G Dendry)

Will Crooks was a local workhouse boy who was so influenced by his childhood experience that he determined to improve the conditions and life chances of future inmates, and particularly its young. He was born into poverty in Poplar on 6 April 1852; son of a disabled father, who, unable to work following an industrial accident, was forced to seek parish relief.

The family of eight was paid two or three shillings a week outdoor relief by the time Will was eight years old, which barely kept them from starvation. Poplar's guardians at that point determined they should be sent to their workhouse, by the Millwall docks.[3]

His experience as a child pauper in the 1860s shaped his thinking, according to biographer George Haw: 'The lad was ravenously hungry all the time he spent in the workhouse. He often felt at times as though he could eat leather; yet every morning when the "skilly" was served for breakfast, he could not touch it.'[4]

Haw recounted that the Crooks' children were kept in the workhouse for two or three weeks before being taken away, by bus with other boys, to the South Metropolitan District School in Sutton. Had the Crooks family moved into Poplar Workhouse nine years later, Will would probably have been despatched to the FGDS itself.

On entering the Sutton children's workhouse, Crooks was separated from his younger brother, and, according to Haws, 'In the great hall of the school he would strain his eyes, hoping to get a glimpse of the lone little fellow among the other lads, but never set eyes upon him again until the day they went home together.'

'Every day I spent in that school is burned on my soul,' recalled Crooks, which according to his biographer, 'he has often declared since.'[5] George Haw was a friend of Crooks in adult life, and observed:

> Sights like those of his childhood, with the shuddering memories
> of his own dark days in the workhouse school made him register
> a vow, little chap though he was at the time, that when he grew up
> to be a man he would do all he could to make better and brighter
> the lot of the inmates, especially that of the boys and girls.[6]

Crooks' career trajectory was dramatic. On leaving the institution he worked initially as a grocer's errand boy, later a blacksmith's apprentice and then an apprentice cooper. After a short spell in Liverpool, he returned to Poplar and found work in the docks.[7]

As a dock labourer, he was a prominent figure in the famous 1889 London dock strike. In the days before the establishment of the Labour party, he was elected, under the Progressive banner, as Poplar's member of the recently established LCC, in 1892.[8] As soon as he was elected, he canvassed the LGB to reduce the property qualification for eligibility for election to boards of guardians, and took advantage of their response, by successfully standing for Poplar's board the following year.

'When he took his seat as a Member in the board-room, where thirty years before he clung timorously to his mother's skirt, he knew that the task of his life had begun,' remarked Haw.[9]

When Crooks was appointed a governor of the Forest Gate establishment in 1897 he was reminded of the problems caused by ins and outs: 'batches of neglected little people in the workhouse. The greater number of these belonged to parents who came into the House for short periods only.'[10]

He observed that, just like his own childhood experience, they got 'no schooling and no training, save the training that fitted them for pauperism.' He soon discovered that 'If they were sent to Forest Gate one day their parents in the workhouse could demand them back the next day and take their discharge, even though they and their children turned up at the gates for re-admission within the next twenty-four hours.'

He was elected chairman of the Poplar board in 1899, soon after it had assumed full responsibility for the Forest Gate institution, and kept the position for 10 years. In 1900, he became the first working-class mayor of Poplar and two years later was elected Labour MP for Woolwich, making him the fourth UK Labour MP. He remained its representative, bar a period of 10 months in 1910, until his death in 1921.

Crooks worked to remove the stigma of the workhouse from the children which, 'Marked out in their childhood as being "from the workhouse", they often bore the stamp all of their life and ended up as workhouse inmates in their manhood and womanhood.' It was his ambition, Haw reported, to make them 'feel like ordinary working-class children. ... [to grow] up like them, becoming ordinary working-men and working-women themselves; so the Poor Law knew them no longer.'[11]

He was a pragmatist and, such was his determination to see the institutions closed, he would vary his case to suit his audience. According to Haw, he would say, 'If I can't appeal to your moral sense, let me appeal to your pocket.' He advocated better value-for-money solutions to deal with workhouse children at a London Guildhall Poor Law Conference, by arguing, 'Surely it is far cheaper to be generous in training poor law children to take their place in life as useful citizens than it is to give the children a niggardly training and a branded career.' He concluded: 'This latter way soon leads them to the workhouse again, to be kept out of the rates for the rest of their lives.'

His efforts were recognised by Mr Dugard, HM Inspector of Schools, who noticed the difference Crooks' impact had had on Forest Gate in his 1906 report. He observed that:

> There is very little (if any) of the institution's mark among the children ... . Both boys and girls are in a highly satisfactory state, showing increased efficiency with increased intelligence on the part of the children ... . They compare very favourably with the best elementary schools.[12]

Crooks actively promoted games and sports for the youngsters, entering them into competitions where they would play alongside non-workhouse children. The boys' football and cricket teams played other board schools and the girls were encouraged to participate in gymnastic training and became proficient swimmers. By 1903, the institution's football team was participating in a local league, and doing well.[13]

One consequence, according to Haws, was that, 'The scholars at Forest Gate began to count for something. They learned to trust each other and to rely upon themselves. They grew up with hope and courage ... . In consequence thousands of them have emerged in the great working world outside, self-respecting men and women.'

Haws met Crooks one evening outside Westminster public baths when he excitedly told his biographer that the Poplar institution had won three trophies in a London-wide gala:

> The first, the London Shield was for boys. Poplar won with 85 marks ... . The second was the Portsmouth Shield ... our girls won that with 65 marks. The third was the Whitehall Shield, for the school ... with the highest number of marks ... . I feel as pleased as though I had done it myself.[14]

Under the leadership of Crooks, much greater effort was put into getting the establishment's youngsters to socialise and perform in public, as a way to boost confidence and morale. In June 1904, for example, the institution's band provided entertainment to a large local cycle meeting on nearby Wanstead Flats and the following year it was performing at an event run by the London Socialists Sunday School League. Four months later it won a cup at a bands' competition at Crystal Palace.[15]

GEORGE LANSBURY

Crooks' fellow local working-class reforming guardian, George Lansbury, was born in Halesworth, Suffolk in 1859, the son of a railway worker and the third of nine children. The family moved frequently during his early childhood and settled in the East End in 1868. He attended schools in Whitechapel and Bethnal Green followed by a succession of manual jobs.

In 1875 he met 14-year-old Elizabeth Brine, whose father owned a saw-mill in Poplar. The couple married in 1880 and four years later emigrated to Australia, where they found life difficult, as they were living in squalor. Aided by Elizabeth's family, the couple returned to Poplar and George joined his father-in-law's timber business. The Australian experience scarred him, and he railed against the false dreams sold to would-be emigrants. Unlike Dr Barnardo, he did not regard enforced emigration to Australia or Canada as an acceptable destination for east London's pauper young.

George Lansbury MP (1859-1940). (Photo: Lena Connell)

In the pre-Labour party era, Lansbury joined the Liberal party and became a political agent, organising parliamentary election victories for Samuel Montague, in Whitechapel, from 1885. He tired of the party's lack of radicalism and resigned from it immediately after the 1892 general election.

He joined the Social Democratic Federation (SDF) and soon became its national political agent, standing successfully as its candidate for the Poplar Board of Guardians, to represent Bromley and Bow, in both 1893 and 1894. He first became a governor of the FGDS in 1895. He stood for the party in the same area at the general election of 1900, but his pacifism, at the time of the Boer War, contributed to his defeat.

A concern for poor law children was a feature in his election addresses in all three of those elections. Like Crooks, he was anxious to see the stigma of the workhouse removed. In 1893, he referred to the fate of the Forest Gate children: 'All children left to the care of the Board shall not be made to feel their dependence is criminal or disgraceful and shall not be marked out by dress or treatment from their fellows.'

He was anxious that they received preparation for post-workhouse life, promising 'They shall receive such an education and training as shall fit them to fulfil the duties of citizenship, and counteract any hereditary tendency to lapse into pauperism.' And again: 'Train and apprentice the boys and girls to useful trades and not as now train them easily for domestic service and the army and the navy, both of which supply the workhouse with a large percentage of adult inmates.'[16]

Lansbury wanted to see the children educated in board schools rather than workhouse institutions, and was clear that enforced emigration should not be an option: 'They shall be ... sent to efficient public schools. No emigration of any child under the control of the Board.'[17]

He revisited the conditions faced by Poplar's Forest Gate children the following year, and was explicit about the reforms required to give them dignity and remove the stigma associated with the workhouse: 'Abolition of uniform. Where possible send the children chargeable to board schools of the district for their daily education.' The children, he argued, should be well fed and stimulated: 'At the district schools insist that the food given shall be sufficient of good quality, and properly prepared. Provide adequate means for recreation.'

In short, his winning manifestos were based on pleas for dignity and respect.

Having served on the Poplar board for two years, he was appointed to the FGSD in 1895. Raymond Postgate, his son-in-law and distinguished biographer, recorded Lansbury's first impression of the place: 'My first view of the school was a most disheartening one. The buildings are ... built on the barrack system – that is, long dormitories for scores of children to sleep in, very little accommodation for recreation.'

He was struck by the lack of self-respect the establishment engendered: 'The time I first saw it the children were dressed in the old, hideous, Poor Law garb, corduroy, hard blue serge, and the girls with their hair almost shaved off, with nothing at all to make them look attractive in any sort of way.' The indignity of the children's appearances was reinforced by the poor nature of the food, which he said was 'quite coarse and I should think at times insufficient'.

It didn't take Lansbury long to identify superintendent Duncan as an obstacle to reform: 'It was apparent that the place was organised and controlled as a barracks. I daresay the superintendent, who had been a military man, was according to his light, quite a decent person, but then his light was deficient.'

Lansbury contrasted the dreary food the Forest Gate children were forced to endure with the epicurean delights the governors experienced. He described to Postgate the scene after his first governors' meeting:

> [A] seven-course dinner was to be served. It was this that made me disgusted of the middle-class men and women who controlled the institution; they could let little girls, who they knew must be starved, stand and wait on them, while they ate chicken, nice soups, sweets etc all at the expense of the rates.[18]

After Poplar took sole control of the institution, Lansbury became chairman of the governors, effectively the Poplar guardians' education committee, and remained so for more than 20 years.

Although they had their political differences, it did not take Crooks and Lansbury long to conclude that incremental and reforming changes in the institution were fine, but not enough. Wholesale and rapid transformation was imperative.

To this end, and conscious of the condemnation of Henrietta Barnett and the Mundella Committee's deliberations, Lansbury concluded that Duncan had to go. He told his son-in-law, 'No sooner did we get control of the school than we appointed a new superintendent and matron, and although neither of them were socialists, they both proved themselves most splendid officials.'[19]

Duncan retired – probably under pressure – aged 67 in 1899, with 'an illuminated address' and a small pension. His last decade at the institution had been a disastrous one: presiding over the fire, the food poisoning outbreak and various bouts of ophthalmia. It was also one of personal tragedy; his wife Harriett died in 1891. He lost little time in remarrying – 24-year-old Forest Gate resident Rosetta Murray – and within a couple of years they had their only child, Leslie.

When he retired, the family moved to Hove and in 1904 he was appointed a member of the council's education committee. The following year he became a poor law guardian, a position he held until his death, five years later.[20] He was elected to Hove Council in 1908, on which he remained for the rest of his life. It must have seemed home from home, as he represented the Vallance ward of the district, the same relatively unusual name shared by his medical officer and clerk at Forest Gate.

He died on 29 June 1910, after a long illness, leaving a 41-year-old widow and 17-year-old son, along with £1,538. They moved back to Forest Gate and the following year were living in Earlham Grove, together with two servants, just a couple of hundred metres from the Forest Lane institution. By now, son Leslie was a civil servant. Rosetta survived Charles by more than 40 years, dying in 1952.[21]

Jonathon Schneer, one of Lansbury's biographers, said that among George's early achievements as chairman of the governors was the delivery of his 1894 election promise to abolish uniforms. He also improved the quality of industrial training, because 'The tailor who taught tailoring was old, so they pensioned him off and got a better one. They had done the same with the bootmaker. In the carpenter's shop they had many improvements.'[22]

The improved conditions that Crooks and Lansbury introduced did not go unopposed. They were regularly accused by other politicians and the local press of extravagance and squandering public money by providing decent food and living conditions. Crooks, as an MP, had to face a parliamentary committee in 1906, convened by J. S. Davy, chief inspector of the LGB, to explain these 'extravagances'. Poplar's guardians were largely exonerated.[23]

However, they were attacked in one exchange when they were asked why they had sanctioned the purchase of Irish cambric handkerchiefs at 3d per piece. They were asked whether they had purchased them for their own use. Lansbury explained that the guardians purchased them and put six in a box, to go with girls as they left for domestic service. Crooks wondered whether the chief inspector thought that it would have been more economical for the girls to use their cuffs.[24]

Lansbury and Crooks stamped out governor self-indulgence around lavish meals and directed the money towards improving food for the children. They were condemned for this in the popular press and accused of extravagance themselves. In tones that may sound familiar to contemporary readers, Postgate commented: 'The *Daily Mail, Daily Mirror* and *Punch* made much of this, portraying Poplar as being profligate spend thrifts, and one cartoon portraying Crooks and Lansbury with cigars in their mouths, ordering a fresh barrel of ratepayers' beer … for their own use – when both were, in fact, non-smokers and tee-totallers.'[25]

Lansbury could point to a record of success during his first four years as chair of the governors. In his 1900 SDF general election address, it stated categorically: 'The changes made at Mr Lansbury's and his colleagues' instigation bid fair to make the Forest Gate School a model in Poor Law education', and proceeded to list them in some detail:

> The food scale has been entirely remodelled. Think of it, men of
> Bow and Bromley – your poor house children did not know what
> it was to have butter on their bread! Now they have even meat
> and a piece of cake with their tea on Sunday.

Self-respect, a hitherto unknown virtue at FGDS, was encouraged by a number of means: 'Mr Lansbury's aim has been to bring them up to be good citizens inferior in no respect to those who do not have so early an acquaintance with destitution.'

Lansbury ensured the children were treated as other working-class children: 'To this end they are properly educated like other children, are taught different trades such as shoemaking, tailoring, engineering etc., for boys and dressmaking, cookery etc. for girls; they have the same holidays as other school children and visitors are allowed once a week.'

Lansbury addressed the over-worked, under-valued position of the teaching staff at the establishment, claiming that, 'The teachers are now efficient, and not a combination of teacher and attendant, as before; consequently, they are better educated for their work.'

The new regime subscribed to the importance of constructive recreation – as highlighted by Crooks above – as an important element in child-rearing: 'Recreation, amusements, and games are provided for the children, and they take to cricket, football etc. with the proper zest children should always feel to play. The boys have a capital brass band, and the singing of the children, once heard is a thing to be remembered.'

In one stirring paragraph about Lansbury, the manifesto set out a philosophy, culture and set of aspirations for the children of Forest Gate which would have been alien to the majority of his former governors. It marked a step change in attitude and was light years away from the prevailing mood of the institution. It would have seemed like a description of heaven to the 40,000 or so children who had passed through the Forest Lane gates before his first entrance:

> Mr Lansbury recently succeeded in carrying a resolution that the children should have a month's holiday at the seaside. To many this will seem going too far. Let us remember therefore the high motives which guide Mr Lansbury in his public work. He does not try to crush the poor down and make their lives as bad and as harsh as possible, but seeks to raise them and make their lives as good and as bright and as happy as possible. He regards the care of the children whom he is elected to protect as a sacred trust. And when we consider the lot of these children, without home ties and home surroundings, many without a father or mother, their lives a monotonous round under the care of strangers, and remember that many unthinking and cruel people are ever ready to cast upon them the stigma of 'pauper', we feel our hearts soften and we cry 'God-speed' to efforts such as these to make the children's lives worth living.

Lansbury did not seek sole credit for the reforms: 'Mr Lansbury has not done all this single handed. In all his efforts he has made in all the works he has done, on the Poplar Board of Guardians and the Forest Gate Schools Committee, he has been loyally and splendidly helped by his Socialist and Labour colleagues.'[26]

The departure of Duncan as superintendent set the scene for a more caring and progressive attitude in the institution. As he was about to resign, the *Tower Hamlets Independent and East End Local Advertiser* was able to report of Christmas activities at the FGDS in 1898: 'A very pretty innovation – which we hope will become an established custom – was made in presenting each child with a greeting card. Sweets, fruits and toys were freely distributed among the children.'

Six months after Duncan's departure, the governors planned the first of what were to become annual summer camps for the Forest Gate boys at

Dovercourt, in Essex. In 1904, the *Essex Guardian* reported that the decision was originally met by trepidation among the officers and suspicion among the boys. Within four years these occasions were eagerly anticipated by staff and children alike and were the highlights of the year for those attending.

Press reports give an indication of the scale and significance of these camps, which would have been inconceivable under the Duncan regime. A 1905 press report said that 200 boys, aged between 10 and 15, went that year and were accommodated in 26 tents that had been made by the tailoring and carpentry departments. Food was ferried in from Forest Gate daily. The boys played games, did exercises and were allowed to go into the village and bathe in the sea with the minimum of supervision. There was a fairground nearby and arrangements were made for them to go on some of the rides. A cricket match was arranged against a training ship that was moored nearby – although not named it was possibly TS *Exmouth*, TS *Goliath's* successor vessel.[27]

The camps were educational field trips, and the children benefitted not only from attending them, but also from the follow up to their field work. On 24 July 1902, the *London Daily News* reported on the outcome of one such trip. It described a London-wide exhibition of school nature study projects at Kew Gardens, attended by the Duke of Devonshire, where one of the participants was the Poplar institution. Describing the display, the article said:

> The school has a stall of marvellous things at the exhibition, some of which have reference to the seaside camp at Dovercourt. Imagine Oliver Twist being sent to the seaside by the Guardians every summer, like 200 boys from the Poplar Poor Law School. There is evidence at the exhibition that they live in tents, go crab fishing, bathing, learn about the ebb and flow of tides and the beauties of country lanes.

The girls did not take part in these camps, because of 'moral concerns', but they were not ignored. Lansbury, it should be remembered, was a strong proponent of women's rights and later the aims of the suffragette movement, and ensured that the girls were able to benefit from visits away from Forest Gate. On 3 September 1904, the *East London Advertiser* was able to report on their equivalent holiday arrangements:

The girls had the permission of the Local Government Board to see 'the sights of London', or at least such are of educational value. They were taken to the Tower, to Covent Garden, to Hampton Court and to the Italian Exhibition [in Earls Court]. Moreover, they paid a visit to the House of Commons where Sir E Flower MP [Conservative mp for Bradford] entertained them to 'Tea on the Terrace'. Some were taken through the streets of London in order to make them acquainted with the ways of the world. All of the girls went for a day to either Southend or Dovercourt. The children are now engaged in writing essays descriptive of what they saw during the holidays.

In other examples of more progressive attitudes at the institution, at the 1903 annual prize-giving event in Forest Gate, the Mayor of Poplar was able to reflect on the advances since he had been one of its governors six years previously. He said that he was:

Extremely pleased to see the many improvements that had taken place [since his time as governor]. There was sufficient proof that good feelings existed between the staff and children and everything was being done for the benefit of the little ones.

Will Crooks responded, on behalf of the governors, declaring that those at the prize-giving 'showed what could be done by love and kindness. It had been a source of delight to him to be present and to see the children looking so happy.'[28] More enlightened attitudes were displayed four months later, when a drill mistress was advertised for the girls. Not only was she expected to be acquainted with a knowledge of exercise, but she had to be able to play the piano and preferably display a competent knowledge of gymnastics.[29]

Important as these reforms were in encouraging a greater spirit of freedom and confidence among the children, they did not address the fundamental problem of the institution. Its size and condition were unfit for the purpose of weaning children away from the dependence and stigma of pauperdom and offering them a realistic chance of future independence.

SHENFIELD BOUND

Crooks and Lansbury were as one with Mundella and the subsequent decision of the LGB: barrack schools had to go. They spent much of their decade in charge at Forest Gate planning that move. As early as 1898, the press reported that Poplar's guardians (with Crooks as chairman and Lansbury chairman of the school's committee) had decided to build replacement establishments in Hutton, near Shenfield in Essex, at a cost of around £100,000.[30]

It took almost eight years to fulfil the plans, against considerable opposition from, among others, Poplar ratepayers, Shenfield residents and the government.

The guardians decided to build accommodation on the large site, with the intention of training girls as well as boys in rural pursuits, in order to keep them out of the over-crowded cities.[31] George Lansbury described the thinking behind the facility, which became known as the Poplar Training School, to a journalist at the time. He said, 'We have carefully gone into the scattered scheme, the cottage-homes and the block system and have adopted what we considered to be the best points in each.'[32]

By 1903 they had decided to build blocks big enough to accommodate 60 boys over the age of 10, or 30 girls and infants. There was to be a gymnasium, infirmary, swimming bath and training facilities, including a dairy farm. It was anticipated that the building costs would be in the region of £120,000, with an estimated £40,000 coming from the sale of the Forest Gate site.[33] The Poplar guardians received approval from the LGB to spend £144,000 on the Hutton project in September of that year, and were authorised to borrow £75,000.[34]

In the event, the sale of the Forest Lane site to West Ham guardians became problematic. Negotiations for the sale stretched into 1907 and a price of £35,000 was agreed.[35] The agreement, however, coincided with an upswing in unemployment and the Poplar guardians were desperately trying to find new workhouse accommodation to cope with the consequential demand. They put the sale on hold for, as it turned out, four years and, having gained the consent of the LGB, turned the premises into a temporary annexe to their main workhouse.[36]

It was only with the introduction of the state pension in 1909 that demand for workhouse accommodation for the elderly declined, and the guardians had enough workhouse capacity in Poplar to sanction the sale of the site to the West Ham union in 1911, at the previously agreed price.[37]

As noted, there was fierce opposition from groups of Poplar ratepayers towards the new Shenfield project, on the grounds of cost. One newspaper reported a meeting of the Poplar Municipal Alliance in November 1905, where a motion was passed which 'emphatically protests against the reckless extravagance of the Board of Guardians and especially in the matter of the Shenfield schools.' A local councillor at the meeting declared that 'the removal of the children from Forest Gate was the most wasteful and extravagant thing the Guardians had ever done.'[38]

The buildings in Hutton were within the rural Essex district of Billericay, many of whose residents were also unhappy about the establishment being erected in their midst. Lansbury was called upon to placate them, and, in passing, confirmed that it would become the largest ratepayer in the village of Hutton, just as the Forest Gate establishment had been within its own area.[39]

This transfer took place in 1907 with little fuss, and led to the closure of the Forest Lane facility as a children's workhouse and its transformation into an annexe for the Poplar workhouse.

Lansbury's achievements had been recognised, if grudgingly, by the Conservative government. Although failure as a socialist candidate at a general election was all he had to show on his national political CV, in 1905, in the dying days of Arthur Balfour's government, he was appointed a member of the Royal Commission on the Poor Law. The appointment was based on his 12-year success as a guardian in Poplar and chairman of the Forest Gate governors, where his achievements did not go unnoticed.

The Royal Commission reported four years later and although largely ignored, it was best known for its minority report, published in the name of Beatrice Webb – a good friend of the Barnetts – with Lansbury as one of its signatories. The minority report has been widely accepted as the blueprint for the establishment of the welfare state. It recommended the abolition of the poor laws, the introduction of a state pension, establishment of a national minimum wage and introduction of national and local public works, to address the scourge of unemployment.

Lansbury, himself, was elected to parliament in 1910, but resigned in 1912 to fight the cause of women's suffrage. In the same year he helped establish and edit the *Daily Herald*. His pacifism kept him out of parliament until 1922, but in the meantime he led the Poplar rates revolt, which in 1921 saw him jailed with 29 fellow councillors, for, effectively, refusing to reduce rates of council pay during the slump following the First World War. On his return to parliament, he was briefly a minister in Ramsay MacDonald's second Labour government and took over as leader of the Labour party after MacDonald defected to head the national government in 1931. He remained leader until 1935, when, once again, his pacifism cost him his position. He died aged 81 in 1940.

Distinguished historian, A. J. P. Taylor described Lansbury as 'the most lovable figure in modern politics'.[40] He cut his political and public service teeth reforming and then closing the children's workhouse in Forest Gate.

NOTES

[1] *THIEELA*, 2 Sep 1899

[2] Barnett, *Canon*

[3] George Haw, *From Workhouse to Westminster – the Life Story of Will Crooks MP*, Cassel and Co, 1907, pp. 8 9

[4] Ibid, p. 10

[5] Ibid, p. 11

[6] Ibid, p. 14

[7] Wikipedia, Will Crooks

[8] Haw, p. 85

[9] Ibid, p. 105

[10] Ibid, p. 119

[11] Ibid, p. 120

[12] *ELO*, 16 Jun 1906

[13] *THIEELA*, 3 Nov 1903

[14] Haw, pp. 121-123

[15] *ELO*, 25 Jun 1904, *Justice*, 26 Aug 1905 and *THIEELA*, 4 Nov 1905

[16] LSE, Lansbury Papers, *Lansbury/1*

[17] LSE, *Lansbury/1*

[18] Raymond Postgate, *The Life of George Lansbury*, Longmans 1951, p. 68

[19] Postgate, pp. 67-8

[20] *Brighton Gazette*, 2 Jul 1910

[21] www.ancestry.com

[22] Jonathon Schneer, *George Lansbury*, Manchester University Press, 1990

[23] Haws, p. 281

[24] Koven, p. 181

[25] Postgate, p. 82

[26] LSE, *Lansbury/28*

[27] *East Anglian Daily Times*, 24 Aug 1905

[28] *THIEELA*, 31 Jan 1903

[29] *THIEELA*, 11 Mar 1905

[30] *Royal Cornwall Gazette*, 15 Dec 1898

[31] Haw, pp. 121-3

[32] *Essex Guardian*, 4 Jul 1903

[33] *ELO*, 4 Jul 1903

[34] *London Daily News*, 19 Sep 1903

[35] *Essex Newsroom*, 5 Jan 1907

[36] *ELO*, 23 Nov 1907

[37] See Chapter 10 for the subsequent history of the site

[38] *THIEELA*, 4 November 1905

[39] *Barking, East Ham and Ilford Advertiser*, 8 Sep 1906

[40] A. J.P. Taylor, *English History, 1914–45*, Penguin 1950, p. 270

CHAPTER 12

AFTERMATH

In 1868, three east London boards of guardians felt that FGSD was a solution for up to 900 of their young pauper residents, but within 40 years the thinking had moved on and it was gradually replaced by a range of other, more appropriate, establishments and solutions. As the preceding chapters have made clear, Hackney was first to leave, in 1876, followed by Whitechapel two decades later, and finally Poplar in 1907.

The futures of children from all three unions were determined by a combination of more enlightened attitudes by their guardians and progressive changes in legislation.

This chapter sketches the fate of subsequent generations of the workhouse children from the three unions, and outlines the fate of the buildings of the one-time children's workhouse.

HACKNEY'S CHILDREN

When Hackney's guardians separated from FGSD in 1876, they joined those of Shoreditch to transform the latter union's children's workhouse in Brentwood into a district school. It was on the outskirts of Romford and 15 miles from Hackney. Shoreditch left the district in 1885, putting Hackney in sole charge of the school, which reverted to separate establishment status.

It was built on a former 31 acre farm, and accommodated up to 500 young people. Most dormitories housed around 30 boys or girls, although there were two very large ones, mainly for the younger children. Everyone had their own clothes and washing kit, and there was a well-regarded infirmary.[1]

Hackney built further extensions, including a swimming pool in 1891, and additional industrial workshops in 1898. By this time the 40-year-old buildings and structure – like those in Forest Lane – were showing signs of wear and decay.

Hackney's workhouse school, Brentwood. (Credit: Mary Evans/Peter Higginbotham collection)

The institution suffered a major scandal in 1893/4, when one of its nurses, Ella Gillespie, was found guilty of 'systematic cruelty'. Her offences included striking children with bunches of keys, beating them with nettles, depriving them of water and then expecting them to drink from toilet bowls, banging heads against walls and demanding children kneel on hot water pipes.

Perhaps the most notorious of her cruelties was the 'basket drill'. She would wake children during the night, get them to place their possessions in wire baskets and march around the dormitory for an hour – receiving a beating if they dropped the basket at any time. She was also accused, perhaps not surprisingly, of being frequently drunk and attempting to secure the silence of visitors to her cruelty by 'treating' them in local pubs and restaurants.

Gillespie was imprisoned for five years for her cruelty.[2] She served three and a half years and soon after her release was employed as matron in a training home, apparently attached to an orphanage in Oxford.[3]

By the 1890s, Hackney adopted boarding out as a practice for looked-after children, and made little use of the enforced emigration of children to Canada.[4]

By 1898, the union had 826 children in its care and tried to place as many as possible in foster homes, both as good practice and in response to the cruelty scandal. The facilities and practices in Brentwood were significantly better than those in Forest Gate. The 1898 survey indicated that 10 of their 32 acres were used for agricultural training and a further five for recreational purposes.

Hygiene was better than in Forest Lane: quarantine procedures for new pupils were more strictly observed and the infirmary was better equipped, resulting in a much lower incidence of ophthalmia. The system of training was more modern, and the boys were taught a wider range of skills; even 'the duller boys' were given agricultural jobs. Arrangements were made to place boys in a variety of employments when they left.

There was a rotation system for teaching domestic skills to the girls and a great external demand for them to be employed as domestic servants when they left. There was an agreement with MABYS for their post-establishment care and supervision. Its feedback suggested that the girls were well equipped for the world of work, and usually prospered.

There were libraries, which were stocked regularly by books donated externally. In the boys' area there was a 'museum', with objects of 'general interest'. The sum of £20 was dedicated to excursions for the children each year, which were organised by the chaplain, and included visits to museums and galleries. Outdoor games were encouraged, and there was an annual sports day. Boys and girls were given supervised walks each Sunday; in addition, about 30 were allowed out of the complex, unaccompanied, on Saturday afternoons.

There were four qualified teachers for boys, whose schoolwork – with the exception of arithmetic – was considered satisfactory. There were three teachers for girls, and their school results were better than those of the boys.

The teachers were all non-resident, so supervision of the children in the home, outside school hours, was left to others. The guardians wished to minimise the numbers of children in the workhouse and were taking steps to reduce the number of ins and outs.

Children new to Hackney's workhouse system were accommodated in 'receiving houses' in nearby Homerton, rather than in the workhouse, itself, prior to their despatch to Brentwood. They were sent to local elementary schools wearing clothes 'similar to that worn by the artisan classes'. They were taken to church on Sundays and to Victoria Park for recreation. The receiving houses were managed by a superintendent 'and his wife'.

Surprise visits were made to Brentwood by Hackney's guardians, on average every two weeks, to check on conditions and act as a deterrent against any potential maltreatment of children.

Hackney was unable to find enough suitable and welcoming homes for boarding out, so established a new cottage homes' site in Chipping Ongar, that could accommodate up to 300 children. It received its first intake in 1905 and the Brentwood establishment it replaced was closed in 1908.

Six 'cottages' were built surrounding a central green – each housing about 52 children. The ground floors were communal areas, with a dining room, study room, day room and kitchen, while the upper two floors housed the dormitories. Staff quarters were located in the central section of the house.

Chipping Ongar hosted a 24-bed infirmary, an administrative building, including the superintendent's quarters and a number of small bedrooms, where the older girls received training as domestic servants. The village had its own school, accommodating 300, in five mixed-sex classes. The under-fives were taught in their cottages and vocational training was given to boys once they reached the age of 14. Girls, in addition to domestic skills, were trained in basic nursing and midwifery.

The number at Chipping Ongar peaked at 369 in 1920, and fell to a little over 200, five years later. The school was renamed the Ongar Public Assistance school in 1930 and operated until its closure at the outbreak of the Second World War, when it was re-badged, yet again, as the Ongar Residential School, for 'mentally deficient boys'.

Reflecting a more compassionate attitude, it was renamed again post war as the Great Stony School, to house children with learning difficulties. It finally closed in 1994, and the buildings converted to residential use.[5]

The Brentwood institution Hackney left in 1908 was initially transformed into a branch workhouse. The Metropolitan Asylum Board took responsibility for it in 1917 to accommodate 300 'sane epileptics'. In 1930, the buildings were taken over by the LCC and transformed into St Faith's Hospital. It was subsequently developed into office accommodation.

WHITECHAPEL'S CHILDREN

Whitechapel left the FGDS in 1897 and sent its children to Grays, which although described as a cottage homes facility, more closely resembled the scattered homes arrangement pioneered in Sheffield four years earlier. The initiative was warmly welcomed by the 1898 survey on grounds of value for money, indicating per capita costs which: 'averaged 8s 1d per child [per week] ... while at the Forest Gate District School scheme the sum is 9s 9d.'[6]

The scattered homes consisted of four pairs of semi-detached houses spread out within the area, each within walking distance of the administrative headquarters.

Most of the houses were intended to accommodate 10 children of different ages and both sexes, while one was built for 20 boys aged 10 years or older. The children attended local elementary schools and wore no distinctive uniforms. The headquarters housed officers' quarters, receiving rooms for new entrants and contained a small infirmary. Overall control of the homes was put in the hands of a 'lady-superintendent', who was a trained nurse with administrative skills.

The job descriptions of the married couple running the institution showed further enlightened thinking. The man was to be responsible for the boys' drill and was also 'to take charge of them after school hours' and 'to take an active interest in their recreation', as well as their good behaviour and cleanliness. It was explicit that he would report to his wife, 'the lady superintendent of the homes', in the execution of his duties.[7] A 1905 advertisement for house parents for one of the homes showed how far expectations and care for the children had moved in less than half a century; it sought homely sounding 'foster parents' for the supervisory role.

There were no plans to have industrial training or bands under the new arrangements because the regular attendees of the elementary schools they attended did not have them. It was feared that Whitechapel children would be stigmatised as workhouse children if they were treated differently – quite a change in attitude from that prevailing in Forest Gate.[8]

The 1898 survey concluded that Whitechapel's guardians were 'keenly alive to the responsibilities of making careful provision for the children under their charge.' The union established a separate 'receiving home' in Mile End, to accommodate up to 42 children; this was a halfway house between the workhouse and the Grays facility after the First World War. In 1925, for poor law administration purposes, Whitechapel was absorbed into Stepney, under whose control it was then placed. The Grays' homes were put under the charge of Stepney's existing Stifford Homes operation, built in that village in 1902.

The Stifford Homes establishment was a more traditional orphanage, accommodating 200 children. It was taken over by the LCC in 1930 and five years later became an approved school for boys. It was transferred to Essex County Council in the 1950s and in 1973 to the London Borough of Newham. By 1979 it had been transformed into a school for the care, treatment and education of upwards of '60 deprived, disturbed and delinquent boys'.[9]

Two of the cottage homes in Grays – Park Cottages and Harold Cottages – are today converted into residential flats. Dene Cottage subsequently became Thurrock Council's treasurer's department, until that was demolished and replaced by flats. Whitehall Lodge was used as a food office during the Second World War and was subsequently transformed into a social services building. These were later demolished to be replaced by High View Gardens.[10]

POPLAR'S CHILDREN

In February 1907, Poplar transferred its 700 pupils to its newly erected training facility – situated within 100 acres and referred to as Hutton Poplars, in the village of Hutton – at a cost of £184,300. It was soon regarded as a flagship provision in meeting the needs for 'workhouse children'.

The buildings were constructed around a large green, with five double cottages for girls and a similar number for boys. The complex also hosted a gymnasium, swimming pool, administrative block and superintendent's house, as well as a laundry training facility. The girls prepared and served their own food as part of their industrial training. Forty acres of the site were used for farming, where children grew much of the food they consumed. Around 500 fruit trees were planted, some of which survive today.

There was no uniform. Girls wore blouses, frocks, print pinafores and jumpers while boys were dressed in knickerbockers and tunics, or trousers and jackets. Initially, it was not without local opposition. Its children were treated badly by villagers and looked upon as unwelcome outsiders; it took some while for these attitudes to mellow.

The boys were taught carpentry, tailoring, boot making and baking in

Poplar's replacement girls' accommodation in Hutton, Essex. (Source: postcard)

small workshops, as well as gardening. They were also encouraged to learn musical instruments so that they could participate in the institution's band, entertain their fellow pupils and possibly graduate to a career in a military band. The girls were trained as domestic servants and were taught needlework, cookery and laundry tasks.[11]

George Lansbury is due much credit for its creation and high standards of design. The buildings were ornate; a member of the House of Lords complaining of their extravagance told his fellow peers that 'the beams in the dining hall would do credit to an English cathedral.'[12]

Other parliamentarians protested that the parquet flooring, teak stairways and central heating meant the institution was more suited for pupils of Eton rather than orphans. But after the fuss died down, the facility attracted praise for its good work. A 1914 government inspection noted that its facilities were 'among the best in Britain' and that its children were 'well cared-for by an efficient staff of specially selected teachers'. A royal visit gave it the establishment seal of approval in 1918.

Part of the Hutton complex was taken over for military purposes during the First World War and the girls were moved to nearby accommodation. In the 1930s, control was passed to the LCC and in the 1950s its farmland was sold off. The facility came under the wing of the Inner London Education

Authority in 1974 following changes in the law relating to looked-after children. Numbers dropped off significantly, as far more emphasis was placed on accommodating children in foster homes. There were only 40 children left on the site in 1980, the last of whom left in 1982.

Most of the buildings have since been demolished, although a small number were refurbished and are now community facilities in the area. The hall, known as Bishops Hill, is currently an adult education facility. Hutton Poplar Hall was restored in 1991 and is presently a hall for hire. Much of the rest of the grounds, once occupied by the school and homes, has been redeveloped for residential purposes.

FOREST GATE'S BUILDINGS

In 1954, the Friends of Forest Gate Hospital published a brochure to mark the centenary of the buildings' construction as Whitechapel's children's workhouse. In passing, its author noted that during that century the building had had one major change of use, at least four separate titles and had been controlled by six public bodies.[13]

Sixty-six years later there has been a further change of use and title and at least three more public bodies can be added to the list of its controllers. The exterior of part of the main building constructed in 1854 remains today, looking much as it did when built.[14]

When Poplar closed it as a children's institution in 1907, it repurposed the site as an annexe to its main workhouse. Additional accommodation for 'sick paupers' was built, at a cost of £8,000. As noted, the introduction of the state pension in 1909 reduced the demand for workhouse accommodation for the aged poor and Poplar looked to close what was becoming a redundant outpost. After some further alterations to the structure, the building was sold to West Ham's guardians, within whose boundaries it was located, in 1911, for £41,000.

West Ham had grown exponentially over the previous 50 years; the population increasing from 33,331 in 1861 to 289,030 in 1911. Its principal workhouse building was located in Langthorne, in what is now Leytonstone, about two miles away. it had originally been constructed in 1841 and was subsequently enlarged. Nearby Whipps Cross Hospital was established as the union's infirmary between 1900 and 1903. Strangely, neither of these two facilities was located within the county borough's boundaries.

West Ham struggled to cope with demands for accommodation for the poor and sick during the economic downturn of the early twentieth century. Its guardians acquired the Forest Lane site to house semi-sick and bedridden patients. It could accommodate 600 people.[15]

According to documents employing terminology of the mid 1950s, the original West Ham patients consisted of 'imbeciles; men, 62, women, 36. epileptics (sane); men, 34, women, 36. chronic bedridden; men, 75, women, 243. sick; men, 50, women, 50. maternity; women, 50.'

The establishment was reopened and rebadged in 1913 as the Forest Gate Sick Home. The official history noted that 'the Great War and the "20s" saw little event of note under the new administration.' Local folklore says it was used as an isolation unit during the outbreak of Spanish Flu in 1919, but there are no records confirming this.

The 1929 Local Government Act replaced boards of guardians with local authority public assistance committees (PACs), and the sick home was transferred to West Ham Council's PAC and renamed, yet again, as the Forest Gate Hospital.

At the time of the transfer there were 500 beds for maternity, mental health and chronic sick patients. In 1931, an additional 200 beds were added, at a cost of £17,000, to meet rising demand. They were for general use, with 75 allocated to what the author of the history described as 'mental defectives coming under municipal care'.

The managers of public institutions in the 1940s tried to disassociate themselves from some of the baggage, imagery and terminology of the old poor law/workhouse traditions. In 1942, responsibility for the hospital was transferred from the PAC to the council's social services committee, and two years later to its public health committee.

During the Second World War, most of the non-maternity patients were evacuated to South Ockenden in Essex. Just as well, as the buildings suffered considerable damage during the Blitz. On 23 September 1940, a high-explosive bomb caused damage to the roof and windows of M Block and another anti-aircraft shell exploded on the temporary kitchen, causing severe damage and necessitating the evacuation of a further 25 patients.

Ten days later another device hit the boiler house, resulting in additional patient evacuations, and the following week yet another high-explosive bomb caused damage near the maternity block. The roadway was entirely

A photo of the (all white) hospital staff 1936. (Credit: Newham archives)

demolished and the external wall of the children's ward badly affected. More patients had to be moved out.

Two further bombs hit the hospital the following week, inflicting serious damage to the kitchen block. The hospital was without heating or lighting, until repairs could be undertaken, resulting in further patient evacuation. The buildings escaped the rest of the war unscathed and remained under the control of the local authority until the establishment of the National Health Service in 1948.

By this time, it was almost exclusively a maternity hospital, and in 1947, at the height of the post-war baby boom, it witnessed the birth of 1,261 children (including six sets of twins and one of triplets). The average number of days 'confinement' was 11.7 days.

The hospital was placed under the wing of the West Ham Group (No 9) Hospital Management Committee of the North-East Metropolitan Regional Hospital Management Board. The NHS continued to develop it as a specialist maternity hospital and by 1950 new wards had opened. During the early 1950s, there were 102 designated maternity and five gynaecological beds – making it the largest unit of its kind in the hospital group. It became an approved centre for the training of midwives.

It was not exclusively a maternity hospital, however, as the regional hospital board sought alternative accommodation for what the centenary brochure called the remaining 'mental and mentally defective patients'.

It only had 116 beds in 1974 and was renamed the Newham Maternity Hospital, becoming part of the newly established Newham Health District, under the umbrella of the City and East London Area Health Authority (Teaching).

Newham General Hospital was opened in 1985, with maternity wards and a special baby care unit, making the Forest Lane Hospital redundant. It was closed by the Newham Health Authority.

After closure, the back of the original main buildings was demolished and replaced by a small housing estate. In 1993, the façade was converted into 110 social housing flats and renamed Gladys Dimson House, after a former Labour Greater London councillor.

Most of the remainder of the former site was developed into Forest Lane Park, between 1991 and 1994. The gatehouse survives as a local community facility, with a small playground attached. The park houses monuments commemorating the 1890 fire and the building's role as a hospital; there are, however, no distinctive plaques on the main building, indicating its original purpose and significant history.

Memorial in Forest Lane Park to the history of the buildings within it. Left, celebrating the institution's role as a hospital; right, a wood carving within the main memorial, remembering the 1890 fire. (Photos: Author's Own)

NOTES

1   Mornington and Lampard, pp. 25-31
2   www.listverse.com/2015/07/11/10-heartbreaking-stories-from-britains-workhouses
3   Steer, p. 76
4   Mornington and Lampard, pp. 25-31
5   www.workhouses.org/Hackney/homes
6   *Derby Daily Telegraph*, 24 Aug 1896
7   www.workhouse.org/whitechapel
8   Mornington and Lampard, pp. 42-43
9   www.british-history.ac.uk/vch/essex/vol8/pp24-35
10 John Webb, Panorama 49, *Journal of Thurrock Local History Society*, 2010, 'Grays Cottage Homes', pp. 36-51

11 https://en.m.wikipedia.org/wiki/Hutton,_Essex
12 *Hansard*, 4 May 1906
13 E. R. Gamester, *History of the Forest Gate Hospital*, published by the Friends of Forest Gate Hospital, 1954
14 www.e7-nowandthen.org/2018/07/nhs-at-70-1-history-of-forest-gate.html
15 Few of the archives of the hospital survive, and many of those which do are closed under the 100-year rule. Those which have survived and are accessible are to be found at the Royal London Hospital Archives in Whitechapel.

CHAPTER 13

CONCLUSION

When the children's workhouse was established in Forest Gate in 1854 it was probably the finest structure in the developing suburb, exuding dignity, confidence and authority, in the manner of so many Victorian public buildings. A passer-by would have been unsurprised to be told it was an English public school. After all, it housed a similar number of youngsters and was set in extensive grounds.

But there the parallels ended. Instead of silver spoons in their mouths, the workhouse youngsters took empty bellies to their new home. In place of Greek and Latin, taught in small groups by highly trained Oxbridge graduates, they were instructed in boot-repairing and laundry tasks, in cramped rooms, by unqualified and often cruel staff. Forest Gate's leavers were as likely to end up in a house of correction as those from public school were destined to reach a house of parliament.

Leavers of both institutions would have moved into the armed forces, one set to join the officer corps and the other, the poor bloody infantry. Yet, victory on the First World War battlefields would have depended as much on the back yards of the Forest Gate school as on the playing fields of Eton.

The total institution was already an anachronism when it opened – untainted by progressive thinking on the care of orphans and abandoned children. The philosophy upon which it was founded was muddled. On the one hand the workhouse children were to suffer the indignity of the 'less eligibility' principles; on the other, they were to be taken away from the 'corruption' of workhouse conditions, to be equipped to lead independent future lives.

They were not treated as individuals with characters to be shaped and personalities developed, but as impersonal numbers to be regimented. There was no encouragement of building self-esteem and developing independence, simply of conformity to authoritarian standards, and acquiescence.

In reality, they were brought up in one institutional setting until those with responsibility for them could pass them either to another (the armed services), or unfamiliar domestic settings, as servants, for others to maintain. It was not until the establishment had been operating for a quarter of a century that any thought was given to the aftercare of those who left, cast out into the world at 14 or 15.

From the outset there was little sympathy or empathy for the plight of the youngsters. They were hidden from public gaze and reared in sterile conditions, in the cheapest ways possible. Throughout its life it was known as a school; variously, a separate, district, industrial – and latterly, pejoratively, a 'barrack' school. In reality it was a children's workhouse, taking the youngsters from as young as two and keeping them off the streets.

The majority of long-stay residents were abandoned children or orphans, incarcerated in an establishment that taught them little beyond the 3 'Rs', basic Christianity and obedience. It housed even larger numbers of ins and outs – transient children – who passed through, often repeatedly, for a few weeks at a time. In its 50-year existence, it was incapable of designing a system of educating them adequately.

The 'industrial training' the youngsters received was little more than the performance of tasks designed to keep the place functioning on a shoe-string budget, and – for the boys at least – of little value once they left. Any training received was incidental to the purpose of the work undertaken – to help the institution operate as cost effectively as possible.

Governments, commissioners, boards, guardians, governors and officers were driven by penny-pinching attitudes and behaviours. Neither they, nor their children, were ever likely to occupy the Forest Gate establishment, and they saw little value in spending beyond the minimum needed to keep it functioning. A low tax bill for those they represented, rather than a decent standard of life for those in their care, was a guiding light.

The miserly mindset resulted in the appointment of cheap, unqualified and unsuitable management and teachers, who blighted the lives of the children. Those governing the establishment did not heed the lessons of the successful TS *Goliath,* that a properly funded and resourced facility, with well-remunerated and motivated staff, could work wonders. Penny-pinching continued for a further 20 years in Forest Lane, to the evident disadvantage of over 20,000 more children.

Governments fiddled at the margins of poor law administration – introducing a plethora of legislation, rules, circulars and guidance notes; moving responsibility from state department to department, changing ministry names, establishing subsidiary bodies and altering funding formulae and regulation – in an effort to improve the way children's workhouses operated. But to little avail; because the underpinning philosophy and logic behind their existence was flawed and unfit for purpose.

There was no overall vision that focused on the needs of the child, although it was surrounded with examples of institutions that offered precisely that. There were the Mettray and Rauhe Haus schemes in France and Germany from the 1830s, reformatory and industrial schools in England from the 1850s, charity-based cottage homes, and a host of other local and national initiatives run by charities, religious institutions and even poor law authorities from the 1870s. Yet none of the good practice developed in any of these was replicated in Forest Gate by the FGDS governors until the very end of the century.

While the children were routinely affected by ophthalmia, their controllers were affected by myopia. Despite a wealth of evidence, from practical experience and the advice of social commentators, they persevered with a clearly old fashioned, unsympathetic regime in which to entrust the care of tens of thousands of destitute children.

Barrack-like schools were not appropriate institutions in which to cultivate already vulnerable, disadvantaged and damaged youngsters into fully fledged, independent citizens.

It is no coincidence that it took the efforts of a small number of empathetic middle-class women and two determined, poverty-scarred, working-class local men, to overthrow the excesses of the FGDS – because they better understood the needs of poor children, and how to meet them, than the detached middle-class men who for so long controlled their destinies.

The dreadful conditions experienced by the Forest Gate District School children and the scandals that plagued the institution were all known to public authorities – the Poor Law Board, the Local Government Board, boards of guardians and governing committees – because their records show it.

But the establishment's desire for meaningful change was virtually non-existent – and it covered up and obfuscated, in order to keep a deficient show on the road. Governors and government departments, and even the local coroner, turned blind eyes to avalanches of bad behaviour: unauthorised beatings, staff indiscipline, negligent management practices, unprofessional medical behaviour, anti-Catholicism, food poisoning, disease epidemics, avoidable fires, adulterated food and simple graft and corruption.

Not a single superintendent was sacked for these offences; though they ensured that many of the lower orders lost their positions. Whistleblowers became scapegoats and were dismissed. Senior officials, guilty of gross misconduct, were simply persuaded to resign, free to inflict their poor behaviour and performance on other poor law bodies – all under the gaze of the government departments, who simply looked away.

The motive for writing this book was never to find heroes and villains, but they leap from its pages. The foresight of Jane Senior, William Bourch-ier and Henrietta Barnett is in direct contrast to the dogged intransigence and self-serving behaviour of Charles Duncan and Thomas Vallance. Working-class heroes emerge, including those who later rose to national prominence, such as Will Crooks and George Lansbury, and those who are scarcely footnotes in history, including Henry Elliott, Charles Hipkins, J. J. Terrett and William Bolton.

A major frustration for me has been the inability to hear directly from the residents of the FGDS about their experiences, and how they affected the rest of their lives. Hardly any memoirs that describe the conditions of the institution and are written from the child's perspective, survive. Few former residents are likely to have felt their wretched experiences were worth retelling or recording. Poor levels of literacy would have inhibited most from committing memory to paper, and potential audiences and readerships, in any case, would probably have been small. Even fewer would have had access to the means to publish, and any recollections written simply for family and for private consumption could easily have been lost or discarded over the intervening century.

In all probability, most former residents are likely to have felt shame at having been brought up in a workhouse and would not have wanted to share their recollections with others. The experience endured in barrack schools was a heavy burden to carry for many, and one that the survivors would have chosen to put to the back of their minds, for fear of reliving painful memories. It is almost a century since my own mother was in a children's home, aged seven and separated from her siblings who were put in other homes. Despite much probing from me over many years, she steadfastly refused to talk about the institution, other than to dismiss it as being a horrible place, from which her abiding memory was looking through the iron bars erected in front of the windows, wondering when her father would next visit.

This book relies heavily on the evidence and observations of outsiders looking in to describe conditions for the 50,000 or so children who lived there. We know large numbers of these children struggled to cope when they left the closed environment for an open world. It is no coincidence that many were groomed for adult life in other institutions, and when they struggled there, would often return to what they knew best – workhouse life as an adult. Much like recidivists today.

Just as there is little first-hand information about living inside the FGDS, we have almost no knowledge of the fate and adult life of the vast majority of its leavers. That which survives concerns, almost by definition, the exceptional rather than the run-of-the-mill former residents.

Map from the1898 survey Our London Poor Law Schools, showing boundaries of East London unions and indicating the destinations of their out-placed children.

I have tried to offer a flavour of the lives of a small number of FGDS children after they departed the institution. This appears in the five shaded text boxes in the book. They, unfortunately, are all second hand accounts, relying on the efforts of: a family historian, an academic and contemporary assiduous note-takers on TS Goliath and at MAYBS.

However, while little is known of the outcome of most of the 50,000 whose lives were shaped by the institution; the reputations of those whose attitudes and behaviours defined the system and damaged the children's lives, such as Jeremy Bentham, Nassau Senior and William Vallance, remain largely unscathed today and honoured in public institutions.

This book began with the observation that the ways in which poor children are treated is a key yardstick for judging the state and values of the nation in which they live. The evidence assembled suggests that for the bulk of Queen Victoria's reign, it was one of callous indifference to the plight of cockney paupers, administered by a detached unsympathetic middle class, more concerned with their private pockets than the public good of those entrusted to their care.

The gatehouse of the former FGDS survives today as a multi-function community centre. It is deeply ironic that one of its principal users is the Magpie Project. This exemplary local charity is dedicated to supporting mothers and young children who, in that deeply hurtful and callous phrase, have 'no recourse to public funds' (or NRPF – in the cold abbreviation of bureaucracy). They are provided with material support, advice, care and attention by the project's dedicated volunteers. The children it supports are the true heirs to those who trooped through the same iron gates 175 years earlier. For some at the bottom of the social pile, little changes over time, while indifference to their plight continues at the very top.

A proportion of the proceeds of this book will be donated to the Magpie Project. You can assist too, by visiting www.magpieproject.org and offering whatever help you can.

APPENDIX

1898: ELSEWHERE

The 1896 Mundella Report on London's children's workhouses attracted controversy, not least from a number of the capital's boards of guardians who published a commentary to address what they felt to be unjust criticisms.[1] They also commissioned a book[2] of pen portraits of London's children's workhouses, in order to contextualise some of the criticism.

The book, published in 1898, was well researched and authored by two distinguished barristers. It offered comparisons for events and developments at the FGDS. It examined all 19 of the London unions' country homes/child workhouses and their annexes, at the very time Whitechapel and Poplar were looking for alternative solutions and, in some way, helped steer the directions they took.

In the late-nineteenth century there were eight poor law unions in east and north-east London: Whitechapel, Bethnal Green, St George in The East (broadly Wapping), Mile End, Stepney, Poplar, Hackney and Shoreditch.

Most of these areas had experienced similar rapid population growth to Whitechapel, Hackney and Poplar from the 1830s, and what follows is a brief account of how each (except the FGSD unions), responded to the growing ranks of dependant young poor, according to the 1898 survey.

The majority had established homes/child workhouses in the Essex countryside; some their own separate establishments, while others combined to form district institutions. Some, notably Hackney, moved their provision from one location and organisation to another.

The only east London unions without Essex facilities were Stepney and Mile End – both at the centre of Barnardo's work in the capital. In practice, the guardians of each left much of care of the destitute children in their areas to charities, and made derisory direct provision themselves.

The Stepney union housed 400 children in a separate institution in Limehouse until 1873, when it decided to send a large number of them to the country. But rather than to any provision in Essex, either under their own auspices, or jointly with other unions, they chose to send their children to the South Metropolitan School in Sutton, some distance away, south of the Thames and inconvenient and expensive for parents to visit.

Mile End did not adopt the countryside homes/child workhouse approach at all, and relied on a school facility in its own borders, in the unhealthy and crowded East End of London, to supplement its reliance on Barnardo's.

There was a considerable variation in the provision and conditions provided by all other east London unions in 1898. In each, attention to the care and needs of the children was considerably in advance of the primitive conditions that prevailed when the Whitechapel child workhouse was first established 40 years earlier. Children's homes were, largely, still being run under the same conditions three quarters of a century later.

SHOREDITCH – COTTAGE HOMES IN HORNCHURCH

These were located approximately one and a half miles from Romford railway station, on an 80 acre estate, purchased in 1886 for £6,300. Five more acres were added later. Shoreditch's children were first removed from its local workhouse in 1848 and sent to an establishment in Enfield. In 1854, they were transferred to the newly created Brentwood institution, which was extended in 1870, and transformed into the Brentwood District School in 1877 when Hackney joined.

That district arrangement was dissolved in 1885 when Shoreditch's guardians sought an alternative solution. They adopted a cottage homes model, located in Hornchurch. It was approved by the LGB in July 1887, at a cost of £48,304, and was opened two years later. An extension, costing £10,000, was added between 1893 and 1895.

In the period between leaving Brentwood in 1885 and moving to Hornchurch, Shoreditch's guardians used Harold Court, in Harold Wood, originally acquired by the Brentwood's managers as an overflow facility for

Some of Shoreditch's cottage homes in Hornchurch. (Credit: Mary Evans/Peter Higginbotham collection)

120 children. The remainder were sent initially to an institution in Edmonton and later to the Plashet children's workhouse (see below).

The Hornchurch scheme comprised 11 detached cottages, each accommodating 30 children, with a separate 14-bed probationary lodge and a superintendent's house, which incorporated office accommodation. There were three groupings, one each for boys, girls and infants.

There were six cottages for boys and five for girls and infants, who were between three and seven years old. The girls came under the control of a house mother, and the boys under the supervision of a married couple, where the husband was also one of the industrial trainers. All the cottages had their own dining room, recreation room, kitchen, scullery, paved playground, offices and garden plots.

There were also workshops, a needle room, swimming baths and a band room. There was an infirmary, with four bright and well-fitted dormitories, together with two day rooms. The buildings were arranged on either side of a broad drive, with a scenic view of the surrounding countryside.

The institution had a reception and infirmary area, for 20 children coming directly from the workhouse, which was erected in 1895. By 1898, only children under three years of age, those awaiting transfer and a few ins and outs were left in Shoreditch's main workhouse. Its guardians were, at the time of the survey, seeking premises nearby for these children, in order to keep them away from its inmates until they could be moved to Hornchurch. There was a probationary period of 14 days in Hornchurch, for quarantine purposes, which the review's authors recommended be increased to 30 days.

Older girls undertook domestic chores and the boys some domestic work in the homes, together with regular work in the gardens. There were no uniforms for any children and an attempt was made to encourage a sense of ownership and individuality in terms of clothing. The union was keen for domestic life to be similar to that of 'the family of a self-respecting man'.

The children had access to a gymnasium, playing fields and swimming baths. Their education was similar to that of working-class children in public elementary schools. The teachers were qualified, certified and non-resident. For the boys, there was industrial instruction in carpentry, engineering, tailoring, painting, shoemaking and in a bake house and gardens.

There were spacious, well-ventilated, school rooms – three for boys, two for girls and one for infants. There was no chapel, but the largest boys' school room doubled up as one. There was a band, formed in 1890, and, as a result, some of the boys moved on to military bands when they left.

Hornchurch had no difficulty in getting girls into domestic service positions. They received some technical instructions in the neighbourhood, in addition to the work experience they received in their home cottages. When leaving, the girls were passed to MABYS, for their care and supervision at work. The boys could usually be placed in jobs in trades for which they had received some industrial instruction. Others were placed into the Homes for Working Boys, established in London in 1870 as an organisation that offered a halfway house between children's institutions and full independence.

Hornchurch was certified to accommodate 381 children, although it seemed unlikely this would be large enough for the future. The guardians, as a consequence, sought to establish a branch facility, as an overflow, in Shoreditch.

Although the Hornchurch establishment had been in existence for less than a decade, the review's authors were able to report that:

From the good work in progress there, it must be apparent that the interests of the children have been, throughout, the first consideration in the minds of the guardians … .

Objections urged against the old schools have no application here; the buildings are not under one roof, the conditions which obtain admit of modification and variation in individual cases, and all the children derive benefit from their home-like surroundings, and the good influences brought to bear upon them in their preparation for their work in the after-life.

BETHNAL GREEN – SCHOOL IN LEYTONSTONE

This 9 acre site, was on the 'outskirts of Epping Forest', less than a mile from what is now Leytonstone High Road railway station. It was established in 1868 on land which was formerly a home of the Buxton family (who were close kin of the Gurneys, who provided the land for the Forest Gate site, and who, like them, were wealthy, philanthropic Quakers).

The child workhouse originally comprised of temporary iron buildings, which were gradually replaced; those surveyed by the report were erected in 1889, at a cost of £65,000.

Before they acquired the Leytonstone facility, Bethnal Green's guardians sent their young poor to establishments in Mitcham (Surrey) and the Central

Bethnal Green's children's workhouse in Leytonstone, today .(Photo: Author's Own)

London District School (Hanwell). When they opened in Leytonstone, they had 118 young in their own workhouse, 191 in Mitcham and 62 in Hanwell.

The certified maximum occupation of Leytonstone was 564, hosting an average of 500, who were despatched to it fortnightly, from the Bethnal Green workhouse.

The accommodation consisted of 12 homes, split between six blocks: half for boys and half for girls and infants. Each home had four dormitories each with 12 beds. In addition, there was a day room, a yard for play and offices. Overall, the sanitary arrangements were deemed to be satisfactory.

There was a house mother in charge of each self-contained home. Her job was to look after the children and see that they were clean and properly dressed and 'to give them as far as possible, the individual care and attention which a mother would give in a good home.'

In addition to the administrative and operational rooms, there was a receiving ward, under the supervision of a house mother, which accommodated 24 youngsters who stayed during their quarantine period.

The schoolrooms were in a separate block and were well fitted out. The boys had one large classroom and two schoolrooms and the girls just one of each. The infants' room was felt to be too small for the estimated 100 who were present at the time of the survey.

The infirmary was in two blocks – one for general sickness and one for contagious diseases – staffed by four trained nurses. There were well-appointed training workshops for the instruction of potential tailors, shoemakers, painters and carpenters, each of which was run by a skilled mechanic.

There was an open-air gymnasium and playing fields, with assistant schoolmasters supervising games. The playing fields were on the small side, the report commented, but as the site adjoined open forest – where the children were able to take almost daily rambles – this was not considered to be a great problem. The children were regularly taken to pantomimes and had an annual excursion to the seaside.

There were four schoolmasters and four schoolmistresses. The recent education department order restricting the pattern of 'half-time' teaching in elementary schools was not mandatory for poor law schools, but the Bethnal Green guardians chose to apply it to their Leytonstone establishment. The result was greatly increased costs, staffing levels and added workloads for teachers.

Bethnal Green boarded out 37 orphan and deserted children to foster parents in 1897, an initiative the guardians were keen to extend. The union took the care of its former pupils seriously. Girl leavers were supervised by MABYS and boys were overseen by a variety of more informal arrangements.

An iron building had been erected in the grounds of the main Bethnal Green Workhouse in the mid-1890s, to accommodate children awaiting transfer to Leytonstone. The survey authors remarked that conditions within it required improvement.

MILE END – LOCAL INSTITUTIONS

Mile End's arrangements within their own patch, the report noted, were unsatisfactory. The children lived in the workhouse, itself, albeit in blocks separated from the adult inmates. For educational purposes, older children attended the local Ben Johnson Elementary School and younger ones were taught by a specially appointed mistress in the workhouse buildings.

The guardians regarded it as socially beneficial for the older children to attend a school outside workhouse premises, particularly as they did not have to wear dull workhouse uniforms. Nevertheless, at the end of the school day, their 200 children returned to their 'home' in either the workhouse or its infirmary.

The children only had a 24-hour probationary period in the main workhouse before joining resident youngsters in the children's quarters, with consequential concerns about the spread of contagious diseases.

These arrangements were about to be replaced at the time of the 1898 survey, with young people moving to a model village site, located on a 100 acre site in North Weald, Essex. The transfer, however, had been held up by the departmental inquiry that the survey was a response to.

In the meantime, some of Mile End's children were sent to the Plashet institution (see below) and others to a facility in Surrey, where the boys received practical training in skills such as carpentry, tailoring and shoemaking and the girls were taught domestic subjects. The Mile End guardians were not sympathetic to the boarding-out system, but they did send a small number of children to Canada, via an emigration programme.

The survey authors noted some progressive measures at Mile End, such as the holding of an annual prize-giving evening, to encourage pride in work. Overall, however, they found the childcare and schooling arrangements to be highly deficient and unsatisfactory.

ST GEORGE IN THE EAST – SCHOOL IN PLASHET

Children from St George in the East went to the Plashet establishment, which was built in 1849. In 1898 it accommodated 143 boys, 113 girls, 30 infants and 10 probationers. There were 11 dormitories; five for girls, five for boys and one for infants. The boys' rooms each had 27 beds, the girls' rooms 19 and the infants' 36.

The institution was originally built on a 17 acre site, 'which at the time was surrounded by open country', and was 'possibly the earliest' to be established by a London board of guardians. Eight acres had originally been laid out for agriculture, with farm buildings, vegetable plots, horses, cows and pigs. In 1889, farming was given up, and 10 acres of the site were sold. The funds raised were used to improve the sanitation and general conditions on the remaining buildings.

Just as the FGDS buildings were showing signs of disrepair and were unfit for purpose in 1898, some of Plashet's even older buildings were proving to be sub-standard. Ventilation and heating in the classrooms, particularly the girls' and infants', were deemed to be unsatisfactory.

Money from the 1889 sale of land had been used to extend day rooms for the children, replace cess pits with more sanitary lavatories and build a new laundry, which allowed for more frequent changes of clothes and bed linen. These improvements provided much more hygienic conditions for the children, who were also given their own towel, toothbrush and hairbrush.

The land sale meant there was no longer enough play sheds for the children, but they were able to make use of 4 acres of adjacent meadow for recreational purposes, and had outside swings and an outdoor gymnasium. The youngsters were also frequently taken to West Ham and East Ham (central) parks.

Although there was no swimming pool, there were weekly trips to baths in Stratford, where the children were given swimming lessons. Entertainers were frequently brought into the establishment, which had a quiet room for children who preferred to read than play. Small plots of land were apportioned for use as gardens and an annual prize-giving day and a trip to Southend, paid for by guardians, were held, in order to raise self-esteem, providing leisure and increase social contacts.

Children faced each other around tables at mealtimes, in contrast to the practice of facing the back of the child in the next row of tables, which was prevalent at Forest Gate. The older girls attended a local school for cookery lessons, and some waited on officers at mealtimes in order to gain work

Site of St George's in the East school in Green Street, Plashet. Later turned into a cinema and now a small market. (Source: postcard)

experience. All received post-institutional support from MABYS on leaving.

Boys received instruction in tailoring, shoemaking and carpentry, but not until they had passed the fourth standard of school attainment. A number were sent to the *Exmouth* training ship. There were two bands and many of the boys went on to join army bands. There was no equivalent to MABYS for boys' post-establishment supervision, other than for those joining the army or navy. A former Plashet boy, the 1898 report noted, had recently been recruited as the institution's own bandmaster.

There was an infirmary, in a separate building, with accommodation for 36 children, including an isolation ward for infectious diseases. Each child was examined medically every fortnight and had their teeth inspected by a dentist once a week. The authors deemed the diet to be suitable, children's health to be good and there were very few cases of ophthalmia. The establishment had a comparatively low death rate.

Girls were no longer required to have close cropped hair and their clothing had improved considerably. Gone were the days of short-sleeved dresses and hats of one pattern; they were now provided with serge dresses with long sleeves and straw hats of various colours.

TS *EXMOUTH* – TRAINING SHIP

TS *Exmouth* was a 200 foot long timber-built vessel, launched in 1854, some 10 years before the widespread adoption of iron-clad ships. It had been a flag ship during the Crimean War and had been on active naval service until 1862, when it was mothballed. It lay idle in Devonport until it was acquired by the Metropolitan Asylums Board in 1876.

The ship was permitted to accommodate 600 boys. It was difficult to get its number of trainees up to capacity, the authors noted, either because of the costs to unions of sending boys there, or because of a reluctance of some establishments to 'part with all their finest "show' boys'". In 1897, 300 boys were discharged, of whom 129 went to the Royal Navy, 112 to the merchant marine and 28 to army bands. Only 28 were sent to their parish workhouses. The previous year, 137 boys from TS *Exmouth* joined the Royal Navy, which was two more than the combined total of all other training ships in the country.

The ship's superintendent (William Bourchier) had become more selective about the condition of boys recruited to TS *Exmouth*, to ensure that they were able, when leaving, to meet Royal Navy height and chest size requirements. TS *Exmouth* continued the use Sherfield House, in Grays as its infirmary. During 1897, a total of 847 boys stayed on TS *Exmouth* – most for very brief periods of time.

TS *Exmouth* took two training trips a year to ports in the west of England, to give the boys seafaring experience, during which time significant numbers left to join the navy. Visitors were welcomed on board on Wednesday afternoons, when the ship was considered to be in good order and clean, as the report confirmed:

> The sturdy, alert and well-disciplined carriage of the boys, too, at once strikes the visitor; and it would be appear almost impossible for anyone to leave the ship ... without a strong sense of having witnessed good work, well done, which pressages, hopefully, for the future of the youngsters whose training has been so manifestly painstaking and thorough.

As with its predecessor ship, TS *Goliath*, boys entered TS *Exmouth* at the age of 12, and their first task was to learn how to mend and patch their own clothes, as well as wash them and take personal responsibility for their lockers and hammocks. They were taught naval skills and, according to the schools' inspector, their schoolwork was satisfactory.

Ninety per cent of the boys on board could swim, and overall, there was a high standard of gymnastic attainment. First aid classes were taught by local visitors, an initiative highly regarded by examiners from St John Ambulance. Musical entertainment was provided regularly by the ships' bands and the boys had access to a library on board. Gymnastics classes were held, and commendably high standards reached.

The superintendent, head teacher and medical officer had all been with the ship for the 22 years since it was commissioned: 'The Exmouth has earned and, we are glad to find, has been rewarded by, continuous success and has won many golden opinions.'

NON-EAST LONDON ESTABLISHMENTS

Other establishments, not based in East London, were covered by the 1898 survey of metropolitan children's workhouses. The list indicates the locality of the main school, and its designation, and in italics and parentheses, any satellite establishments it ran. They were: Anerley – North Surrey District School (*Wainwright House, Broadstairs*); Ashford – West London District School; Banstead – Kingston and Chelsea District School (*Marlesford Lodge, Hammersmith*); Edmonton – Strand Union separate school; Hanwell – Central London District School; Hornsey Road – St Mary's, Islington separate school; Leavesden – St Pancras separate school (*Eastcliffe House, Margate*); Mitcham – Holborn separate school; Southall – St Marylebone's separate school; Sutton – South Metropolitan District School (*a) Brighton Road, b) Banstead Road, c) Witham orphan home, d) Herne Bay convalescence home*); Tooting – Westminster separate school; West Norwood – Lambeth separate school.

NOTES

[1] *Criticism of the Report of the Departmental Committee,* King and Son, Westminster, 1897
[2] Mornington and Lampard

TIMELINE

━━━━━━

This timeline is of key national (in medium typeface) and local (**in bold**) events that helped shape the history of the Forest Gate children's workhouse and its buildings.

1601   Poor Law Relief Act (what later became known as the Old Poor Law). Parishes become responsible for relieving their own poor through local taxation, the poor rate. It could be spent on either 'outdoor relief' – cash or payments in kind – or accommodation for the 'impotent' poor.

1713   Knatchball's Act, allowed parishes to establish workhouses.

1766   Hanway Act, paved the way for London's pauper children to be located in the country, away from workhouse influences.

1782   Gilbert's Act, allowed groups of parishes to form 'unions' to run workhouses.

1834   Poor Law Amendment Act, established the framework and philosophy for the administration of poor law over the next century, created poor law unions and created the Poor Law Commission.

1838   James Kay-Shuttleworth proposed establishment of district schools in the country.

1844   Poor Law Amendment Act, repealed and updated the Hanway Act, permitting London poor law unions to establish children's workhouses in rural areas.

1847   Poor Law Board replaced Poor Law Commission.

1854   **Whitechapel children's workhouse established in Forest Gate.**

1865   Union Chargeability Act, determined the formulae for boards of governors to fund joint initiatives, such as the FGDS, which was to plague its entire existence.

1867   Metropolitan Poor Law Act, facilitated the establishment of district schools by London boards of guardians and established the Metropolitan Asylum Board.

1868   **Hackney and Poplar guardians joined forces with Whitechapel to establish the Forest Gate District School (FGDS).**

1869   Metropolitan Poor Law Amendment Act.

1869   **FGDS acquired training ship, TS *Goliath*, under the terms of the 1869 Metropolitan Poor Law Amendment Act.**

1871   Poor Law Board (PLB) replaced by Local Government Board (LGB), at national level.

1873   Jane Senior appointed Britain's first civil servant, to report to the LGB on conditions in children's workhouses, particularly from a female perspective.

1874 Senior's report published.

1875 TS *Goliath* destroyed by fire, killing 22.

1876 Henrietta Barnett, with Jane Senior, established Metropolitan Association for Befriending Young Servants (MABYS).

1877 Hackney left FGDS.

1877 Large-scale outbreak of ophthalmia at FGDS.

1877 Henrietta Barnett became Britain's first, and FGDS' only, female children's workhouse governor.

1884 Henrietta Barnett established the Children's County Holiday Fund.

1888 A second large-scale outbreak of ophthalmia at FGDS.

1890 Fire on New Year's Day at FGDS killed 26.

1893 Food poisoning outbreak at FGDS killed two and affected 132 others.

1893 Will Crooks and George Lansbury first elected to Poplar Board of Guardians.

1894 Henrietta Barnett's brother-in-law, E. A. Hart, began a campaign against district schools, through his position as editor of the *British Medical Journal* (*BMJ*).

1894 Local Government Act abolished ex-officio guardians and children's workhouse governors.

1895 Large-scale outbreak of scarlet fever at FGDS.

1896 Following scandals at FGDS and pressure from the *BMJ*, the government established the Mundella Committee, to examine the operation of London's children's workhouses, which hastened their demise.

1896 Will Crooks became FGSD governor, the first ex-children's workhouse boy to achieve the status; George Lansbury soon followed him.

1897 Whitechapel left FGSD, putting the establishment under the sole control of Poplar Guardians.

1897 Lansbury became chairman of Poplar Guardian's Education Committee, effectively the children's workhouse governing body.

1898 Publication of *Our Poor Law Schools – Comprising Descriptions of the Schools.*

1902 Education Act replaced local school boards with local education authorities.

1905–1909 Royal Commission on the Poor Law.

1906 Poplar closed Forest Lane children's workhouse and transferred the residents to country homes in Hutton.

1906–1908 Forest Lane buildings and site vacant.

1908–1911 Buildings used as an annexe to Poplar workhouse.

1911 West Ham Guardians bought the land and site, and converted them largely to hospital provision.

1930 Boards of Guardians abolished, replaced by local authority Public Assistance Committees.

1940 Four nights of heavy Blitz bombing on the hospital during the Second World War resulted in the large-scale evacuation of patients.

1948   With the establishment of NHS, the Forest Lane facility became a maternity hospital.

1986   Forest Gate Maternity Hospital closed; Newham General Hospital opened.

1993   Many buildings on the site demolished to make way for a housing development. Forest Lane Park established.

BIBLIOGRAPHY

ARCHIVES

London Metropolitan Archives

Minutes of the governors' meetings of the FGSD, July 1868–March 1898, in 15 volumes: FGSD/001 – FGSD/015

Minutes and correspondence relating to *Goliath*, March 1870–March 1876, in three volumes: FGSD/016 – FGSD 018

An incomplete set of governors' annual reports for the FGSD: FGSD/019

A small collection of correspondence of the FGSD's superintendent, for the period August 1895–August 1896, in three volumes: FGSD/020 – FGSD/022

The admission and creed registers relating to the FGSD 1854–1897, in 16 volumes: FGSD/023 – FGSD/038

Staff records relating to the FGSD, 1868–1897, in three volumes: FGSD/040 – FGSD/042

The Henrietta Barnett papers, and in particular notes towards chapter five of her unpublished, untitled autobiography, *Be-friending the Friendless*, can be found *at LMA/4063/006*

Minutes of the Poplar Guardians' Forest Gate School Visiting Committee Vol 1, 1897: POBG83.1 LMA

London School of Economics

George Lansbury papers

National Archives

The register of paid officers and staff appointed to the Forest Gate schools, 1857–1907: MH9/22

Correspondence between the PLB, later LGB, and the FGSD between 1868 and 1900, in 11 volumes: MH27/101 – MH27/111

Tower Hamlets Archives

Press cuttings of William Vallance: LCX00309

Royal Commission on the Poor Laws, 1907, evidence given by Will Crooks MP: LC 7999

OFFICIAL PUBLICATIONS – CHRONOLOGICAL

*Report of the General Board of Health as a Preliminary Enquiry into the Sewerage, Drainage and
  Supply of Water and the Sanitary Conditions of the Inhabitants of the Parish of West Ham* (1855)
*Report by Mrs. Senior on Pauper Schools, Appendix to Third Annual Report of the Local Government
  Board – 1873–4* (London 1874)
*Enquiry into System of the Maintenance and Education in the Metropolitan Poor Law Schools, Mundella
  Report* (1896)
Report of the Metropolitan Poor Law Schools Committee, Minutes of Evidence (London 1896)
Criticism of the Report of the Departmental Committee – King and Son, (Westminster 1897)

NEWSPAPERS/JOURNALS

Aldershot Military Gazette, The
Army and Navy Gazette
Barking, East Ham & Ilford Advertiser, Upton Park and Dagenham Gazette
Bentley's Miscellany
Brighton Gazette
Broad Arrow, The
Chelmsford Chronicle, The
Clerkenwell News, The
Croydon Advertiser, The
Daily News, The
Derby Daily Telegraph, The
East and South Devon Advertiser
East Anglian Daily Times
East London Observer (ELO)
Essex Guardian
Essex Halfpenny Newsman
Essex Herald
Essex Standard, The
Evening Standard, The
Forest Gate Weekly News
Globe, The
Grays & Tilbury Gazette
Hackney and Kingsland Gazette
Hampshire Telegraph and Sussex Chronicle
Household Words
Illustrated Times
Justice
London Daily News (see Daily News, above)
Manchester Evening News
Marylebone Mercury
Morning Advertiser

Morning Post, The
Night and Day, a monthly record of Christian Mission, ed Dr Barnardo 1877-1888
Northern Times, The
Pall Mall Gazette
Panorama – Journal of Thurrock Local History Society
(Portsmouth) Evening News, The
Royal Cornwall Gazette, The
Scotsman, The
Sheffield Daily Telegraph
Shipping and Mercantile Gazette
Shoreditch Observer
Stratford Express, The
Stratford Times and South Essex Gazette, The
Tablet, The
Times, The
Tower Hamlets Independent and East End Local Advertiser (THIEELA)
Transactions of the National Association for the Promotion of the Social Sciences, 1882
Westminster Gazette, The
Wilts and Gloucestershire Standard

BOOKS

Barnett, Henrietta Rowland, (1919), *Canon Barnett: His Life Work and Friends*, Vol 1, John Murray

Barnett, Henrietta Rowland, (1933), *Matters that Matter*, John Murray

Bready, Wesley, (1935), *Dr Barnardo, Physician, Pioneer, Prophet*, Allen and Unwin

Brown, Arthur, (1982), *The Chartist Movement in Essex And Suffolk*. Department of History, University of Essex

Brown, Arthur, (1990), *Meagre Harvest: The Essex Farm Workers' Struggle Against Poverty 1750–1914*, Essex Record Office

Carradice, Phil, (2009), *Nautical Training Ships – An Illustrated History*, Amberley Press

Chaplin, Charlie, (1954), *My Autobiography*, Simon and Schuster

Clifford, Jim, (2017), *West Ham and the River Lea – A Social and Environmental History of London's Industrialized Marshland 1839–1914*. U.B.C. Press.

Davenport-Hill, Florence, (1889), *Children of the State*, Macmillan and Co

Haw, George, (1907), *From Workhouse to Westminster – The Life Story of Will Crooks MP*, Cassell and Co

Fenn, R. J., (1876), *The Burning of the Goliath*, Shaw and Sons

Fishman, William, (2001), *East End 1888*, Cromwell Press

Fraser, Neil, (2012), *Over the Border – The Other East End*, Function Books

Fry, Katharine; Pagenstecher, Gustav, (1888), *History of the Parishes of East and West Ham*, privately published

Gamester, E. R., (1954), *History of Forest Gate Hospital*, Friends of Forest Gate Hospital

George, Dorothy, (1966), *London Life in the Eighteenth Century*, Penguin

Hammond. J. L.; Hammond, B, (1932), *James Stansfeld – A Victorian Champion of Sex Equality*, Longmans

Higginbotham, Peter, (2012), *Workhouse Encyclopaedia,* The History Press

Higginbotham, Peter, (2017), *Children's Homes – A History of Institutional Care for Britain's Young,* Pen and Sword

Higginbotham, Peter, (2019), *Workhouses of London and the South East,* The History Press

Koven, Seth, (2014), *The Match Girl and the Heiress*, Princeton University Press

Lansbury George, (1936), *Looking Backwards and Forwards*, Blackie

Limbrick, Gudrun, J., (2014), *Leaving the Workhouse: The Story of Victorian Orphanages*, Word-Works

Marriott, John, (2012), *Beyond the Tower – A History of East London,* Yale University Press

Mornington, Walter; Lampard, Frederick, (1898), *Our London Poor Law Schools: Comprising Descriptive Sketches of the Schools* – Eyre and Spottiswood

Neal, Wendy, (1992), *With Disastrous Consequences – London Disasters, 1830–1917*, Hisarlik Press

Newham, L. B., (1986), *West Ham 1886–1986*

Oldfield, Sybil, (2008), *Jeanie, An Army of One: Mrs Nassau Senior 1828–1877, The First Woman in Whitehall*, Sussex Academic Press

Palmer, Alan (1989), *The East End – Four Centuries of London Life,* John Murray

Pelly, Derk, (2001), *Upton Connections: 1732–1916: A Story of Families*, Pentland Books

Postgate, Raymond., (1951), *Life of George Lansbury*, Longmans

Ross, Alexander, M., (1955), *The Care and Education of Pauper Children in England and Wales*, PhD Thesis. University of London (www.core.ac.uk/download/pdf/1882891.pdf)

Schneer, Jonathan, (1990), *George Lansbury*, Manchester University Press

Steer, Rosemary (2020), *Children in Care: 1834–1929: The Lives of Destitute, Orphaned and Deserted Children*, Pen and Sword

Taylor, A. J. P., (1950), *English History, 1914–45*, Penguin

Tyler, Paul, (2007), *Labour's Lost Leader: The Life and Politics of Will Crooks*, Tauris

Wagner, G., (1979), *Barnardo*, Weidenfeld and Nicolson

Watkins, Micky, (2005), *Henrietta Barnett in Whitechapel: Her First Fifty Years*, Hampstead Garden Suburb Archive Trust

White, Jerry, (2003), *Rothchild Buildings – Life in an East End Tenement Block, 1887–1920*, Pimlico

Williams, A. E., (1943), *Barnardo of Stepney*, George Allen and Unwin

Williams, Peter, (2019), *West Ham and its Fire Brigade – An Illustrated History, 1800–1965*, E. B. Books

WEBSITES

www.britishnewspaperarchive.co.uk – Subscription site for access to over 30 million pages of British newspapers

www.calkin.co.uk – Details of Bourchier portrait

www.civilservant.org.uk – A non-government website, authored by an ex-senior UK civil servant, providing objective current and historic data about the British civil service

www.E7-NowAndThen.org – Forest Gate local history blog, edited by this book's author

www.formerchildrenshomes.org.uk – Dedicated to sharing memories and information about former children's homes, orphanages, cottage homes and other institutions for children

www.hbschool.org.uk – Henrietta Barnett School

www.oxforddnb.com - Oxford Dictionary of National Biography

www.spartacus-educational.com – Free British educational history site

www.wikipedia.com – Online encyclopaedia that needs no introduction

www.workhouses.org.uk – Invaluable resource for detailed histories of individual workhouses and poor law institutions, run by the indefatigable Peter Higginbotham

INDEX

Illustrations in *italics*, references in notes preceded by n.

Lightning Source UK Ltd.
Milton Keynes UK
UKHW011037200821
389165UK00001B/42